The Great Lovers

The Great Lovers

ANDREW EWART

PICTURE RESEARCH
MARION GEISINGER

Hart Publishing Company, Inc. • New York City

Contents

LIST OF ILLUSTRATIONS

THE DUKE OF WINDSOR AND WALLIS SIMPSON

ACKNOWLEDGMENTS

BROWN BROTHERS   220 West 42nd Street, New York, N.Y.
279, 282, 288, 294-295

CULVER PICTURES, INC.   660 First Avenue, New York, N.Y.
44-45, 110, 158, 163, 180, 182-183, 281, 285, 290, 316, 323, 348, 354

EUROPEAN PICTURES SERVICE   39 West 32nd Street, New York, N.Y.
298, 308, 312, 318, 329 (2), 373, 377

GRANGER COLLECTION, THE   37 West 39th Street, New York, N.Y.
74, 113, 114, 120, 155

WALTER HAMPDEN MEMORIAL LIBRARY   16 Gramercy Park, New York, N.Y.
240, 251

HISTORICAL PICTURE SERVICE   2753 West North Avenue, Chicago, Illinois
36, 48, 56, 153, 175, 179, 184, 185, 198, 220, 230

LORD CHAMBERLAIN, ST. JAMES'S PALACE   London SW1, England
133

MANSELL COLLECTION, THE   42 Linden Gardens, London W2, England
167, 205, 210, 249, 252

METROPOLITAN MUSEUM OF ART, THE   Fifth Avenue at 82nd St., New York
101

MUSEUM OF THE CITY OF NEW YORK   Fifth Avenue 103rd to 104th St.
New York, N.Y.
246

NATIONAL MARITIME MUSEUM   Greenwich, London SE 10, England
126-127, 136-137, 144-145

NATIONAL PORTRAIT GALLERY   Trafalgar Square, London SW 1, England
143, 164, 201

NEW YORK PUBLIC LIBRARY   Fifth Avenue at 42nd Street, New York, N.Y.
61

PIX, INC. 236 East 46th Street, New York, N.Y.
336-337 (3), 347, 357, 358, 364-365, 395, 396, 397, 398-399

PAUL POPPER LTD. 24 Bride Lane, Fleet Street, London EC 4, England
368

PROFESSIONAL PICTURE SERVICE 147 West 42nd Street, New York, N.Y.
23, 25, 28, 35, 38, 41, 51, 52, 53, 71, 73, 76, 78, 80-81, 82, 85, 86,
85, 86, 95, 99, 102, 106, 123, 124, 129, 131, 134, 139, 140-141, 90, 216,
219, 225, 229

RADIO TIMES HULTON PICTURE LIBRARY 35 Marylebone High Street,
London W 1, England
192-193, 236, 242, 363, 374, 381, 387

TURKISH GOVERNMENT TOURISM AND INFORMATION OFFICE 500 Fifth
Avenue, New York, N.Y.
57, 58, 59

UNITED PRESS INTERNATIONAL 220 East 42nd Street. New York, N.Y.
189, 261, 266-267, 268, 274, 293, 303, 306, 310-311, 320, 344-345,
339, 351, 352, 355, 391, 392, 393

WIDE WORLD PHOTOS, INC. 50 Rockefeller Plaza, New York, N.Y.
286, 300-301, 304-305, 325, 331, 360, 361

The
Great Lovers

Preface

"Love is not all; it is not meat nor drink
Nor slumber nor a roof against the rain. . . ."

Yet love has brought—and lost—all these things and more. Love has changed the course of empires, literature, and art.

There are those who have valued love above a crown, above fame, above lucre, above children—and even above sanity.

Though love be the stuff of legend, it is also the stuff of life. Behind the fantasies of films, novels, plays, and paintings there stand real flesh-and-blood men and women—pulsating hearts that found the greatest adventure of all.

The halo of love can envelop anyone—a slum girl, a head-strong princess, a ruthlessly ambitious general, a harlot, a pro-fessorial president, a homely bluestocking, a no-nonsense business-man. The love of each of these won a place in history.

There was Nell Gwynne who peddled oranges in the theatre pits of Restoration England and rose to bear a king's sons. There was the dark genius of Dostoevsky who felt compelled to portray his willful young mistress in so many of his novels.

Even in our own century a king fell in love, and his passion had repercussions heard around the world. Contemporary Carib-bean calypso recalls that—

"It was love, and love alone
Caused King Edward to leave his throne."

17

This volume makes no pretension to being all-inclusive. Yet few will gainsay the assertion that the loves set forth on these pages are among the most renowned passions of all time. The stories of these loves will brighten the tomes of history and enrich the understanding of all of us.

Larger than life—each fully alive—here are THE GREAT LOVERS!

The
Great Lovers

Antony
and
Cleopatra

Cleopatra, Queen of Egypt, undoubtedly has the distinction of being the most written about woman of all time. Books by the hundred, plays by the score, ballets by the dozen, and film after film have examined every aspect of her character and personality. Most of these works are based not on fact but on imagination. Her life attracted the genius of Shakespeare and Shaw, even though they used her triumphs and defeat only as a vehicle for their poetic imageries and dramatic powers, as did many lesser men.

She owes all this interest through the ages, not entirely to her unsurpassed beauty or seductive charms, but to her conquest of two mighty Romans, Julius Caesar and Mark Antony, and to the part she played in reshaping the history of her world. For Cleopatra employed her ability to excite and rouse men's senses as an instrument of national policy, and she employed her charms to bend to her will the rulers of the Mediterranean world. Yet she lived for only thirty-eight years, and she died by her own hand.

With Julius Caesar under her spell, the daughter of the Ptolemies nurtured the dream of becoming empress of the world. But this vision was shattered by the daggers of the Ides of March. After Caesar's murder she fled from Rome back to the throne of Egypt with Caesarion, her son by Caesar, but without the treaty of alliance she had promised her people. For two years she worked to restore the lost confidence of her subjects. At the same time, she kept a sharp eye on the struggle for power going on in Rome. Mark Antony and Octavian finally emerged after the bloody civil war as the two main rivals for supremacy.

Cleopatra well knew that the future of her country, no less than her own, depended on the outcome of this rivalry, so she decided to take an active hand in the game. She had to make a choice between the two rivals for power, and she had to stake her all on that choice. Perhaps the fact that Antony was outstandingly handsome, with a gay and lighthearted attitude towards life, influenced her final decision; but it seems more likely that, as most shrewd judges of the political scene believed, he had greater practical advantages too.

CLEOPATRA   A sculptured head, now in the British Museum, which conveys the fabled beauty of the Egyptian queen.

Thus when Antony sent an ambassador to invite the Queen to meet him at Tarsus in Cilicia, she saw that her chance had come to ensnare in her net the next ruler of Rome. Artfully ignoring the reason behind the invitation—to answer the accusation that she had given aid to Antony's enemy in the late wars—she set out to dazzle the Roman with all the splendors of Egypt. She would not merely pay Antony a visit, she would fit out an expedition to mark the occasion.

She ordered her personal fleet to be made ready, and she filled twelve ships with gifts of gold and jewels. Her own regal galley had sails dyed in the purple of Tyre, its decks covered with costly draperies. From the bridge of the ship rose a golden shell under an awning of gilt embroidery.

Cleopatra at once began to prepare herself for the encounter. Slaves bathed and anointed her body with the oil of Sidon, massaged her hands with lotion, polished her fingernails with powdered mother-of-pearl, and carmined her toenails. Her hair was dressed in the latest fashion by a Persian attendant; her eyes and face were made up with all the many skills of her beauticians. Gorgeous robes were brought in and spread out before her. She chose an emerald-colored tunic, fastened at the shoulders by pearl clasps, which left bare her arms and bosom over which a transparent veil was draped. Huge pear-shaped pearls were attached to her ears, and her arms were adorned with precious bejeweled bracelets. Finally, she slipped her feet into sandals of soft white kid soled with thin gold. The Queen of Beauty was ready for the Temptation of Mark Antony.

ANTONY   A bust of the Roman general in the Vatican Museum

The noble Roman watched the golden galley float down the Cydnus and glide into the pool of Tarsus. He heard the music of fifes, flutes, and harps as it was wafted ashore on the light breeze. When the royal vessel came to rest beside the quay, Mark Antony caught his first sight of Cleopatra reclining on a purple couch under a golden canopy. Beautiful boys representing cupids fanned her with ostrich feathers. Scented smoke, redolent of incense and cinnamon, drifted from the galley and teased his nostrils.

Mark Antony was more than impressed by the elaborate display on the Cydnus—he was overwhelmed. He sent his envoy to welcome Cleopatra, and invite her ashore to dine with him. She sent back her warm appreciation of the invitation, but she insisted that on this first evening of their meeting, he must come aboard her craft as her guest.

Mark Antony accepted with alacrity. And when he went on board he, too, was arrayed in his military best, and wore a silver breastplate embossed with an Homeric scene. His officers followed, thinking, no doubt, that the ladies of Rome were mere novices in the finer arts of self-display. Cleopatra took Antony by the hand, leading him to the banqueting cabin where twelve couches circled the royal dais. Golden tapestries hung from the wall, and the floor was ankle deep in scattered flowers.

Their revelries lasted for five days and nights. Cleopatra had spared no expense to confound her important guest with her lavish display and opulence. The word of the wits went round that "Venus was come to feast with Bacchus, for the common good of Asia." For behind the glittering show lay a deadly serious purpose—to persuade Antony to conclude an alliance with Egypt against Octavian (Caesar's adopted son), and to support her own son, Caesarion, as his father's rightful successor in Rome.

Antony quickly fell captive to the Queen's voluptuous charms and brilliance of mind, luxuriating in both the pleasures of the flesh and the magic of her society. Needless to say, he readily accepted her invitation to join her again before winter came.

At their reunion, Cleopatra set out to receive Antony in Alexandria with such pomp and splendor that her spectacle at Tarsus seemed but a circus sideshow by comparision. The streets of her city were decorated with ceremonial arches and were even carpeted for the occasion. To receive him, she stood on the top step of the royal palace, flanked by mitred priests swinging censers. Lining the steps were dignitaries of her court arrayed in full magnificent regalia. When Antony appeared, she cast a laurel wreath before him. He fell upon one knee, saluted her first in the Roman fashion; then, more exuberantly, with outstretched arms. Together they entered the palace, Antony holding her hand in his.

This meeting, however, like the first, had a serious political purpose. Its short-term objective was to conclude an alliance between Rome and Egypt which would allow Antony to draw on the rich treasury of Cleopatra. With the guaranteed support of her fleet and army for his campaign, he could expect to sweep Octavian from his path.

Together they hatched a much more ambitious project: when he was undisputed master of the Roman world, he would proclaim himself Divine Emperor with Cleopatra as his Empress. They would then found a dynasty which would hold the world in thrall into the distant future. There can be little doubt who was the architect of this cosmic design. In his life of Antony, Plutarch, greatest of the ancient biographers, has described in detail their riotous life together in Alexandria. It was hardly surprising that Cleopatra soon found herself pregnant. In due course, she gave birth to twins—a boy and a girl who were solemnly titled Alexander the Sun, and Cleopatra the Moon—another indication of the direction in which their ambitions were heading.

Antony was now completely infatuated. But he could not go on wining and making love forever—especially since his wife Fulvia was not content to sit around idly in Rome until the great man saw fit to return to her. Fulvia organized an expedition against Octavian which he had no difficulty in defeating, and Antony's wife

was forced to flee to Athens.

At last Mark Antony realized that his position in Rome was in serious danger. After a reluctant farewell, he left Alexandria for home in the spring of 40 B.C. Four years were to elapse before Cleopatra was to set eyes on him again.

Again and again in that period the Queen must have felt abandoned and betrayed. First came the news of Fulvia's death in Greece, quickly followed by a peace treaty signed at Brindisi between Antony and Octavian.

A heavier blow was to follow—Antony's marriage to Octavia, his rival's half-sister. This was treachery indeed! It is recorded that the Queen's fury was terrible to behold; in order to calm her, her doctors had to drug her into a state of unconsciousness. Now she set about educating her son Caesarion as the future ruler of her people, and devoted herself to the affairs of state which she had neglected during her dalliance with Mark Antony. Determined to consolidate her dynastic heritage, she reorganized her army, refurbished her fleet, and restocked her shipyards. She also restored the famed Library of Alexandria which had been seriously damaged by fire.

CLEOPATRA   *This bas relief in the Temple of Hathor, dedicated to the Egyptian goddess of love and joy, stands on the bank of the Nile near Thebes. The bas relief pictures Cleopatra in the guise of Isis, goddess of earth-giving produce.*

Meanwhile relations between Antony and Octavian steadily worsened. Antony could scarcely bear to live in the same city as his rival, whom he persistently underestimated both as a soldier and a man. Finally, Mark Antony took up quarters in Athens and adopted the Greek way of life and dress, discarding the Roman toga.

Things went very well for him in Greece. He was immensely popular with the Athenians who treated him like a demigod, and he conducted a successful military campaign against the Parthians. Absorbed in his new wife who was with child, he must have held Cleopatra very far from his thoughts. He even felt self-confident enough to risk a trial of strength with Octavian; and to that end, fitted out an expedition of three hundred ships. The clash between them seemed inevitable when Octavian decided to negotiate. He, too, was building a fleet, and he was not quite ready for the showdown.

Antony looked around for new worlds to conquer, new glories to achieve. He proposed to crush Persia, and so enlarge Rome's empire that the Romans would have to acclaim his as the sole ruler. Campaigning in Persia, however, required immense treasure. Naturally, his thoughts once again turned to the Queen of Egypt and her vast storehouse of riches.

He broke up camp in Greece, packed his wife Octavia off to Italy, set up new quarters in Antioch, and despatched an envoy to invite Cleopatra to join him and negotiate an alliance. She did not hesitate—but laid down inexorable conditions. The first was that Antony must marry her. This was no romantic decision—it was coldly political.

Indeed, Antony found the Cleopatra he greeted in Antioch a remarkably changed woman. She was now thirty-two, even more alluring than before, but tempered by the fires of experience as a ruler and the skepticism of a woman betrayed. This time she brought no expensively decorated royal galley of love, but a mind steeled for hard bargaining. This time she was not escorted by a bevy of beautiful Egyptian girls and cupid boys, but by her Minister of State and his staff. Even more disconcerting to the impatient Antony, he was kept waiting for two days before she would agree to sit down at the conference table with him. When she did, she dictated the terms of the treaty. In addition to the marriage clause, she demanded that Antony recognize Caesarion in his written will as the legitimate heir to the Egyptian throne. The treaty was to concede Egypt's sovereignty over a considerable stretch of the coast of Syria and the Lebanon, part of the Jordan valley, slices of Samaria and Galilee, and the island of Cyprus. In return for all this, Cleopatra would place all the resources of her country at the disposal of Mark Antony.

The treaty was signed in Latin, Greek, and Egyptian. It represented a fantastic triumph for Cleopatra, for it restored Egyptian power to what it had been in the greatest days of the Pharaohs, fourteen centuries earlier.

Three days after the signing of the treaty, the marriage of Cleopatra and Mark Antony was solemnized in the Palace of Antioch. She was seated on a square of ivory inlaid with ebony; he on a purple cushion studded with gold stars. With the golden spatula which through the ages had been used to anoint the kings of Egypt, she anointed Antony on head and mouth. Then the Egyptian High Priest and court officials prostrated themselves before their Queen and her Consort, kissing the ground and their feet. The High Priest placed a crown on the head of each, and scribes drew up a contract on papyrus declaring that the twin children of the newly wedded pair—Alexander the Sun and Cleopatra the Moon— had been legitimatized by the marriage. To mark the occasion, Cleopatra ordered the minting of special coins which bore the heads of herself and her consort.

Antony passed that winter in Antioch raising an army of 100,- 000 men, including 60,000 Italian legionaries, for his expedition to Persia. He marched out to war in March of 36 B.C.

Cleopatra escorted him as far as the Euphrates River. She had intended to see the campaign through by his side, but she found she was again with child and was forced to return to Egypt for the birth. On the way, she stopped at Jericho for a meeting with King Herod who had concocted a plot to have her murdered, but then thought better of it. Instead, Herod loaded her with costly gifts and himself escorted her to the Egyptian frontier.

Cleopatra settled down in Alexandria to await her child and news of great victories from the east. Instead, the news was of unrelieved disaster. Antony was forced to make a retreat as ignoble as any in military history—it lasted nearly a month and cost him 24,000 men.

He barely struggled back to his headquarters in Syria with the remains of his once great force, and immediately sent for Cleopatra. Plutarch, recording all this, adds that Antony behaved like a man possessed, drinking with mad abandon, and continually scanning the horizon to catch the first glimpse of the purple sails that would bring his queen to him.

At last she arrived in her royal galley, leading a string of cargo boats crammed with uniforms, weapons, and gold to reequip and pay Antony's tattered and defeated soldiery. Realistically, she urged him to abandon any fanciful dreams of eastern conquest and concentrate on the inevitable clash to come—the one with Octavian.

At the same time, news reached Antony that his Roman wife Octavia was now in Athens with reinforcements for his army, as well as money and supplies. Octavia urged Antony to renew his campaign in the east, and wipe out the stain of the catastrophe. Thus Antony's two wives were pressing him in the same way, but in very different directions.

Cleopatra, however, had two tremendous advantages over Octavia. First, she was by his side; and secondly, she was a vastly better politician. The Egyptian Queen realized that Octavian was using his half-sister to persuade Antony to undertake yet another disastrous campaign in order to finish Antony forever in the eyes of the Roman people. Cleopatra, therefore, made use of every feminine artifice to persuade her husband to do her bidding.

CLEOPATRA AND JULIUS CAESAR   In this painting, the seductive queen graces the salon of the mighty Roman general. Some six years before her affair with Antony, the Egyptian queen had beguiled the great Roman emperor and had borne him twin sons.

Plutarch records that she "feigned to be dying for love of him; she starved herself to look ill. When he entered her room, she fixed upon him her eyes full of adoration; and when he left, she sighed in languor and seemed about to swoon away. She looked at him with eyes full of tears which she wiped surreptitiously, turning away her head as if to conceal her sorrow."

It comes as no surprise to learn that she won the day. Antony sent orders to Octavia in Athens to return immediately to Rome, and to resume her duties as a good wife should. Cleopatra quickly recovered her high spirits, taking Mark Antony back to Egypt with her. There she used her hold over him to advance the status of her country in general, and her capital Alexandria in particular. Moreover, she never missed an opportunity to convince him that the ultimate trial of strength must be between himself and Octavian.

The day of reckoning could not be long delayed. During Antony's long absence, Octavian had made himself undisputed master of Rome and of Italy, of all Gaul, Spain, and of two African provinces. He could call upon an army of forty legions. And since he had brought a period of peace and tranquility to a troubled empire, he was the most popular man in Rome. He was now twenty-seven—the adopted son of the great Julius Caesar. The only possible barrier to his supreme power was Mark Antony.

Happily for Octavian, his rival was now cavorting with a foreign queen already detested in Rome. Had not this same foreign enchantress also ensnared the godlike Julius?

CAESAR AUGUSTUS   This statue of the Roman general, also known as Octavian, stands in the Vatican Museum. The title "Augustus" was conferred upon him by the Roman Senate, in recognition of the wide reforms he instituted, and his establishment of the Pax Romana (Roman Peace). He is accounted to be one of the greatest of Roman rulers. Octavian is reputed to have said, "I found a Rome of brick, and left it of marble."

Octavian was as eager to be rid of Antony as Cleopatra was to sweep Octavian from her path to glory. The Egyptian beauty now saw herself as the founder of a vast new empire. She was already in command of all the realm of Alexander the Great save only Greece, Macedonia, and Thrace, and she now held sway over all the ancient kingdoms of the Pharaohs.

The two worlds were bound to hurl themselves upon each other. But first came the maneuverings and the battles of words. Antony proclaimed Cleopatra Queen of the territories in the east, a move that was denounced by Octavian in the Senate.

Octavian went further, reproaching his rival for dishonoring his lawful wife by openly preferring a foreign mistress. Antony retaliated by accusing Octavian of having a whole series of lovers, and of organizing infamous orgies.

ANTONY AND CLEOPATRA ON COINS   *This drawing done by P. Sellier from an ancient Roman silver coin was reproduced in Volume 3 of V. Duruy's "Histoire des Romains", published in Paris in 1882. These likenesses have little resemblance to the idealized sculptures shown in earlier pages in this chapter.*

Meanwhile, both sides feverishly prepared for war. Cleopatra took charge of the military and naval organization; she had come to realize that Antony was more interested in attending wine festivals than war conferences.

She also became more and more suspicious of her lover's real intentions. She discovered that he was secretly communicating with Octavian to negotiate yet another truce between them.

Then she made what was, to her, the most shocking discovery of all. Her spies reported an exchange of letters between Antony and Octavia, which showed that he was anxious to use his Roman wife as a mediator in the crisis. He was now fifty, a wine bibber, and growing too soft and lazy for heroic feats of arms. Cleopatra, nonetheless, was determined to screw his courage to the sticking point. After all, he was her only hope of overthrowing the might of Rome, and of achieving her ambition to be mistress of the world.

Now Octavian played his trump card. He had obtained the will of Mark Antony from the guardians of Rome's official documents. He called a special sitting of the Senate to denounce his rival. "It was obvious," he said, "that Cleopatra had corrupted Antony's mind by the use of philtres and love potions which had ruined his character and sapped his will. . . . Surely no Roman worthy of the name would make himself the consort of a foreign queen against Rome." He went on to sneer at the preparations for war being made in Egypt. "These are not being conducted," he said, "by Mark Antony, but by a General Staff consisting of a eunuch, a lady-in-waiting to Cleopatra, and the Queen's hairdresser. These are the military advisers to the noble Antony. Only a man completely bewitched by a woman could sink to such a level and abandon so completely his dignity and honor."

Then he flourished before the astonished Senate Mark Antony's will which he proceeded to read out. In that document, Antony had declared Caesarion to be Julius Caesar's true and legitimate son, and Antony had bequeathed large sums of money to his own three children by Cleopatra. The will also provided that

"should he die in Rome, his body should be carried in solemn pro-cession across the Forum, but afterwards be conveyed to Cleopatra in Alexandria and be buried there." Octavian suggested that Antony was bereft of his reason, and that the Senate should deprive the Egyptian Consort of his public offices in Rome.

Octavian also demanded a formal declaration of war against Cleopatra, Queen of Egypt. The Senate so decreed.

The issue between West and East was finally determined—as most schoolboys have been compelled to learn—by the great naval engagement at Actium on the west coast of Greece in the year 31 B.C., one of the decisive battles of the world. According to Plutarch, as the critical stage of the battle was reached, Cleopatra should have sent her naval squadrons in to help the hard-pressed Antony. In-stead, she gave the signal to retreat, and headed her flagship for the open sea—and Egypt.

On discovering that he was being deserted by his beloved ally, Antony forgot the battle and all that was at stake for him; he could think only of his mistress who was running away without even saying good-bye. He staggered about his ship, beating the air like a man demented, shouting "Cleopatra! Cleopatra!" Then, still wrap-ped in his scarlet cloak, he boarded a five-oared galley and chased after the Queen's purple-sailed flagship which had been named the *Antoniad*.

THE BATTLE OF ACTIUM   *An engraving by Herman Vogel show-ing the Egyptian queen aboard her barque during the disastrous encounter.*

When at last he caught up with her, the Queen took him aboard, neither of them speaking a word. Antony sat in the prow for two days and two nights, refusing to eat, clutching his head in his hands. Thus the two lovers who would rule the wide world fled from the scene of battle, leaving the day—and the entire civilized universe—to Octavian.

Back in Egypt, where Cleopatra claimed that the resounding defeat was a glorious victory, Antony built himself a little hideout by the sea near the Pharos lighthouse, where he sulked all alone. With unflagging courage and energy, Cleopatra went scouring Asia and Africa for alliances and armies—knowing that sooner or later the long arm of Octavian would reach out for them both. She was not prepared to sit and await her capture. She even got ready a gigantic escape operation, a fantastic project to drag her entire fleet across the desert to the Red Sea. She is also said to have tried out various poisons on condemned criminals to find out which would be the most effective for her, if fate decreed her death. She was clearly leaving nothing to chance.

When Octavian was quite ready, he began a cat-and-mouse game with Cleopatra. He sent a secret envoy to assure her that he bore her the most friendly sentiments, and would allow her to retain her throne and part of her exchequer, on one unnegotiable condition that she must prove to him that Antony was dead.

She rejected this offer with contempt, and it was probably as well she did, for the ancient chroniclers agree that Octavian had no intention of keeping his part of the bargain. What he was really after was to take Cleopatra and her children alive and then parade the captives in Rome. Octavian sought the delight of seeing his enemy publicly humiliated, and then ignominiously put to death.

The sands were now running out swiftly for the trapped couple. When Octavian reached Alexandria with a fleet, the Egyptian navy surrendered at once. As soon as the Roman forces landed, Antony's cavalry capitulated. Alexandria quickly fell to Octavian's mercy.

OCTAVIA   A portrait in the Louvre Museum in Paris.

What followed was the stuff beloved by tragedians. A false report reached Antony that Cleopatra had taken her life. He tried to commit suicide by falling on his sword, but missed the heart and lay critically wounded. The news that Cleopatra was alive roused the dying Antony who demanded to be carried to her. As she wept over her dying lover and their dead dreams, he implored her to seek terms from their enemy. Then he called for a goblet of wine, and drinking, died in her arms. A modern moviemaker could not have invented a more touching death scene; but according to classical historians, that is exactly how it happened.

There remained one last act in the double tragedy—the death of Cleopatra. Within minutes after Antony breathed his last, Cleopatra was put under house arrest by the emissaries of Octavian. She was under guard, with only her lover's body for company, in the great mausoleum which she had had built, according to the custom of Egypt's rulers, for her own tomb.

At first, Octavian was gracious. He allowed her to give Antony honorable burial, and she performed the complicated funeral rites over him. After that ordeal, she fell ill with fever and exhaustion. She was now thirty-eight. The tremendous strain of the past months was taking its full toll.

Octavian announced that he would pay her a visit of condolence. At first, she tried to bargain with him for her life and her throne—some said to charm him—even offering him a bundle of Julius Caesar's love letters as a bribe. But she found him coldly polite, and uncooperative. He did, however, grant her request to visit Antony's tomb on the following day. By this time, she must have been well aware that Octavian planned to turn her death into a Roman holiday.

Cleopatra ordered her ladies-in-waiting to dress and make her up to look her most regal. When she had finally approved her appearance, she sent Octavian a request to permit her body to be buried alongside that of Mark Antony. Octavian, realizing that his victim meant to elude his grasp, rushed to her mausoleum, to find her lying serene in the sleep of death, wearing a magnificent dress of white silk, and adorned with all her royal ornaments.

It is said that a peasant was admitted to her presence carrying a basket of figs in which lurked an asp, a tiny snake whose bite brings instant death. When Octavian examined her body, two tell-tale bites reputedly were found on her left arm.

So ended what we have all been taught to believe was one of the greatest love stories in the history of mankind. And indeed, with so many classical ingredients for high romance and deep tragedy present in its unfolding, it may seem churlish to cast the stone of doubt. But it is reasonable to put a more realistic interpretation on the actions and behavior of the two chief characters in this drama. It may be less romantic—but more accurate—to assess Queen Cleopatra as one of the ablest heads of state of her day. When she came to the throne, Egypt was a vassal of Rome, the glories of the Ptolemies were all in the past, and their empire had disintegrated. Cleopatra set out to make her country great again. As capable and intelligent as she was alluring, Cleopatra shrewdly realized that her personal and sexual magnetism offered her a potent weapon in gaining ascendancy over the most powerful man on earth—Julius Caesar. When his assassination wrecked her plans, she did not abandon her designs, but with astute calculation, set about finding the next most likely Roman to help her implement her objectives. How could she know that, compared with Caesar, Mark Antony was a featherweight, a good and brave commander at his best, but a vain and pleasure-loving playboy by nature, not the man to carry out the grand design of one born to rule all mankind—merely a handsome mediocrity.

Whether Antony truly loved Cleopatra or not is difficult to know. He enjoyed her, was captivated by her, and came to depend on her. But after their first passionate affair, he abandoned her for four years without a word or a message. Then, in need of her wealth, he picked up his affair where he left off. Even when he was about to launch his last great attack against Octavian, he was still

DEATH OF CLEOPATRA   In this picture by August Von Heckel, the Egyptian
queen has thwarted the vengeance of Augustus. She and her handmaiden have committed suicide. A trusted servant weeps over her body, while her arch enemy Augustus
Caesar stands with clenched fist, having been denied his revenge.

conniving with his Roman wife.

Perhaps one had best leave those two intriguing characters to mythology, where they have provided countless generations with a plot many dramatists have been unable to resist.

Justinian and Theodora

It was an improbable love story—the prostitute from the streets of Alexandria and the shepherd boy from Bulgaria. Together they restored the lost grandeur of the Roman Empire, won back the Eternal City from the barbarians, rebuilt the burned-out magnificence of Constantinople, and bequeathed to the world a code of laws still in use today. Improbable, but it all happened, in the sixth century A.D.

47

Constantinople, first built by Constantine and later to be know as Byzantium, was regarded in the sixth century as the new Rome, since Rome itself had fallen to the invading Goths. Flanked by the Bosporus and the Sea of Marmora, Constantinople had become the cornerstone of Byzantine culture and the heart of a new world. The Byzantine Emperors considered themselves the rightful successors to the great Caesars. Power was divided between the Emperor and the Christian Church headed by the Patriarch. Ornate churches had replaced the old temples. The imperial palaces were marvels of precious stone, silver, and mosaic. But the heart of this lovely city was corrupt. Alongside the glorious buildings and splendid monuments were brothels and gaming-houses. Pimps and hired assassins were everywhere, and it was dangerous to venture out of doors after dark.

In this city, Theodora plied her trade. She was only eighteen but had a lifetime of vice behind her. The daughter of a circus trainer of bears who had been hugged to death by one of his charges, she had been apprenticed in a brothel at the age of twelve. She had learned her erotic business so well that she was taken over by a celebrated madam, Antonina, and groomed into a top-class courtesan. In a magnificent house in the most fashionable quarter of Constantinople, she entertained the most distinguished and wealthy clientele. One of these regular visitors was appointed governor of Benghazi, and he persuaded Theodora to become the governor's lady there. But she quickly tired of being cooped up in the women's quarter of their official residence, and she ran away after having an affair with a young secretary. She bribed her way onto a ship bound for Alexandria, and landed at that Egyptian port, broke and hungry.

THE EMPRESS THEODORA   *A painting by Val Prinsep.*

After a while on the streets, she was taken in by a rich merchant from Antioch who housed her, but deserted her when she became pregnant.

Theodora was determined to get back to her native Constantinople. She joined a touring company of actors and actresses who took her along the coast of Syria. On the way, she had her baby, a son whom she named John. She reached Antioch to seek out the father, only to find he had died. So she left the boy on his grandmother's doorstep. Theodora had just turned eighteen.

During Theodora's three-year absence, Constantinople had acquired a new Emperor. This was Justin, an illiterate soldier who had left his native Bulgaria for the glittering capital of Byzantium. He had found success in the Imperial Guard, and had become commander of that select corps under the Emperor Anastasius.

In the midst of a palace revolution and bickering rival factions, Justin had managed to seize the throne in A.D. 518. He had been shrewd enough to realize that in all the intriguing, he needed a thoroughly reliable assistant. He had therefore sent back to Bulgaria for his nephew, Peter Sabbatius, on whom he lavished all the education and training that his money and power could command. Peter proved an apt pupil; and the former shepherd boy worked himself into a powerful court position. He was the undisputed heir apparent when Theodora came into his life.

Several different stories describe Theodora's first meeting with Peter Sabbatius. Theodora herself encouraged the fable that her Prince had discovered her in a quiet house in a residential street of Constantinople while she was demurely spinning wool and praying to the saints. But unfortunately for Theodora's story, Byzantium's court historian was also a gossip writer. This man, Procopius, was unimpressed with Theodora. He even made a point of collecting all possible tidbits about her former notorious life. Even worse, he put them down in his secret records and published his notes as soon as the Emperor and his controversial Empress were safely entombed in their vaults.

JUSTINIAN MEDALLION   *The Emperor, in this likeness, is dressed in complete military armor. Encircling his head is the conventionally stylized Imperial halo. The Latin translated inscription reads "Our Lord Justinian, Perpetual Augustus."*

THE EMPEROR JUSTINIAN   *This mosaic portrait of the em-*
peror—the best likeness of him in existence—is located in the apse of
the Church of San Vitale which he built in Ravenna.

According to Procopius, Theodora got a letter of introduction
from one of the actresses in the itinerant troupe which had brought
her and her illegitimate child back toward Constantinople. Her
problem was: how could she get near enough to the Prince to give

him the note? Theodora apparently wheedled her way past the guards, scrambled up a vine into his private apartments, "and so beguiled him with her seductive glances and provocative expressions" that he read her letter.

THE EMPRESS THEODORA   *Companion to the mosaic portrait of Justinian (opposite page) is this contemporary picture of Theodora and her court, also located in the apse of the Church of San Vitale.*

In any case, Theodora was soon installed in the palace where she began to fill in the considerable gaps in the Prince's sex education. She was, however, clever enough to see that he needed more than a mistress. He was then thirty-nine and knew little of life outside the court. Theodora convinced him that she was an expert on people—actually a fairly accurate claim. He came to depend more and more on her counsel and common sense, and he soon found her indispensable both in and out of bed. He installed her in an exquisite little house called Hormisdas, conveniently connected by a little-known stairway to the back entrance of the palace. The lovers often sneaked off together for secret trips on the Sea of Marmora.

Once the heir to the throne was in her power, Theodora concentrated on the all-important task of persuading him to marry her. Several obstacles hindered her: first, the Empress Euphemia; next, the Church and the Army; but most awkward of all, the law which explicitly forbade the nobility of the country from marrying actresses or prostitutes.

Nature removed the first obstacle: the Empress died. Theodora then concentrated on the Patriarch. She invited that unworldly dignitary to Hormisdas, and charmed him into believing that she was a gracious and misunderstood girl. Then old Justin fell ill; and his heir, suitably prompted by Theodora, persuaded him to sign a decree which authorized men of all ranks to marry the women of their choice, regardless of occupation. That achieved, the couple decided to risk the disapproval of the Army. They arranged a private and secluded wedding ceremony.

Theodora saw to it that her marriage settlement made her a partner in all her husband's business affairs. By an adroit maneuver, Peter Sabbatius took advantage of Justin's failing health to have himself nominated co-Emperor—"to preserve the status quo." He also took the name of Justinian. His maneuvering was just in time, for Justin died that same summer (527), and Justinian's elevation to the throne was automatic.

So the harlot became the Empress of Byzantium. For the first time in the history of Byzantium, Emperor and Empress were crowned together. When Court and Church saw Justinian and Theodora sitting side by side on the double throne, there was no doubt that the two would be co-rulers. A week after the Emperor had been anointed by the Patriarch in the Cathedral of St. Sophia, Theodora, too, was anointed and consecrated there.

The Empress, extremely sensitive about her notorious background, organized an army of spies to keep her informed of all the jokes and malicious gossip being spread about her in the city. At court she devised elaborate rituals to do her honor. Nobles admitted to her presence had to prostrate themselves before her and kiss her feet; they had to address her as "Basilissa," the ancient Greek title for *mighty queen,* and address her husband as "Basileus." She set great store by the insignia of the Purple Shoes, symbols of royal power which only the Emperor and Empress could wear. These shoes were believed to bestow fertility upon the Basilissa, for the Byzantines regarded the sole of the foot as having special sexual significance.

The ever-critical Procopius had a field day when Theodora turned her energies toward reclaiming fallen women. He wrote:

It was but natural that the Basilissa should exert herself in favor of her former colleagues. Five hundred prostitutes who used to ply publicly for trade around the Forum for a modest fee have been compulsorily invited by the Empress to join a new convent, "The Repentance," on the far shore of the Bosporus, as a well-deserved retreat for meditation. It appears, however, that monastic meditation is not entirely to the taste of such damsels, and many of them have chosen to cut short their chances of redemption by jumping into the sea at night.

However, Theodora was responsible for encouraging Justinian to begin the monumental work of codifying the complex tangle of

Roman law. He entrusted the task to Tribonian who set up a commission of jurists to weed out obsolete laws, to condense others, and to arrange the result in chronological order in one volume—the *Justinian Codex,* from which even today's laws have evolved. Jus-

THE HAGIA SOPHIA   This outstanding example of Byzantine architecture was erected by Justinian during the years 532-537. Most of the original artwork in this magnificent building was painted over when the church was turned into a mosque after Constantinople fell to the Turks in 1453. Hagia Sophia (Holy Wisdom) is now a museum of Byzantine art. Much work by the Turkish Government has been done to restore the original decoration.

EXTERIOR OF HAGIA SOPHIA   *The main dome, rebuilt by Justinian after a series of earthquakes, was completed two years before his death. It is 102 feet in diameter and 187 feet high. After the Turkish conquest, four minarets were added during different eras. The building remains the outstanding example of early Byzantine architecture.*

tinian thus won distinction as one of the outstanding lawgivers of all time.

It seems clear that Justinian was henpecked, and the wits of Constantinople were not slow to seize on the situation. Indeed, it is said to have been a contributory cause of the revolt against the

Palace in A.D. 532. Justinian had become known as "the Empress's consort" and nasty little ballads were heard all over the city:

*"Now Justinian the brave
Is become a woman's slave."*

It was also rumored that the Emperor was impotent. Theodora

THEODORA AND JUSTINIAN   These closeups show in detail the mosaic artwork on the previous pages.

had given him much, but not an heir. There were also more deep-seated causes of the mounting discontent—among them unemployment and the rising cost of living.

An ugly mob gathered. They burned and pillaged the homes of the wealthy, and then marched on the Palace. "Burn the golden brothel!" was their cry.

Theodora rose to the occasion. Dressed in a golden mantle and a gown of Tyrian purple, she stepped out on the balcony and faced the demonstrators. Her beauty and haughty courage stopped them short. Shrewdly, she promised them all bread and circuses in the city's sports arena, the Hippodrome. The crowd dispersed.

Theodora ordered an unprecedented spectacle to be organized in the Hippodrome for January 18, 532. She offered free food and drink, chariot races, gladiator combats—everything to attract the greatest possible audience. After the last event in that jam-packed stadium, the Commander-in-Chief of the Imperial Forces marched in at the head of his toughest battalion of mercenary troops and gave the order to slaughter the spectators. At the end of the day, they counted 30,000 dead.

Though the capital has been devastated, Justinian's throne was saved. Again prodded by Theodora, the Emperor began to build an even more beautiful city over the ruins. Again he chose his man well; the architect Anthemius proved to be a genius. The new St. Sophia became the glory of the Christian world.

But their greatest triumphs were to come. Together, Theodora and Justinian planned to reconquer the Roman Empire from the barbarians. Theodora probably helped select the man for that formidable task—Belisarius, the general who had married her old teacher in the arts of the courtesan, Antonina. The lucky pair had found yet another genius, for Belisarius lives in military history as one of the greatest tacticians of all time.

First, he wrenched back from the vandals the former Roman possessions in North Africa. He brought stupendous treasures to Constantinople, including the priceless furniture from King Solomon's Temple.

Justinian then assigned Belisarius his major challenge—to win back Italy from the Goth kings. After a brilliant campaign, the great soldier conquered the Eternal City for his Emperor who was now truly a Caesar.

By this time, Theodora was meddling in every aspect of the

ANCIENT HIPPODROME   *This engraving of the hippodrome of Theodora's day was published in Venice in 1600, the
artist having drawn from a fifteenth century representation.*

Empire's affairs. She even appointed her own Pope in Rome.

Then Constantinople was scourged by bubonic plague, and
Justinian himself fell ill. Theodora took his place at all official
ceremonies, and spent each night at his bedside. The Emperor was
completely dependent on his "Gift from God," the literal mean-

ing of her name. He recovered from his illness, but his mind was impaired. Theodora was now the undisputed power in the Empire.

Her power corrupted her even further. She became domineering, magalomaniac, cruel. Belisarius, the popular hero, threatened to dim her luster, so she chose to humiliate him. She maneuvered with his wife Antonina who had grown tired of him, and Theodora contrived to deprive Belisarius of his command, and confiscated two-thirds of his property. She timed her stroke well: people were too busy burying their dead and escaping the plague to defend their general. It was ironic, though, that the man who defeated the barbarians should submit meekly to disgrace at the hands of a power-mad woman.

But Theodora was finally out-maneuvered by another woman. She had interfered even further with Antonina's family affairs by trying to force a marriage between her own nephew and a daughter of Antonina and Belisarius. Her former partner in vice frustrated that design, and decided to cut Theodora down to size.

One day, an old man from Antioch sought an audience with the Empress. He had reared Theodora's illegitimate—and only— son. The son, John, was a musician, a handsome, strapping youth, now seventeen. His guardian had brought him to Constantinople to re-unite him with his mother, and to secure a glittering future for him. John, who did not know the secret of his birth, stirred all the long-suppressed maternal feelings in Theodora. She insisted that her secret should not be revealed to him, but she made him her private flute player, and found a way to see him every day.

Soon she realized that the impressionable youth had fallen in love with his Empress and patroness. Because of her tender affection for him, he imagined that his passion was reciprocated. The vengeful Antonina knew all about their clandestine meetings, and put the worst construction upon them. She alerted Justinian's spies. Upon overhearing what they thought to be lovers' endearments, they reported back to the Emperor. Justinian was beside himself with rage and grief. He ordered the young man's immediate arrest and gave secret instructions: John was to be tortured and put to death that same night.

Justinian's officer relayed the orders to the Palace executioner, but considered it diplomatic to let Theodora know what was to happen. Horrified, she quickly told Justinian the true identity of young John, and demanded his immediate release.

A sprightly officer was sent racing down the ten floors to the dungeons to stop the torture. The Emperor and Empress clattered after him. The execution chamber was tucked far away behind a labyrinth of stairways and passages, and the dungeons had been built so that the screams of the damned could not be heard. When Theodora arrived, the only sound was the heavy breathing of the executioner who was wiping the blood off his sword.

This, her son's death, was the greatest tragedy of her reign, and significantly changed her way of life. She had been plotting for Justinian to accept the luckless John as their heir apparent. Now there was no possibility that she would give the Emperor an heir. Her arrogant spirit crumpled, and she turned to religion for solace, building magnificent churches, including the Church of the Apostles by Anthemius, and concentrating on leaving splendid memorials of herself as the greatest of all the Empresses.

In the spring of the year 548, she sought peace and serenity on a small island on the Sea of Marmora. There, she died of cancer at the age of forty-seven. Her last request was in keeping with her old self: "Bathe my body in oil of roses, and sprinkle it with rare perfume."

Justinian, of course, was utterly lost without her. He kept all her court favorites in power, and carried on her policies as though by divine command. He mourned her until the day of his death.

The last word on Theodora, however, was spoken by the Orthodox Church: it made her a saint.

Charles II
and
Nell Gwynne

King Charles II of England, while married to a barren queen, kept scores of mistresses and acknowledged fourteen illegitimate children. Marguerite de Carteret, Lucy Walter, Catherine Pegge, Barbara Villiers, Louise de la Valliere and Louise de Perroncour de Querouaille—to mention but a few of his paramours—are now nearly forgotten. One of his favorites, however, has become a legend. Reared in a brothel, and formerly employed as a pothouse

wench, orange-seller, actress and whore, she nevertheless attained the royal bed. Who has not heard of Nell Gwynne?

Nell Gwynne's reputation has endured for three hundred years, and each century has adapted her story to the mood of the age. In her own time she was the subject of hundreds of anecdotes, lampoons, plays, memoirs and histories—most of them ribald. Then, by Victorian times, attitudes changed. Victorians saw her as "sweet Nell of Old Drury," the classic moral example of a child who rose from slum to palace and died repenting her sins.

All the available evidence suggests that Nell was proud of being a royal whore—and made no secret of it. When her great rival for the King's bed, Louise de Querouaille, was created Duchess of Portsmouth, Nell wore "an exceeding rich suit of clothes" to confront her. The new duchess said patronizingly, "Nelly, you are grown rich, I believe, by your dress; why, woman, you are fine enough to be a queen." "You are entirely right, madam," replied Nell, "and I am whore enough to be a duchess." And she once told her two sons by Charles that they were "princes by their father for their elevation, but they had a whore for their mother to their humiliation."

THE KING'S MISTRESS   *This painting of Nell Gwynne depicts the beauty in the full flower of her youth.*

Today, any mention of Nell Gwynne is still reasonably certain to produce a chuckle, a grin, or a knowing wink—but no malice. How is it that "pretty, witty Nell" is still held in affection? According to one of her twentieth-century biographers, Arthur Irwin Dasent:

> *English men, and women too, have always entertained a peculiar liking for Mistress Nell, whilst rightly withholding their sympathy from such kittle cattle as Barbara Villiers and Louise de Querouaille, her two principal rivals in the King's affections. They, though of better birth and exposed to fewer temptations, are remembered, if at all, as having been two of the most rapacious and unscrupulous harpies who ever disgraced an English court.*
>
> *On the other hand, Nell's invariable kindness to the poor and needy—the class from which she sprang—after she had been raised from grinding poverty to comparative affluence, has been the mainspring of the remarkable interest which has centered round her name.*
>
> *Successive generations have extended to her an indulgence seldom conceded to the fair and frail in any age or in any country. . . . There is abundant evidence that she had a generous and a tender heart, frequently exerting her influence with the King (to whom she was not only sincerely attached but consistently faithful) for good and worthy objects. . . .*

According to her horoscope, which is still preserved in the Bodleian Library, Oxford, Ellen Gwynne was born at 6 A.M. on Saturday, February 2, 1650. Her birthplace is in doubt, as London, Hereford and Oxford all claim the honor—but she was probably born in or near Covent Garden, at a small house in a squalid alley called the Coal Yard, Drury Lane. Little is known of her father, but her mother was a thoroughly disreputable character. Old Madam

Gwynne was an enormously fat woman who smoked and drank to excess and in her youth had been "skilled in acts of gallantry." She kept a bawdy-house in the Covent Garden district until Nell set her up in a respectable Chelsea residence. In July, 1679, after a hearty debauch, Madam Gwynne fell into a stream and was drowned.

Nell is quoted as saying that she was brought up "in a bawdy-house to fill strong waters for the guests." In mid-seventeenth-century London it was a feat for a slum child to survive, and at thirteen Nell had a lifetime of experience behind her—serving ale and brandy, selling herring and fruit in the streets, outwitting pick-pockets and fending off seducers.

Shortly after the Restoration of King Charles, two theatrical companies, the Duke's Company and the King's Company, estab-lished theatres in Lincoln's Inn Fields. The King's Company pros-pered and set up a larger theatre off Drury Lane. Here, thirteen-year-old Nell plied her celebrated trade of selling small oranges to the gentlemen who paid half-a-crown to sit on the backless benches of the pit. If she needed further education in the arts of badinage and profanity, Nell got it in the pit of the King's Theatre, working six days a week and augmenting her small earnings by obliging the gentlemen after hours. Determined to get out of the pit and onto the stage, she learned to read—but not to write. She took lessons in dancing, singing and elocution. Since there was a desperate short-age of actresses, Nell soon got her chance—no doubt by way of the "casting couch." Soon she became one of the most acclaimed com-edy stars of her day.

Although the stage was a considerable step up from the pit, acting was in those days still a disreputable occupation for ladies. Like many other successful actresses, Nell was happy to leave when a suitably wealthy man offered to keep her. Nell's admirers had one thing in common—their Christian names. First, there was the actor Charles Hart, a tall, handsome fellow; next there was Charles, Lord Buckhurst; and finally, Charles II—whom Nell once remarked was her Charles the Third. Dasent gives this account of her first meeting with the monarch:

> *Nell's personal appearance at this time—she was now seventeen—must have been extremely attractive. She was of middle height, exquisitely formed, with the smallest foot and the neatest ankle in all the town. Her hair was bronze-red, sun-kissed with streaks of gold, her luxuriant tresses falling in silken waves over shapely, snow-white shoulders. Her eyes were of the darkest imaginable shade of sapphire blue, her mouth a perfect Cupid's bow, revealing when she smiled two rows of small but evenly-matched pearly teeth. She had a complexion like the wild rose, a skin of satin and a well-shaped, if, as some say, a tip-tilted nose.*
>
> *But perhaps the greatest beauty of her face, and it is one that is seldom or never found in those of plebeian birth, was that her eyebrows and eyelashes were dark, in striking contrast to her warm red hair.*

Young Villiers, the Duke of Buckingham, escorted Nell to a play in the rival theatre, the Duke's, one afternoon. King Charles sat in the next box, incognito. Charles, to Villiers' embarrassment, struck up conversation with Nell, then invited both to supper where he made sure that his brother, the Duke of York, occupied Villiers' attention while he himself monopolized Nell. Dasent describes the scene:

> *They made a merry party of four at a neighboring tavern, where Charles, who could make himself well-nigh irresistible to women once his desires were aroused, paid such marked attention to Nell throughout the evening that the quick-witted girl could not fail to perceive the inner meaning of his gallantry.*
>
> *When the tavern-keeper, unaware of the rank and*

THE LAUGHING AUDIENCE   *Hogarth, the master
satirist, affords a glimpse of the theatre of Nell Gwynne's day.
Miss Gwynne must have often seen such faces when she acted in
the Theatre Royale.*

quality of his guests, presented his bill to the King as the senior member of the party, Charles fumbled in his pockets only to find that he had not enough money with him to discharge it. The Duke of York being found to be equally impecunious, Villiers had to pay the reckoning, not only for himself and his inamorata, but for all four.

Nell, amused beyond measure at the comicality of the situation, burst into fits of laughter and, mimicked to perfection the King's tone and usual mode of expression, "Odds fish! But this is the poorest company that ever I was in before at a tavern."

Instead of being angry with her for laughing at him, Charles was so captivated by her high spirits that he promptly imagined himself to be head over heels in love. No doubt he had thought much the same dozens of times before, but so rapidly did this new-born passion develop that, before the party broke up, he declared his royal will and pleasure to be that Nell should retire from the stage at the earliest possible moment, and place herself under his protection.

Samuel Pepys the diarist—himself an unsuccessful admirer of Nell—notes for January 11, 1668, that "the King did send several times for Nelly, and she was with him. . . ."

In Restoration England, freed from Puritan repression, King Charles and his Court went on a gigantic debauch, with whoring and gaming the favorite pastimes. Many of the wealthier citizens followed the royal pattern. Keeping a mistress was a popular practice, and the husband who resented his wife's extramarital activities was regarded as a spoilsport. Other people, who clung to Puritan attitudes, regarded the two major disasters which overwhelmed London during 1665-67—the Plague and the Great Fire—as a judgment of God on the wicked city. The theatres were shut down and the Court retreated to Oxford.

SAMUEL PEPYS, ESQ. *Pepys'*
lusty and untrammeled diary, a record
of the daily life and reflections of an
ambitious, observing, and fun-loving
young man, extends from 1660 to
1669, and gives a graphic picture of
the early Restoration period.

In May, 1670, the fruits of Nell's royal liaison became apparent—and she named her first-born Charles. Moved by her
pleading, the King set her up in a small house at the east end of
Pall Mall—one of the poorest dwellings in the neighborhood. Nell
was still his whore; she had not yet achieved the decent status of
mistress. She tried desperately to get her son acknowledged, and
she badgered the King for dignities and pensions, but Charles did
nothing. Then Nell changed the situation dramatically by doing
something no royal favorite had dreamed of doing—she went back
to the stage. The King's Company made her doubly welcome at Old
Drury—now they could cash in on her notoriety as mother of a
royal bastard. The sly topical allusions were too much for Charles.
He negotiated the leasehold of a house on the better side of Pall

Mall, the house Nell was to live in for the rest of her life. She had now arrived as a mistress. She gave sittings ("naked, leaning on a bed with her child") to the fashionable portrait painter, Sir Peter Lely, and the King made many visits to his studio. In 1671 her second son was born. She named him James, after Charles's brother, later James II.

Nell tried all she knew to win honors for her sons and herself, but in court intrigue she was only an amateur compared to her chief rivals for the King's favors, Barbara Villiers and Louise de Querouaille. Both Villiers and de Querouaille had wheedled the rank of duchess out of the weak and easy-going Charles. But in December, 1676, a warrant was passed for "a grant to Charles Beauclerc, the King's natural son (by Nell) and to the heirs male of his body, of the dignities of Baron of Heddington, Co. Oxford, and Earl of Burford in the same county, with remainder to his brother, James Beauclerc, and the heirs male of his body." And the King granted both children the right to wear the royal arms crossed with a bar sinister. At last, after six years of her scheming, pleading and wheedling, her first-born was a peer of the realm and Nell could claim to be the equal of the court ladies. She had another great ambition, though—to be a countess in her own right. Poor Nell was to die without achieving that status, but on January 5, 1684, her son was exalted to the title of the first Duke of St. Albans with all rights and privileges vested in that rank. Her second son, James, died after an accident in France at the age of eight.

CHARLES II

GOD·SAVE THE KING

CHARLES Y̆ 2ᵈ BY THE GRACE OF
GOD KING OF ENGLAND SCOTLAND
FRANCE & IRELAND Defender of y̆ faith
Began his Reign over his subiects the 30 of Ianuary 1648
at the which time the Bloody Regicides so barbarously Murdered his father

This preferment of her elder son dramatically changed the attitude of the Court toward her. She was no longer shrugged off as a rough-tongued comedienne, but accepted by all her aristocratic neighbors at the better end of Pall Mall and St. James'. True, some of the King's diehard Ministers were reluctant to acknowledge her new status as the mother of a royal duke, and a few haughty ladies were outraged at the appearance in their midst of a former actress and orange girl. The Dowager Duchess of Richmond once told the King that "she could not abide to converse with Nell and the rest of that gang." Charles sharply informed her that those he "lay with were fit company for the greatest woman in the land." And the wife of the Keeper of Whitehall Palace dared to call Nell "whore" to her face. Nell replied swiftly that if anyone else had called her so she would not have objected, but it afflicted her to be called so by one who had been "an old notorious whore even before whoring was in fashion."

There is, too, a famous story of her footman whom she found one day bleeding and disheveled. She asked him to explain his sorry condition. He told her: "I have been fighting, madam, with an impudent rascal who called your ladyship a whore." "Blockhead!" said Nell. "At this rate you must fight every day of your life. Why, all the world knows it!" "Do they so?" cried the footman. "Well, they shan't call me a whore's footman for all that."

NELL GWYNNE'S LODGINGS IN DRURY LANE
This watercolor, executed in 1850 by J. Findlay, must be some-what apocryphal for the scene was drawn some 200 years after Nell Gwynne had her lodgings in the inn known as the Cock and Magpie.

When it became known that she was giving a birthday party for the King, Lady Shrewsbury hinted that she would welcome an invitation. "No, no," said Nell. "One whore at a time is enough for His Majesty." She had to beat off many contenders for the royal bed. One of these was another actress, Moll Davis, and it is said that she and Nell at one time used to take turns to accommodate the lusty Charles. But Nell decided to eliminate the other. She invited Moll to supper before visiting the King and put a powerful purgative in her food—with predictable consequences.

Without doubt her natural wit and rumbustiousness captivated Charles II, who loved her in his own wavering fashion. Remarkably, she retained her hold on his capricious affections for seventeen years despite the comings and goings of a succession of high-born ladies, the intrigues of courtiers and politicians against her, and the libelous pamphleteering of poets and playwrights who could not resist the target. King Charles was considering a plan to reward her long and faithful service to the Crown by making her the Countess of Greenwich, thus granting her heart's desire. But the years of wenching and hard drinking caught up with him. John Evelyn, the aristocratic diarist of that day, writes of Sunday night, February 1. He witnessed "the inexpressible luxury and profaneness" of the Court at Whitehall with King Charles "sitting and toying with his concubines, Portsmouth (Louise), Cleveland (Barbara), et cetera." (The words "et cetera" refer to Nell, whose name Evelyn could rarely bring himself to write.) The party broke up, and Nell kissed her royal lover. She was driven across the part to her house in Pall Mall, blissfully unaware that she would never see him alive again.

NELL GWYNNE   *This portrait by the Dutch artist, Sir Peter Lely (1618-1680), amply conveys the voluptuous attraction of the famed beauty.*

THE ORGY AT THE ROSE TAVERN   *A satirical print by William Hogarth, which
is as remarkable for the characters' lack of manners as for their unbridled sensuality.*

While dressing the next morning, the King suffered a fit. For four days he lay in extreme agony while physicians tried all possible means to ease him. His mistresses were kept in an antechamber while the Queen, his close friends and some of his natural children knelt by the bedside. He spoke tenderly to all and murmured to his brother, the Duke of York, that he was sorry to be so long a-dying. He commended his children to his brother's care. Then he added a phrase which has come down the centuries: "Let not poor Nelly starve." He died on February 6 in the twenty-sixth year of his reign, the fifty-fourth of his life. A few hours later his brother was proclaimed King James II.

JAMES, LORD BEAUCLERC   One of Nell Gwynne's two sons by Charles II. (The other son was titled the Duke of St. Albans.)

No one is accorded less sympathy than a dead king's mistress. Nell, who had just turned thirty-five, found a pack of creditors howling at her doors. Her annual £5,000 pension ceased with Charles' death. Her unlimited credit, too, was now ended.

James II was an honorable man, though not generous, but he was surrounded by priests and Nell could not appeal to him in person. After smuggling messages to him through the Keeper of the Privy Purse, she received assurance that the new King would take care of her business in due time. But he was occupied with affairs of state, including a spring session of Parliament. Nell would obviously have to wait, though her creditors could not. She mortgaged what she could, borrowed what she could, and raised some £6,000 on her jewels and plate, but was still approximately £700 short of satisfying the creditors. In May she sent King James a note which began: "Had I suffered for my God as I have done for your brother and you, I should not have needed either of your kindness or justice to me." Upon this reminder, the King sent her a considerable sum of money with "kind expressions and assurances for the future."

Nell was delighted. She replied: "This world is not capable of giving me a greater joy and happiness than your Majesty's favor. . . . All you do for me shall be yours, it being my resolution never to have any interest but yours, and as long as I live to serve you, and when I die, to die praying for you." But she could not refrain from mentioning the dead Charles. "He told me before he died," she said, "that the world should see by what he did for me that he had love and value for me. . . . He was my friend and allowed me to tell him all my griefs, and did like a friend advise me and told me who was my friend and who was not." In September she had another pleasant surprise from King James. He paid off the £700 that she still owed. In addition he gave her a Treasury note for £1,300 to be drawn at once, and in December two cash payments of £500 out of the Secret Service funds. And he settled on her a pension of £1,500 a year from January 1, 1686.

She did not enjoy it for long. Early in March, 1687, she was stricken with apoplexy which paralyzed one side of her body. Like her lover, Charles II, she suffered from what was euphemistically called "the gallant disease," contracted from one of her early lovers and now reaching its final stages, with hardening of the arteries and high blood pressure. Clergymen surrounded her; they urged repentance, confession and piety. Nell was only vaguely aware that she had sinned. She had been a whore in an age when whoring was a recognized trade. She had loved pleasure, but she had given much, too, both as entertainer and lover. She was, however, prevailed upon to repent. In her will, she remembered everybody. She gave small bequests to the poor of St. Martin's Church and added a request to her son, the Duke of St. Albans, that he "lay out twenty pounds a year for the releasing of poor debtors out of prison every Christmas Day." She also bequeathed £50 for the use of the Roman Catholic poor of the parish—to show charity to those who differed from her in religion.

CHARLES II   In this oil on canvas by John Michael Wright (1625-1700), the King of Great Britain and Ireland, 1660-1685, is dressed in his robes of office. His Majesty holds the Orb of England, and wears a formal periwig.

GIN LANE   This print by the famous William Hogarth depicts quite clearly the London from which Nell Gwynne sprang. The lines over the tavern door reflect upon the evils of drink.

Nell clung tenaciously to life through the summer and autumn of 1687, but on November 14 she died. She was buried three days later in the chancel of St. Martin's with pomp befitting the mother of a royal duke. Dr. Tenison, rector of St. Martin's, preached his funeral sermon on the text: "Joy shall be in Heaven over one sinner that repenteth, more than over ninety and nine just persons who need no repentance."

And so Nell Gwynne was given over to legend. One of her recent biographers, John Harold Wilson, sums her up thus:

> *Friendly and kind, witty and giddy, honest and loyal, Nell was above all ambitious and hard-working. By nature humorous, pleasure-loving and frankly carnal, she chose prostitution as an honorable and lucrative profession in an age when the successful courtesan was socially approved. Brought up in the rough schools of bawdy-house and Restoration theatre, she quickly grew skilled in the art of pleasing, and with honest realism she employed her skill to get far more out of life than her birth and breeding warranted. Although she never attained her ambition to be a countess, she kept the affections of King Charles II for seventeen years against formidable competition, founded a line of noble descendants entitled to wear the bar sinister on their shields and left a son rich in dignities and property. She earned every bit of her success.*

Napoleon
and
Josephine

She was christened Marie-Joseph-Rose Tascher de la Pagerie, but to the French at the height of Napoleon's success she was Our Lady of Victories, to her enemies she was "the lewd Creole," and to Napoleon himself—she was Josephine. Born on June 23, 1763, on a plantation on the slopes above Fort-Royal Bay on the Caribbean coast of Martinique, she was destined to be crowned Empress of France.

JOSEPHINE   *A portrait of the Empress by Baron Francois Gerard, Napoleon's court painter, convincingly records her fabled beauty.*

When Napoleon first set eyes on her in 1795, she was in her thirty-second year, with one marriage, two children, and many affairs behind her. Her husband, Alexandre de Beauharnais, had lost his head to Robespierre's guillotine, and she had narrowly escaped the same fate. But now the Terror was over and a right-wing counterrevolution was under way. Paul Barras, an elegant, scheming, and unscrupulous politician, whose mistress she had been for a year, was appointed commander-in-chief of the Army of the Interior. He chose Napoleon Buonaparte as his second-in-command; and together, the ruthless pair mowed down the mobs with grapeshot and restored order in Paris. When Napoleon ordered all citizens of Paris to disarm, Marie-Rose (as she was then known) sought his permission to retain her husband's sword for her son Eugene. This Buonaparte granted, and she called on him to thank him for the gesture. Napoleon fell in love with her at first sight. He was then 26.

To him, she seemed to have all the social accomplishments that he lacked. He was gawky and shy in distinguished company; she was elegant, graceful, and at ease. He was an outsider; she belonged. Whether Napoleon knew of her year with Barras or not —and Barras later claimed that he did—he had set his heart on having her, and the world was to learn that what Napoleon wanted, Napoleon usually got.

Nine days after his "whiff of grapeshot" had pacified Paris, he was a lieutenant-general; and ten days after that, a full general commanding the Army of the Interior. Clearly, he was marked for greatness.

Marie-Rose was flattered by his ardor—and impressed by his prospects. On February 9, 1796, she agreed to marry him. A fortnight later, he was appointed commander-in-chief of the Army of Italy, and the marriage arrangements were accordingly speeded up. The ceremony was held in a town hall on March 9; Barras was one of Napoleon's two witnesses.

Napoleon was nearly two hours late for his wedding, so engrossed was he in his plans for the campaign in Italy. There were no relatives present from either side. He had not dared to tell his family in Corsica that he was going to marry a stranger to them; and Marie-Rose was afraid to bring either her son Eugene or her daughter Hortense, lest they show open hostility to her bridegroom. Both gave their ages as 28—he gallantly, for he was not yet 27; she discreetly, for she was approaching her thirty-third birthday.

One immediate consequence of the marriage was a change in her name from Marie-Rose to Josephine, his pet name for her; and a change in the spelling of his name—the Italian Buonaparte became the French Bonaparte. Although he was most anxious to placate her children, he only succeeded in terrifying Hortense by pinching her ear affectionately; Eugene remained respectful but suspicious.

Their honeymoon lasted 36 hours, then he was off to convert the ill-equipped and undisciplined rabble—the French Army of Italy—into an effective fighting force. He had 30 thousand men in tatters to pit against a combined Austrian and Sardinian force of 60 thousand; yet he was so offhandedly confident, he told Josephine to join him in Milan as soon as he had captured that city. In the meantime, he wrote passionate love letters addressed to Citizeness Bonaparte:

> *Every moment takes me farther from you, my adorable love, and at every moment I find less strength to be parted from you. You are the constant object of my thoughts and my imagination exhausts itself in wondering what you are doing. If I see you sad, my heart is torn and my anguish increases; if you are gay and foolish with your women friends, I reproach you for having quickly forgotten our painful separation three days ago—then you are fickle and unmoved by deep feelings. . . . Ah! do not be gay, but a little melancholy, and, above all, may your soul be as free from sadness as your beautiful body from sickness. . . .*

His first love letters, known to historians variously as the *Honeymoon Letters,* the *Letters of Delirium,* or more prosaically, the *Letters from Italy,* have become as famous as the story of his feats of arms. Their tone is sometimes savage, sometimes tender; sometimes enraptured, sometimes tormented; sometimes philosophical, sometimes erotic. They are much more than the outpourings of a first love; they are the expression of a powerful intellect, and the manifestation of a personality that was to dominate the century and hold the entire world in awe. They were scrawled on top of anything that came to hand—a camp table, perhaps a map box; and they were written by the light of a campfire in a nearly illegible script which was the despair of all who tried to decipher his scrawl.

He wrote at least twice a day during his Italian campaign; yet of these letters only 42 have survived. They are unique for they offer a glimpse of a man of supreme genius in his unguarded moments before he became aware of posterity. In a way he was never to repeat, he reveals in these letters his inner self, without a trace of self-consciousness. And these letters, above all, illustrate the doubts, jealousies, and suspicions that plagued Napoleon the Lover before Josephine lost him to history.

The following epistle was written at Nice on March 30, 1796:

Not one day has passed that I have not loved you, not one night that I have not clasped you in my arms. I have not drunk so much as a cup of tea without cursing the call of glory and ambition which have wrenched me from you who are my life, my soul. In the midst of military affairs, at the head of my troops, in my inspections of the camps, my adorable Josephine holds undisputed sway over my heart, possesses my mind, engrosses my thoughts. If I travel away from you with the swiftness of the torrent of the River Rhone, it is only in order to see you again the sooner. If in the middle of the night I arise from my bed to work, it is only because I may thus advance by some few hours the moment of the arrival of my beloved.

And yet, in your letter dated 23–26 Ventome [13-16 March] you address me formally as "You" [Vous]. "You" thyself! Ah, wicked one, how could you have written that letter? How cold it is! And besides, begun on the thirteenth, not completed until the sixteenth—a lapse of four whole days. What were you doing all that time that you could not finish a letter to your husband? Oh, my darling, that formal "You" instead of the familiar "Thou," those four lapsed days, make me rue my formerly indifferent heart. . . . "You!" "You!" Ah, what will it be two weeks from now?

My soul is saddened, my heart enslaved, my imagination frightens me. . . . You love me less; you will find consolation elsewhere; someday you will cease loving me. Then tell me so. I should at least know how I have merited the misfortune. . . .

I ask of you neither eternal love nor fidelity, but only truth, utter honesty. The day upon which you should say "I love you less" would be the last day of my love—or the last day of my life. Were my heart so base as to love unrequited, I would gnash it between my teeth. . . .

Ah, Josephine! Remember what I have told you before: Nature created my soul strong and resolute, yours She wrought out of gossamer and lace.

Have you left off loving me? Forgive me, light of my life: my mind must encompass projects vast in scope, but my heart is given over utterly to you, and it is assailed by fears which make me wretched. Adieu! Ah, if you love me less, it can only be that you have never loved me. Then I should become indeed an object of pity.

P.S. The war, this year, is no longer recognizable. I have ordered the issuance of meat, bread, and forage to

*my troops. My armed cavalry will soon be on the move.
My soldiers manifest an inexpressible confidence in me.
You alone cause me anxiety. You alone, the delight and
torment of my life. A kiss for your children—whom you
do not even mention. But that, Pardieu! would cost you
the writing of a letter half as long again. And that would*

*HUMBLE BEGINNINGS   This building in Ajaccio on the island
of Corsica is reputed to be the house in which Napoleon was reared.*

NAPOLEON AS FIRST CONSUL

mean that all those visitors arriving at ten o'clock to pay their morning call would be deprived of the pleasure of your company! Women!!!

Before going to Nice where his bedraggled army awaited him, he stopped at Marseilles to conduct another difficult campaign—that of persuading his mother and family to accept his marriage to Josephine. In his impatience to wed, he had committed a grave offense in the eyes of his family—he had not asked formal permission of its head, his eldest brother Joseph, nor had he warned his mother of his intention. She was a tough, unbending Corsican traditionalist who had often ridden beside her husband in punitive forays, and had borne 12 children before she was widowed at 35; to her, Napoleon's choice of this frivolous Parisian spendthrift was disastrous. It took him three days of argument and every sort of persuasion before his mother would agree to answer the dutiful daughter-in-law letter which he had brought her from Josephine. The reply was composed by the three daughters and reluctantly signed "Mme. Letitzia Buonaparte."

But if his mother's letter to his bride was stiff and formal, his must surely have compensated for it. He wrote:

My incomparable Josephine, away from you there is no happiness. Away from you the world is a desert. . . . You have taken more than my soul; you are the only thought in my life. If I am weary of the burden of my work, if men disgust me, if I am ready to curse life itself, I put my hand on my heart, your portrait beats there: I gaze at it and love is for me an absolute happiness and all is smiling, except for the time that I am absent from my sweetheart. . . . To live for Josephine, that is the story of my life.·. . . Farewell, farewell, I lie down without you, I shall sleep without you. I beg you, let me sleep. For many nights I have felt you in my arms, but—but it is not

you. Soul of my existence, write to me by every courier,
I cannot live otherwise. . . .

Living for Josephine was hardly to prove the whole story of
Napoleon's life, but he brought to love the same all-consuming con-
centration that he brought to battle. She, on the other hand, grew
to love her fiery, unpredictable Corsican so much that he filled her
entire existence. While he was proving to France that he was a military genius by fighting six battles in a fortnight with his threadbare
soldiers and exacting a surrender from the Sardinians, she was in
Paris, feeling poorly. Perhaps she was pregnant? He would have
been overjoyed, for he took time off from marching and fighting to
tell her: "A souvenir from my incomparable wife and a victory from
destiny: those are my desires. A unique, complete souvenir, worthy
of him who thinks of you at every moment."

He kept imploring her to join him, but at first the Directory
refused to give her permission, lest her presence distract him from
his military duties. As usual, he solved the problem by a resounding
victory. After defeating the Sardinians, he turned on the Austrians,
drove them before him, won the bloody battle of the Lodi Bridge,
and swept into Milan—all within one week. On May 21, the Directory informed him that they no longer objected to Josephine's
joining him. Although her pregnancy was a false alarm, the journey
she faced was nonetheless long and rough. For a variety of reasons,
she did not set off until June 26. Napoleon fumed at the delay, and
suspected that she was either ill or unfaithful. Finally he could
restrain himself no longer, and dashed off this letter to her:

My life is a constant nightmare. A deadly presenti-
ment prevents me from breathing. I no longer live. I have
lost more than life, more than happiness, more than re-
pose. I am almost without hope. I am sending you a cou-
rier. He will stay only four hours in Paris and then will
bring me your reply. Write me ten pages. . . . You are
ill, you love me, I have upset you, you are pregnant and

NAPOLEON AS GENERAL   The great tactician leads his army
to the Battle of Jena. The painting was done by Horace Vernet.

*I do not see you. . . . I have wronged you so much that I
do not know how to make amends. I accused you of remaining in Paris. You were ill there. Pardon me, my dearest; the love which you inspire in me has taken away my
reason; I shall never regain it. . . . My forebodings are so*

deadly that I think of nothing except seeing you, to press
you for two hours against my breast and we die together.
. . . I dare not tell you not to undertake the long, hot
journey if you are able to. Come by short stages, write to
me every night and send the letters ahead of you. In your
letter, my dearest, be sure to tell me you are convinced
that I love you beyond anything that can be imagined;
that you are persuaded that every moment of my life is
devoted to you; that not an hour passes when I do not
think of you; that it has never entered my head to think of
other women; that in my eyes they are all without grace,
without beauty, without wit; that you, you alone as I see
you and as you are, can delight me and absorb all the
faculties of my mind; that you have conquered every
part of it; that my heart has no corner that you have not
seen, no thoughts which are not subordinate to you; that
my strength, my arms, my spirit are all yours; that my soul
is in your body and the day that you changed or ceased to
be would be the day of my death; that Nature, the world,
is beautiful for me only because you dwell in it. . . .

When she did reach Milan—her retinue including her ill-
tempered pug, Fortuné—Napoleon was not there but farther south,
overseeing the siege of Mantua. On his return there was a passionate reunion, broken off each day by urgent calls to arms. Between visits to the front he wrote her:

Ever since I left you I have been sad. My happiness is to
be with you. Ceaselessly I recall your kisses, your tears,
your sweet jealousy; and the charms of the incomparable
Josephine constantly light a bright, burning flame in my
heart and my senses. . . . I thought I loved you days ago,
but since I have seen you I feel that I love you a thousand
times more. . . . Ah! I beg you to let me see some faults
in you! Be less beautiful, less gracious, less loving, above

CORONATION   *Napoleon and Josephine before the great*
Gothic portico of Notre Dame cathedral in Paris.

all, less good; never be jealous, never weep; your tears
drive me mad, burn my blood. . . . A million kisses, even
to Fortuné, despite his ill nature. . . .

Already Napoleon's ambitions, like Hitler's in our time, were
becoming global—"Today Europe, tomorrow the world." But England stood in his path to universal power. He considered an invasion

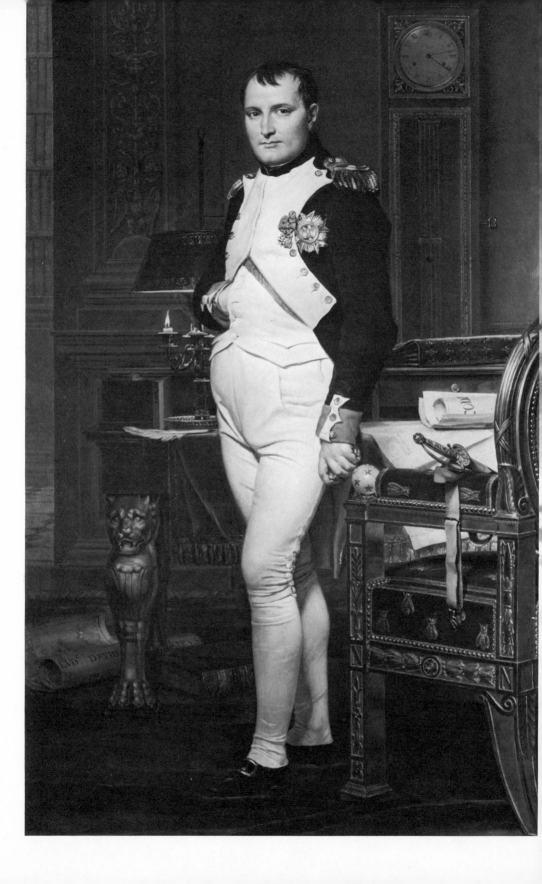

of Britain, and even inspected the suitability of northern ports, to that end, but finally decided that such a project would be foolhardy. Better to cut off the enemy from her vast wealth across the seas, particularly from India. Accordingly, he had himself appointed commander-in-chief of the Army of the East and, in May, 1798, he sailed for Egypt.

Josephine pleaded to be allowed to accompany him but he would not hear of it. She was apprehensive about a long parting—and with good cause, for Napoleon had involved himself in a liaison with Pauline Foures, wife of one of his officers, and even spoke of divorcing Josephine should his mistress be with child by him. Moreover, Josephine found herself in the hands of his hostile family who were lining their pockets through the great man's influence, and who bitterly resented her as an interloper. They did their best to discredit her, sending him secret messages alleging her infidelity.

Josephine, realizing that her marriage was at stake, determined to get to Egypt. But just as she was organizing her voyage, the news came that Admiral Nelson had destroyed the French fleet at the Battle of the Nile. Napoleon was cut off from France! In the end, it was he who eluded the British blockade and reached Paris for the confrontation with her.

The scene in their home on Rue de la Victoire, must have been worthy of Hollywood, with his family making every kind of allegation against her, and she vainly trying to gain access to his rooms. Eventually, she lay prostrate and sobbing outside the door of his bedroom with her two children by her side, the boy Eugene now 18 and the girl Hortense 16. At last, Napoleon admitted them. Soon the children departed, and the tortured couple were reconciled, Napoleon sending his family packing, to nurse even greater hatred against the triumphant Josephine.

NAPOLEON IN HIS STUDY   *This famous canvas was painted by Jacques L. David.*

Now France was suffering great hardship under the relentless British blockade of the seas and was clearly on the verge of another revolution. Napoleon was the obvious choice as strong man. After plot and counterplot, he emerged as First Consul. His fiery passion for Josephine as a lover was cooling, but he was coming to appreciate her considerable qualities as a wife and hostess. "I only win battles," he said of her, "but she wins me hearts." She also proved an ideal go-between among the old revolutionaries and the royalist émigrés.

Her extravagance, however, was on a colossal scale—during his absence in Egypt she had run up debts totaling one million, 200 thousand francs. She would only admit half that sum to Napoleon, who, although furious, agreed to provide the 600 thousand francs. Curiously enough, although he was as closefisted in money matters as most of his family, he was happy to indulge her in building up a fashionable and glittering court. On his appointment as First Consul he set up their official residence in the Tuileries which he renamed "The Palace of Government."

Napoleon was determined to be the sole ruler of France, but he knew—and said—that his power depended on his glory, and his glory on his victories. He needed another victory, and he got it by defeating the Austrians at Marengo, in June, 1800. In August he was declared Consul for life, and he began to live like a king with Josephine very much his consort. He ordered the palace of Saint Cloud to be restored at a cost of three million francs and he took Josephine on a triumphal tour of the northern provinces. He also acquired a mistress or two—and she acquired four ladies-in-waiting.

His power over the people was not secure, and all hope of restoring the monarchy by military action was extinguished. Desperate men talked of assassination as the surest way of ridding France of Napoleon, especially as it now seemed certain that Josephine would never give him an heir. After one murder plot had been quelled, his supporters began campaigning for a change in his rank —he must be given a hereditary title and the right to name his successors. In 1804, the Senate "persuaded" him to accept a new Constitution which accorded him the title of "Emperor of the French Republic," with Josephine as Empress. "I am going to impose on you a command which you will have much pleasure in obeying," he told her. "I wish you to be dazzling in jewelry and richly dressed."

His family at once began a concerted campaign to persuade Napoleon to divorce Josephine before the Pope came to Paris to crown him. They urged him to marry a foreign princess who could give him an heir. They even introduced tempting bait in the form of a girl who seemed to them to possess all the qualities that had attracted him to Josephine, with another added—youth. This was Mme. Duchatel, who was 20, and married to a man twice her age. The ruse succeeded, for Napoleon quickly became infatuated with the lady, and Josephine was sufficiently ill-advised to surprise them together. He drove his Empress from the room in a fury, pursued her to her bedroom, roared that he was tired of her spying and that it was time he had a wife who could give him children. He ordered her to leave Saint Cloud at once, and he sent for her son Eugene to take her away. He told Eugene that he was determined to divorce Josephine.

When his great rage subsided, he began to consider the effect a divorce would have on public opinion, especially if he was known to be the guilty party. He even got around to hinting that Josephine should ask *him* for a divorce, but she promptly dissolved in tears. Gradually it dawned on him that the situation had been contrived by his own family, and he decided to teach them a lesson. He would make amends to her by an unprecedented gesture. Not only would Josephine accompany him to his coronation as his wife, but he would endow her with more than the courtesy title of Empress—he would crown her Empress by his own hand so that she would be seen to share his power. And his family would be forced to be in attendance—to see the woman they despised ennobled by his side.

Her finest hour began at noon on December 2, 1804, in the cathedral of Notre Dame.

CORONATION OF JOSEPHINE   *All the pomp of the Napoleonic court—clerics, nobles, and the military establishment—are set forth in this formal painting. After he had crowned himself, Napoleon places a crown on the head of the queen.*

A French writer described the scene:

> *[Napoleon] looked with an air of complacency at the Empress as she advanced toward him; and when she knelt down—when the tears which she could not repress*

fell upon her clasped hands as they were raised to Heaven,
or rather to Napoleon—both then appeared to enjoy one
of those fleeting moments of pure felicity which are
unique in a lifetime.

*The Emperor performed with peculiar grace every
action required of him during the ceremony, but his manner of crowning Josephine was most remarkable. After
receiving the small crown surmounted by the cross, he
had first to place it on his own head, and then transfer it
to that of the Empress. When the moment arrived for
placing the crown on the head of the woman whom popular superstition regarded as his good genius, his manner
was almost playful. He took great pains to arrange this
little crown which was placed over Josephine's diadem;
he put it on, then took it off; and finally, put it on again,
as if to promise her that she would wear it gracefully and
lightly.*

What the hundreds of thousands who cheered their new
Emperor and Empress through the streets of Paris did not know
was that, in the greatest secrecy at midnight on December 1, in the
chapel of the Tuileries, Josephine and Napoleon were married by
his uncle, the Cardinal Fesch. The Pope had made it clear to them
that he could not officiate at the coronation of a man and woman
who in the eyes of the Church were living in sin. Their town-hall
marriage of eight years before was not acceptable to His Holiness.

Although Josephine was now at the zenith of her glory, a sinister shadow was spreading across her life—their childlessness. The
Bonaparte family were certain that she would never give Napoleon
the heir he so desperately wanted, and they renewed their insidious
campaign to persuade him to divorce her. She, on her part, encouraged him to doubt that he was capable of paternity; but he was not
convinced, and he embarked on a series of affairs to prove the contrary. At last he was satisfied that one of these mistresses—Eleonore
Denuelle—was pregnant by him. Now the idea of divorcing Josephine became more attractive. Still he hesitated, for he could not
rid himself of the nagging doubt that he would be separating himself not only from the only woman he had ever loved, but also from
his good omen—Our Lady of Victories.

There followed his great victory at Jena, and his utter defeat of the Prussians in Berlin. Then he was off to Poland, chasing the Russians.

In Warsaw, he became infatuated with Marie Walewska, the lovely young wife of an aging Polish nobleman. Josephine got wind of this affair, and wrote petulantly to him. He replied: "I love only my little Josephine, sweet, pouting, and capricious, who can quarrel with grace, as she does everything else, for she is always lovable except when she is jealous—then she becomes a regular termagant."

After the peace of Tilsit, he returned to Paris and Josephine; and once more he fell under her spell, although he also renewed his amorous affairs. Inevitably, with much talk from his family about "securing the dynasty," the thought of divorce was again thrust into his mind. Eventually, he sent a go-between, Fouché, to sound Josephine out.

When she upbraided Napoleon for this trick, he denied it. "We must not be angry with Fouché," he said. "It is enough that we are determined to reject his proposal, and you know well that I could not live without you." Then, as an afterthought, he went on: "Of course, if such a thing *did* happen, it would be for you to help me to make the sacrifice. I should count on your love to save me from the odium of a forced separation. You would take the initiative, would you not? You would appreciate my position, and have the courage to renounce me?"

"You are the master," she told him, "and you shall decide my fate. If you should order me to quit the palace, I would obey instantly, but the least you can do is to give me that order plainly. I am your wife; I have been crowned by you in the presence of the Pope, and I will not voluntarily renounce these honors. If you divorce me, all France shall know that it is you who send me away, and the country shall be ignorant neither of my obedience nor of my profound grief."

This scene ended with them sobbing in each other's arms. But he kept brooding on the subject of divorce. He still loved her, but

he was determined to found a dynasty. He told one of his ministers: "If I had the misfortune to lose her, reasons of State would compel me to marry again—but I should only be marrying a womb. She alone can be my life's companion."

In the year 1808, he was busy negotiating alliances with the rulers of Germany and with the Czar, but Josephine suspected that he was also looking for a suitable wife from one of these royal families. When he did eventually find the moral courage to tell her, he had the great victory of Wagram behind him. It was the night of November 30 and they had just dined together in the Tuileries. Over coffee he dismissed all others, then took her hand, and pressed it to his heart. "My dear Josephine," he said in a well-rehearsed speech. "You know how I have loved you. To you alone I owe the only moments of happiness that I have enjoyed in this world. But my destiny cannot be controlled by my wishes. My dearest affections must yield to the interests of France."

NAPOLEON'S FAREWELL TO JOSEPHINE   The artist,
E. Pagliano, has captured the utter despair of the rejected Empress.

She interrupted him, muttering that she understood, and then collapsed. Napoleon had to call servants to carry her to her bedroom. He summoned Josephine's daughter Hortense and told her: "The decision is made. It is irrevocable. All France desires the divorce and loudly demands it. I cannot oppose my country's will and nothing will move me—neither prayers nor tears."

To this Hortense coldly replied: "You should not be surprised at my mother's tears—it would be more surprising if, after 15 years of married life, she shed none. But I am convinced that she will submit, and we shall all go, remembering only the kindness that you have shown us."

Josephine had need of all her considerable courage in the weeks that followed, as Napoleon prepared the public for the shock of the divorce by diminishing her official privileges.

There remained one final ceremony of refined cruelty: on the night of December 15, before the high officials of the Empire, the assembled households of the Imperial Family, and the gleeful Bonapartes, Napoleon read a lengthy statement which ended with this flourish:

> *God knows how much it has cost my heart to take such a decision. But there is no sacrifice beyond my courage when I am shown that it is of value to the welfare of France. I must add that, far from ever having reason for complaint, I can on the contrary only congratulate myself on the attachment and tenderness of my much-loved wife: she has embellished 15 years of my life: the memory will always remain engraved on my heart. She has been crowned by my hand; it is my desire that she should retain the rank and title of crowned Empress, but above all that she should never doubt my affection, and that she should always regard me as her best and dearest friend.*

If the crowning was her finest hour, this must have been her most anguished. She was handed a statement of renunciation to

THE DIVORCE OF THE EMPRESS JOSEPHINE   *The artist, H. Chopin, in depicting the proceedings has captured the restrained anguish of the Queen.*

read out before the glittering assembly but no words would come. Instead, she collapsed sobbing in her chair, and the Secretary of State to the Imperial Household intoned it for her. It said:

With the permission of my august and dear husband, I have to declare that, having no longer any hope of bearing children who could fulfill the needs of his policies and the interests of France, I am pleased to offer him the greatest proof of attachment and devotion that has ever been given on this earth. I am indebted in everything to his beneficence; it was his hand that crowned me and,

*in the elevation to that throne, I have received nothing
but proofs of affection and love from the French people.
I believe that I should show my gratitude for all these sentiments by consenting to the dissolution of a marriage
which henceforward would be an obstacle to the welfare
of France, which would deprive it of the happiness of
being one day governed by the descendants of the great
man so evidently raised up by Providence to efface the
evils of a terrible revolution and reestablish the altar, the
throne, and social order. But the dissolution of my marriage will alter nothing in the feelings of my heart; the
Emperor will always have in me his dearest friend. I
know how much this action, dictated by political con-
siderations, has grieved his heart, but we both glory in
the sacrifice that we make for the good of the country.*

The following February Napoleon signed a treaty of marriage
between himself and the Archduchess Marie-Louise of Austria.
The Empress Josephine was given the estate of Navarre, and virtu-
ally banished from Paris. Napoleon had no wish to be embarrassed
by the presence of the old and the new in his capital city.

But when final defeat and humiliation came to "the great man
so evidently raised up by Providence," Marie-Louise was quick to
desert him. Josephine, hearing of his abdication and exile to Elba,

THE FALLEN MONARCH   *This familiar canvas by
Paul Delaroche depicts Napoleon I after his abdication.*

said: "If it were not for her, I would join him myself." But that, of course, was impossible, and she returned to Paris and Malmaison, her home in the days of glory, where she died on May 29, 1814, a month before her fifty-first birthday. Paris, then occupied by Napoleon's enemies, gave her a magnificent State funeral.

Twelve months after Waterloo, Napoleon returned to wander through the house and gardens. "Poor Josephine," he said—and his words can stand as her epitaph—"She was truly more replete with charm than any other person I have known. She was a woman in the fullest meaning of the word: variable and vivid, and with the best of hearts."

Lord Nelson and Emma Hamilton

More than a century and a half has passed since the death of Horatio Nelson at the Battle of Trafalgar—time enough for the scandal of his love affair with Emma, Lady Hamilton, to have died down; time enough for the world to realize that his association with her made him a greater, not a lesser, man.

In his day, Nelson was venerated even more than Winston Churchill was in his time. And the public expected its hero to be a

117

saint. To many, therefore, in high places and in low, it seemed incredible that the conqueror, in his years of glory, should himself be conquered by a low-born woman of easy virtue, and that he should have permitted himself to become a figure of fun because of his overwhelming love for her. As a result, he has been too much extolled and she too little understood. It is time to correct the imbalance.

The future Lady Hamilton was born a blacksmith's daughter, at Hawarden, Flintshire, on April 26, 1765. Her father, Henry Lyon, apparently died that same year. Emma, who was christened Emily, spent her childhood in extreme poverty. At thirteen, she entered domestic service in a doctor's household. Two years later —by that time a ravishing beauty—she went to London with her mother, where she was hired by a celebrated quack and mountebank, Dr. Graham, to sell his "cures" to gullible customers.

Emma caught the eye of a young rake, Sir Henry Fetherstonehaugh, who made her his mistress and installed her at his mansion, Up Park, on the Sussex Downs. When she learned that she was to become a mother, the gallant Sir Henry cast her out—at the age of sixteen. She returned, disgraced, to her grandmother's home in Hawarden. In despair, she wrote of her plight to the Hon. Charles Francis Greville, second son of the Earl of Warwick, whom she had met at a shooting party at Up Park. To her delight she received an encouraging reply, to which she in turn responded, as follows:

> *Yesterday did I receive your kind letter. It put me in some spirits for, believe me, I am allmos distracktid. I have never hard from Sir H [Fetherstonehaugh]. I have wrote 7 letters and no anser. What shall I dow? Good God, what shall I dow. . . . I cant come to toun for want of mony. I have not a farthing to bless my self with, and I think my friends looks cooly on me. I think so. O.G. what shall I dow? What shall I dow? O how your letter*

affected me when you wished me happiness. O.G. that I was in your posesion or in Sir H. what a happy girl would I have been! Girl indeed! What else am I but a girl in distres—in reall distres? For God's sake, G. write the minet you get this, and only tell me what I am to dow. Direct same whay. I am allmos mad. O for God's sake tell me what is to become on me. O dear Grevell, write to me. Write to me. G. adue, and believe me, yours for ever Emly Hart.

This letter, its style and spelling notwithstanding, apparently intrigued the Hon. Charles; and on impulse, he determined to play Pygmalion with its author—a decision which was to have remarkable consequences. In 1781, he set Emma and her mother up in a modest establishment in the country, in Edgware Row, allowing them £150 a year for household expenses, plus an annual personal allowance for Emma of £50. Greville was then aged thirty-two, a devoted companion to his highly distinguished uncle, Sir William Hamilton, the British Ambassador to Naples and an internationally acclaimed archaeologist.

Emma was well satisfied with her life in Edgware Row, and soon she was whole-heartedly in love with Greville. He wrote of her in 1784, three years after their association began:

She does not wish for much society, but to retain two or three creditable acquaintances in the neighborhood she has avoided every appearance of giddiness, and prides herself on the neatness of her person and the good order of her house. . . . She has vanity and likes admiration, but she connects it so much with her desire of appearing prudent, that she is more pleas'd with accidental admiration than that of crowds which now distress her. . . . She never has wished for an improper acquaintance; she has dropt everyone she thought I could except against. . . .

EMMA HAMILTON AS NATURE   This oil on canvas (c. 1782) by
*John Romney was commissioned by Charles Greville while Emma was his
mistress.*

Emma set about improving her scanty education, especially in music and art. She became highly skilled in singing, dancing, and acting. The painter John Romney, a friend of Greville, found her appealing, and his *Diaries* record some 300 occasions when she sat for him during this period. "While she lived under Greville's protection," the painter noted solemnly, "her conduct was in every way correct, except only in the unfortunate situation in which she happened to be placed by the concurrence of peculiar circumstances. . . ." The "unfortunate situation" was her daughter, Little Emma. Since Greville had resisted all Emma's pleas that the girl be allowed to live at Edgware Row, she had been left to Emma's grandmother to rear.

Greville was ambitious, but he saw little chance that his political career would advance, or that his finances would improve unless he was named his uncle's heir. Sir William Hamilton's wife had died childless in 1782. An idea for securing his own future took shape in Greville's mind: why not provide Sir William with a delectable mistress—someone with whom he could not possibly consider marriage, but whose attentions would keep him from seeking a wife elsewhere? The ideal choice was under Greville's own roof in Edgware Row.

Greville began to build up Emma's qualities to his uncle. He extolled her charms in a remarkable series of letters to Sir William through the year 1785, but his uncle was slow in rising to the bait. At last Greville came straight out with it:

> *I know you love variety and are a general flirt. . . . I know that your heart is neither callous to friendship nor to beauty. . . . I am from frequent experience convinced that I can judge for you and you for me. . . . If you did not chuse a wife, I wish the tea-maker of Edgware Row [Emma] was yours. . . . I do not know how to part with what I am not tired with. I do not know how to contrive to go on, and I give her every merit of prudence and mod-*

eration and affection. She shall never want, and if I de-
cide sooner than I am forced to stop by necessity, it will
be that I may give her part of my pittance. . . . I should
not write to you thus if I did not think you seemed as par-
tial as I am to her. She would not hear at once of any
change, and from no one that was not liked by her.

Hamilton stalled at first: "As to E," he wrote from Naples,
"was I in England and you was to bring your present plan to bear,
and she would consent to put herself under my protection, I would
take her most readily, for I really love her. . . . [But] I see so many
difficulties in her coming here, should you be under the necessity of
parting with her, that I can never advise it."

But Greville kept up his propaganda campaign, and at length
Hamilton succumbed. Emma was persuaded that it was to Greville's
interest and to her own that she should go to Naples. She agreed in
the belief that Greville would join her there within a few months
and bring her home. Hamilton, for his part, promptly paid his
nephew's accumulated debts. In 1786, therefore, Emma went off
to Naples—and to a destiny that no writer of fiction would have
dared to invent. First she became Sir William's mistress; five years
later, on September 6, 1791, she became his wife in a ceremony
performed at Marylebone Church, in London, with the permission
of King George III.

Emma was now living in a new world, meeting the great social
and literary figures of the day. Everyone was attracted by her beauty
and her unaffected manner. She won a reputation for her "living
statue" portrayals of Helen of Troy, Cassandra, Andromache, and
other classical heroines. Goethe, the German poet, eulogized her
in glowing terms; and even the Duchess of Devonshire, a celebrated
society beauty, was enraptured by these performances. "Everything
she did," wrote the Duchess, "was just and beautiful." The
Duchess, however, could not resist the waspish comment that
Emma's ordinary conversation, "though perfectly good-natured and

EMMA'S EARLY PROTECTOR
The Honorable Charles Greville.

unaffected, was uninteresting, and her pronunciation very vulgar."
Sir William had no such complaints: Six months after their marriage, he wrote:

> *Our situation is enviable. Lady Hamilton has nothing
> to do with my public character, but their Sicilian
> Majesties are so good as to receive her, and she has gained
> the hearts of all, even of the ladies, by her humility and
> proper behavior. . . . She knows that beauty fades, and
> therefore applies herself daily to the improvement of her
> mind.*

FERDINAND I, KING OF THE TWO SICILIES

By February 1793, England was at war with revolutionary France; and in September of that year, the first British ship of the line arrived at Naples on operations. The ship was the *Agamemnon:* her captain, Horatio Nelson. Sir William described Nelson to Emma as a small man who could not boast of being handsome but who would one day, Hamilton thought, astonish the world. Nelson, who was then thirty-four, had first taken to sea at the age of twelve. For years he had been waiting impatiently for an appointment that would help him make his name. Now the war with France had given him that chance. "I have never before entertained an officer in my house," Sir William told his wife, "but I am determined to bring him here." The invitation, duly issued and accepted, was to lead to one of the most remarkable *ménages à trois* in history.

Nelson's first visit to the Hamiltons was brief, but he forged a lasting friendship with Sir William, even though the Ambassador was thirty years his senior. In the five years that elapsed before Nelson and the Hamiltons met again, they kept up a regular correspondence. Meanwhile, Emma became the favorite and most trusted confidante of Queen Maria Carolina. In fact, it was through her influence with the Queen of the Two Sicilies that Nelson was able to obtain supplies for his fleet at Naples—then officially neutral— during the Nile campaign. (For this achievement, and at Nelson's suggestion, Emma was later decorated by the Czar.) Nor had Nelson been idle. His tremendous victory at the Battle of the Nile, on August 1, 1798, restored British supremacy in the Mediterranean and ended Napoleon's dream of conquest in the East.

Seven weeks later, Nelson returned to Naples. Lord and Lady Hamilton were overjoyed to welcome the hero of the hour, but found him physically greatly changed from the vigorous young officer they had received at the beginning of the war. Nelson had lost the sight of one eye, at Calvi in 1794; his right arm had been amputated in 1797, as a result of a wound received at Santa Cruz de Tenerifi; his hair was nearly white; his slender frame was bowed with suffering and responsibility, but his zest for action had in no

PREPARING TO HOIST NELSON'S SIGNAL   *Immediately preceding the Battle of Trafalgar in 1805, Nelson issued this signal which has since become famous:*

"England expects that every man will do his duty." This scene aboard the "Victory" was painted by T. Davidson.

way abated. Although he had received still another wound in the engagement at Aboukir Bay—he had been struck above the right eye by a piece of shrapnel—Nelson was eager to engage the French once more.

Emma set to work to nurse him, while Sir William relieved him of some of his administrative duties. At Nelson's urging, the Hamiltons helped to persuade King Ferdinand to lead an army from Naples in a bid to free the Papal States from French occupation. This expedition was an ignominious failure, however, and the French advanced on Naples unopposed.

It was now Emma's turn to show her mettle. She and her mother smuggled the royal family away from Naples by an underground passage, and led them safely to the harbor where Nelson's ship was waiting. On the stormy crossing to Sicily, six-year-old Prince Albert died in Emma's arms.

For two months Nelson stayed with the Hamiltons in Palermo, and it was from their home that he directed the blockade of Malta and Naples. Sir William, nearing his seventieth birthday, was failing physically in the trying Sicilian climate and becoming petulant. There is little doubt that Nelson and Emma, thrown together more and more, began their affair in Sicily. Ever since his victory at the Nile, Emma had made no secret of her devotion to Nelson. Her transition from hero-worshipper to lover was probably inevitable. From the Palermo interlude on, for the rest of Nelson's hectic life, he and Emma were passionately united. Sir William silently condoned a relationship which he was powerless to prevent. As long as he lived, he gave no hint of the slightest bitterness toward Nelson or toward Emma, who continued to run his home for him as before. All three, it would appear, had agreed to accept the situation with equanimity and to keep up appearances.

Emma was now at the peak of her achievement and position: she was the wife of a senior diplomat of a major power; she manipulated a queen, albeit one in exile; and she was the mistress of an acclaimed hero. The penniless illiterate of Hawarden had come a

MARIA CAROLINA *The Queen of the Two Sicilies was the sister of Marie Antoinette.*

long way. Then her world began to shift under her feet.

In June of 1799, the French agreed to an armistice with the Papal States. Nelson and the Hamiltons returned to Naples, and King Ferdinand was restored to the throne of the Two Sicilies. Soon thereafter, Lord Keith, the newly appointed commander of the British Mediterranean Fleet, ordered Nelson to Minorca, to defend the island against a threatened attack. Nelson demurred, claiming that the Ballearics were in no danger but that conditions in Naples required his continued presence. Historians generally agree that Nelson's appraisal of the situation was correct; but the fact remains that he *was* insubordinate—and that Emma was in Naples. The rumor spread that the hero of the Nile had disobeyed his superior officer in order to stay by the side of his mistress—a rumor that acquired teeth and fangs when it was learned that Emma was once again pregnant, after an interval of eighteen years. There is no question that the child was Nelson's.

In the fall of 1800, Sir William was recalled to London; and in November, the Hamiltons set sail—with Nelson—for England. The mood of the travelers can only be imagined; Nelson had to look forward to the reproaches of his wronged wife; and Emma, to the hostility of London society.

Her child was born on January 30, 1801—a girl who was christened Horatia. The infant was promptly smuggled off to a wet nurse in Marylebone.

The circumstances of the child's birth were wrapped in secrecy, concealed for years even from the girl herself—indeed, the truth did not come out for half a century. Meanwhile Nelson had become second in command of the Northern Fleet. In the four months that elapsed before his stunning victory at the Battle of Copenhagen, the lovers frequently corresponded about their daughter. They referred to her as Horatia Thompson, under the pathetic pretense that they were discussing the child of a young subaltern in Nelson's ship. But however they tried to conceal their liaison, no matter how unworthy their stratagems, it is clear that

EMMA LADY HAMILTON
A miniature found in the cabin
of Lord Nelson after his death.

they were overwhelmingly in love, bound fast together by a force stronger and more enduring than steel. Nelson regarded their union, although unconsecrated, as indissoluble; and Emma was never unfaithful, even to his memory.

In an affair of such intensity, with both parties in the public eye and both married, someone was bound to get hurt. The chief sufferers in this case were Nelson's wife and the daughter Emma bore him, who was never acknowledged by her father. Until Horatia was born, Nelson maintained the facade of a marriage; after the child's birth, he continued to provide for Lady Nelson but he rejected her. "I have done all in my power for you," he wrote, "and if I die, you will find I have done the same. Therefore my only wish is to be left to myself, and wishing you every happiness, believe that I am your affectionate Nelson."

Lady Nelson professed "astonishment" at the note. She made no attempt to win her husband back, and took no steps to divorce him. She had her revenge in preventing the lovers from marrying. She cut herself off from his family, most of whom went over to Emma's side, referring to Lady Nelson as "Tom Tit." No quarter was asked, and none was given. Lady Nelson was implacable, and the lovers were pitiless.

By contrast with the wronged wife, the injured husband was generous and uncomplaining. Hamilton even insisted on paying half the annual expenses of Merton Place, the small estate in Surrey which Emma bought in Nelson's name as a quiet retreat for her hero. Astonishing as it seems, Sir William worshipped the man who had cuckolded him and the woman who had betrayed him. Indeed, when he died, on April 6, 1803, it was in Emma's arms, and with Nelson's hand clasping his! Hamilton left Emma an immediate gift of £300 and an annuity of £800. A codicil to his will, signed only a week before his death, contained a remarkable tribute to Nelson:

> *The copy of Madam Le Brunn's picture of Emma in enamel, by Bone, I give to my dearest friend Lord Nelson, Duke of Bronte, a very small token of the great regard I have for his Lordship, the most virtuous, loyal and truly brave character I ever met with. God bless him, and shame fall on those who do not say Amen.*

HORATIO, VISCOUNT NELSON   *The Vice-Admiral was 42 years of age when he posed for this portrait executed by Hoppner in 1801. The painting is now in St. James Palace in London.*

LETTER FROM LADY HAMILTON TO LORD NELSON   *Written from Canterbury on October 8, 1805, the letter reads: "Dearest Husband of My Heart, You are all in this world to your Emma—may God send you victory, and hasten soon to your Emma, Horatia, and paradise, my sir, for when you are here it will be paradise. My own Nelson, may God prosper you and preserve you for the sake of your affectionate, Emma." The missive was returned to Lady Hamilton unopened for Nelson was dead upon its arrival.*

Hamilton did not know, when he signed the codicil, that his wife was pregnant again, for the third and last time. Emma was not yet forty and still a beauty, although her girth had increased, for she ate with relish and had developed a fondness for porter. When the child was about to be born, Nelson was at sea on H.M.S. *Victory*. The thought of separation from his beloved gave him a "raging fever." "Call him what you please," he instructed her, "but, if a girl, Emma." The child, whose sex we do not know, apparently was stillborn.

War with France formally resumed on May 18, 1803, and Nelson was soon off about his favorite business—chasing the French fleet. His service took him from Emma for two years, but his devotion never wavered. "I have not a thought except you and the French fleet," he wrote her, "and I will embrace both so close when I can lay hold of either one or the other that the Devil himself should not separate us." He devoured her letters and treasured a lock of her beautiful hair. Even as he sat signing orders he took time off to write to her: "My life, my soul, God in heaven bless you." Each day he drank her health "and darling Horatia's."

When Nelson returned to England, after two years of hunting and harrying the French fleet but never quite catching up with it, he came ashore to public adulation, but made straight for Merton and Emma. He had spent only twenty-five days in England when Pitt pressed him to assume command of the *Victory* once more. Emma said she would not stand in his way. "Brave Emma!" said Nelson. "If there were more Emmas, there would be more Nelsons."

An excerpt from his notebooks dated September 13, 1805, reveals his frame of mind:

Friday night, at half-past ten, drove from dear, dear Merton, where I left all that I hold dear in this world, to go to serve my King and Country. May the great God whom I adore enable me to fulfill the expectations of my country, and if it is His good pleasure that I should return, my thanks will never cease being offered up to the throne of his mercy. If it is His good providence to cut short my days upon earth, I bow with the greatest submission, relying that He will protect those so dear to me that I may leave behind. His will be done. Amen. Amen. Amen.

Other evidence abounds that Nelson must have had a strong

THE BATTLE OF COPENHAGEN   *Ignoring his senior officer's command to cease fire, Nelson put his telescope to his blind eye, saying that he did not see the officer's signal. The Danes were defeated. As a result of the victory, Nelson was made a* viscount *and was given command of the Channel fleet.*

presentiment of personal doom. On October 19, from his ship anchored off Cape Trafalgar, he penned this letter to "My dearest beloved Emma, the dear friend of my bosom". . .

> *The signal has been made that the Enemy's Combined Fleet are coming out of port. We have very little wind, so that I have no hopes of seeing them before tomorrow. May the God of Battles crown my endeavors with success; at all events, I will take care that my name shall ever be most dear to you and Horatia, both of whom I love as much as my own life. And as my last writing before the Battle will be to you, so I hope in God that I shall live to finish my letter after the Battle. May Heaven bless you, prays your Nelson.*

His last public document was a codicil to his will, witnessed by two of his captains. This read as follows:

> *October the 21st, One thousand eight hundred and five, then in sight of the Combined Fleets of France and Spain, distant about ten miles.*
>
> *Whereas the Eminent Services of Emma Hamilton, Widow of the Right Honorable Sir William Hamilton, have been of the very greatest service to our King and Country, to my knowledge, without her receiving any reward from either our King or Country, first that she obtained the King of Spain's letter in 1796 to his brother, the King of Naples acquainting him of his intention to declare war against England, from which letter the Ministry sent out orders to then Sir John Jervis to strike a stroke, if opportunity offered, against either the arsenals of Spain, or her Fleets. That neither of these was done is not the fault of Lady Hamilton, the opportunity might have been offered.*

LETTER FROM LORD NELSON TO LADY HAMILTON   *The letter reads:*
*"My Dear Lady Hamilton, I have kissed the Queen's letter. Pray say I hope for the
honor of kissing her hand when no fears will intervene. Assure her majesty that no person has her felicity more than yourself at heart, and that the sufferings of her family will
be a tower of strength on the day of battle. Fear not the event, God is with us. God bless
you and Sir William. Pray say I cannot stay to answer his letter. Ever yours faithfully,
Horatio Nelson."*

THE BATTLE OF TRAFALGAR   *Nelson was killed in this confrontation, bu*
his Mediterranean fleet defeated the combined forces of France and Spain and ende
Napoleon's sea power.

Secondly, the British Fleet under my command could never have returned the second time to Egypt, had not Lady Hamilton's influence with the Queen of Naples caused letters to be wrote to the Governor of Syracuse, that he was to encourage the Fleet being supplied with everything, should they put into any port in Sicily. We put into Syracuse, and received every supply, went to Egypt and destroyed the French Fleet.

Could I have rewarded these services I would not now call upon my country; but as that has not been in my power, I leave Emma Lady Hamilton, therefore, a Legacy to my King and Country, that they will give her an ample provision to maintain her Rank in life. I also leave to the beneficence of my country my adopted daughter, Horatia Nelson Thompson; and I desire she will use in future the name of Nelson only.

These are the only favors I ask of my King and Country at this moment when I am going to fight their Battle. May God bless my King and Country, and all those who I hold dear. My relations it is needless to mention: they will, of course, be amply provided for.

This writing was heavy with foreboding—indeed, as Captain Blackwood, one of his witnesses, left the *Victory* to rejoin his own ship, Nelson told him they would never meet again. A few hours later Nelson was fatally wounded by a French bullet.

To the shame of his King and country, the codicil was never honored. Of course, the matter was highly delicate; men in power discussed the pros and cons at great length; and as can be imagined, in great secrecy. Responsibility was shuffled back and forth, but no one would accept it as his particular duty to see that the hero's last wishes were followed.

Emma was not one to accept this state of affairs quietly. She tried endlessly to use Nelson's codicil as a bludgeon to compel the

SIR WILLIAM HAMILTON

THE DEATH OF NELSON   *The scene was painted by A. W. Devis (1763-1822).*
Among Nelson's last words were, "Take care of my dear Lady Hamilton."

authorities to do her justice. Her complaint of merit unrewarded became an obsession, and she grew more and more extravagant in stating her case. Moreover, she insisted on living as lavishly as ever. Nelson had left her Merton, a legacy of £2,000, and the income from the £4,000 which he settled for Horatia's maintenance. But Emma needed more. Even if the government had observed Nelson's wishes, she would no doubt have found her pension inadequate.

Emma lived on for more than nine years after Trafalgar, years of disintegration, disappointment, and decline. Beset by a horde of parasites, she kept Merton for three years, then moved with Horatia to Heron Court in Richmond. Her debts mounted; then came the money lenders, the inevitable flight from creditors, and the ultimate degradation—a year in debtors' prison.

In the summer of 1814, taking advantage of a respite in the war with France, Emma and Horatia sailed for Calais, with £50 between them. They settled in the village of St. Pierre, two miles outside the port. It was there that, in January 1815, Emma died of jaundice, made fatal by over-drinking. While Nelson lay in glory in the crypt of St. Paul's Cathedral his Emma was buried in the little village cemetery of St. Pierre. Her life was summed up by Dr. William Beatty, once surgeon on H.M.S. *Victory,* who wrote of her:

> *Few bend them at thy bier, unhappy one!*
> *All know thy shame, thy mental sufferings, none,*
> *All know thy frailties—all thou wast and art:*
> *But thine were faults of circumstance, not heart.*

Robert Browning and Elizabeth Barrett

Neither had been in love before they met, yet they came to be called "The Immortal Lovers," for they were truly soul mates. She was a semi-invalid, dominated by her possessive and self-righteous father, and he was a handsome and healthy young man, still totally dependent on his family. Both were rapidly establishing reputations as poets.

Robert Browning was 32 when he first saw Elizabeth Barrett's volume, *Poems*. A month later, he wrote his first letter to her. When her correspondence with him began, she was 38, and already convinced that the best years of her life were over: ". . . my face was so close against the tombstones that there seemed no room even for the tears."

When she received her first letter from Browning, she replied at once, for she had long admired his poetic genius. They shared the same religious convictions, a common interest in humanitarian causes, and an enlightened devotion to literature. However, Browning was fond of opera and the theater; both of these were closed to her because of her father's religious prejudices. Browning played the piano and organ, and often visited London art galleries, whereas Elizabeth had "seen and heard nothing of pictures and music." In her first letter, she wrote that they had "great sympathies in common and I am inclined to look up to you in many things, and to learn as much of everything as you will teach me."

An immediate bond was forged by their poetry. "You cannot understand," he wrote, "what a new feeling it is for me to have someone who is to like my verses, or I shall not ever like them after!" They made valuable criticisms of each other's work.

A stream of correspondence now poured from New Cross on the Kent Road where Browning's parents had moved, and Wimpole Street in central London where Elizabeth's father, Edward Moulton Barrett, had taken up residence.

Browning began pressing Elizabeth to allow him to call on her. She hinted that one day his request would be granted: ". . . if you think that I shall not *like* to see you, you are wrong, for all your learning. But I shall be afraid of you at first."

Two months passed before he repeated his request, but he added: "I ask you *not* to see me so long as you are unwell . . ."

Then came the reply for which he had long been waiting: "If you care to come to see me, you can come." But she warned him that he might not receive "the least straw of pleasure," for "there is nothing to see in me, nor to hear in me—I never learned to talk as you do in London."

To appreciate just how great an act of courage and will this was on her part, it is necessary to sketch in the extraordinary family setting in which Elizabeth Barrett existed. She was the eldest of 12 children of a man who has been described as "one of those tyrannical, arbitrary, puritanical rascals who go sleekly about the world, canting Calvinism abroad and acting despotism at home."

That she was a prodigy can be understood from her own revelation that, at the age of four, her "great delight was pouring over fairy phenomenons and the actions of necromancers." At nine, she wrote an epic; and at 10, tragedies. By the age of 12, the study of metaphysics was her "highest delight," and she felt edified and exalted by Locke! At 15, she had two poems published—both lamenting the loss of freedom in modern Greece.

Mr. Barrett, who had been born and reared in Jamaica where his family owned plantations, regarded his wife and children just as much his chattels as were his West Indian slaves. Although their shackles were invisible, they were none the less real. Mr. Barrett was that most odious example of nineteenth-century Englishman, the religious autocrat with a bent for liberalism and social reform. When this pious hypocrite, whose money was amassed from the sweat of black Jamaicans, decided it was time to establish his large family in a suitable residence, he scorned an English manor, preferring the castle of Hope End in Herefordshire. It was a mass of spires and crescents, clustering around domes and minarets, and nestling within 400 acres of landscape set off by an oak grove.

The despot of Hope End would often join his captive brood in games and gallops on his broad acres. The children had no lack of toys or delicacies, but their father exacted immediate and absolute obedience in return for his favors. He relegated his wife to the status of a childbearing machine, while he played the king, with Elizabeth as his favorite princess, and Edward, his first son and heir-apparent, as his prince.

Elizabeth was an endearing child of fragile beauty. She idolized her father, until she was old enough to see what a ruthlessly selfish monster he really was. She tells how he delighted in lifting her up to the chimney piece, standing her on it, and commanding: "Straight up now, like a hero!"

Like many rich men who imagined themselves liberal, Mr. Barrett had a varied library. Although he did not forbid his children to browse, he censored what they read. When Elizabeth showed that she had an omnivorous appetite for literature, he warned her: "Don't read Gibbon's history; it's not a proper book. Don't read *Tom Jones*—and none of the books on *this* side." And Elizabeth obeyed his every command. There was, however, enough on the *other* side to keep her occupied, including Tom Paine's *Age of Reason,* Voltaire's *Philosophical Dictionary,* and Hume's *Essays.* After a diet of Voltaire, the young prodigy closed her nightly prayers with: "O God, if there is a God, save my soul—if I have a soul."

She devoured all the permitted books and drew all her joy from a life of the mind and imagination. She had a solitary, shutoff childhood, made all the more so by the fact that, at 15, she was assailed by a weakening illness which turned out to be tuberculosis.

Her brother Edward was her constant companion on woodland walks, and he shared all her adolescent secrets. She had now outstripped her tutor, and her capacious mind needed contact with a man of wide learning. She was to find him in a blind scholar named Hugh Stuart Boyd who lived in Great Malvern.

Boyd, who was steeped in classical literature, was an apparently inexhaustible fount of knowledge for the girl's receptive mind. They quickly forged a friendship filled with tender sympathy and understanding on the one side, and a protective affection on the other. She read to him from Aeschylus, Euripides, and Plato.

Later she was to write of Boyd:

You were older,
And more learned, and a man!
Yet that shadow, the enfolder
Of your quiet eyelids, ran
Both our spirits to one level;
And I turned from hill and lea
And the summer sun's green revel,
To your eyes that could not see.

In 1828, when Elizabeth was 22, her mother died. It was the first of a long series of misfortunes for Mr. Barrett, misfortunes that he bore like the Old Testament figure he was. The year 1832 brought a financial slump which hit him hard, and he decided to sell Hope End. He did not, however, take his family into his confidence until he had arranged an alternative home in Sidmouth. He announced this devastating change in their lives in his usual peremptory fashion, warning his children against any show of emotion. They spent their last evening in the spacious residence playing cricket with him.

Sidmouth was to be only a temporary expedient until Barrett could manage something more suitable. Then came the bill to abolish slavery, which seemed an act of calculated treachery to the pious plantation-owner. He declared that they might as well hang lead weights on the island of Jamaica, and send it at once to the bottom of the sea. Nonetheless, he sent his son Edward to the West Indies to look after his interests during the chaotic period before the emancipation. Elizabeth, however, rejoiced over the Abolition Bill.

It took the Barrett family three years to escape from Sidmouth. They moved to Baker Street in London—another of Mr. Barrett's temporary expedients, which also lasted three years. At last they moved into their permanent home at 50 Wimpole Street; and at last, Elizabeth showed signs of making contact with the world of people rather than with the world of books.

She was now in her thirties, and without much hope of finding love. Her poetry was well received by literary London; and she was occasionally lured to dinner tables where she met such great names as William Wordsworth and Walter Savage Landor.

But the fog and rain of a London winter gravely weakened her health, and Mr. Barrett was persuaded to let her go to an aunt in Torquay for fresh air and nourishing food. Her dearly loved brother Edward joined her. He, too, was convalescing—from a love affair, roundly vetoed by his father.

When Edward was about to return to Wimpole Street, Elizabeth pleaded with him to prolong his stay. Although Mr. Barrett disapproved, he grudgingly gave his permission. It was a decision that was to have shattering consequences, for Edward was drowned while yachting.

Elizabeth's grief almost killed her. She was full of self-recrimination, blaming her selfish love for Edward's death. Her father's hard silence did nothing to ease her. For months, her life hung in the balance. She later wrote that it was ". . . the only time I have known what absolute despair is." She did not return to Wimpole Street for 15 months, and then against medical advice. The doctors now warned her that she must resign herself to an invalid's life.

Like Elizabeth, Robert Browning was a precocious child; but unlike her, his early adventures in the foothills of Parnassus met with ridicule. The elder Robert Browning was a superior clerk in the Bank of England. He was as proud of his son's talent as Barrett was of Elizabeth's, but there the similarity between the two fathers ended.

Browning senior was by inclination a scholar. His early hopes of becoming an artist were frustrated by his parents who sent him off to a lucrative plantation position in St. Kitts in order to drive all the "artistic nonsense" out of his head. There, he developed such a loathing for slavery that he quit his plantation job to become a schoolteacher. He then returned to England to have it out with his outraged father. He was found a job in the Bank of England.

ELIZABETH BARRETT BROWNING   *Portrait of the reknowned English poetess at age 53, painted by F. Talfourd.*

Browning senior determined that his son would never experience his frustrations. So he set about building up a massive library
in his home in Southampton Street, Camberwell. With reading, his
intellectual appetite expanded; he became a scholar in Hebrew and
Greek, and became well versed in Italian and French literature. If
great achievement was to be denied him, all things must be made
possible to his son. Hardly was the boy weaned before Browning
senior began the work of schooling his son's genius.

Young Browning was lulled to sleep with a classical ode. He
was encouraged to paint as soon as he could hold a brush; he was
given a music master the moment his interest in music was manifested. When his father took him for a walk, not a minute was
wasted; Robert would trot beside his scholarly pater listening to a
reading from some great author. The boy lapped up every tittle of
knowledge. Fortunately, he was robust as well as intelligent.

He was 20 when he wrote *Pauline;* it was published in 1833,
and the printing costs were paid for by an aunt. The name Robert
Browning did not appear on the title page, nor, indeed, did the
publishers know the author's identity. The book's appearance in the
world of literature was met by indifference or worse. "This is a
dreamy little volume without an object, and unfit for publication,"
said the *Literary Gazette.* The *Edinburgh Magazine* shrugged it off
as "a piece of pure bewilderment." The cruelest blow of all for
Browning was a detailed attack on the poem by the brilliant John
Stuart Mill. From that time on, Browning never again mentioned
his first-born literary effort without a chill of horror.

Young Browning then decided to travel abroad to purge himself of his humiliation. He was a singularly attractive youth with
ivory-tinted skin and long and wavy dark hair. He moved with
grace; held his head high.

On his return to England, he thought of entering the diplomatic service and applied for a post in Persia. This came to nothing.
He then buried himself in his father's library; and for six months,
he wrote with abundant energy. The result was *Paracelsus.*

This time, his father paid the printing costs. And this time, the name Robert Browning appeared on the title page.

The critics now rushed to acclaim "a brilliant new poet." The year was 1835.

One year later, they were acclaiming yet another literary find when *The Romaunt of Margret* by Elizabeth Barrett was published.

By 1840, the Brownings abandoned Camberwell, which had become urbanized, and they moved to an old-fashioned, three-stories house at Hatcham.

Often Browning had wondered at having "for many years now made up my mind at the impossibility of loving any woman." He tried to compensate for this lack with intellectual friendships; and

ROBERT BROWNING
Portrait of the poet at age 38,
executed by Lowes Dickinson.

he sought to satisfy his restlessness in travel. He sailed to Naples in 1844, and during that slow voyage he wrote *"The Good News from Ghent to Aix."*

During his stay in Italy, the publication of Elizabeth Barrett's *Poems* caused a literary sensation in England. Browning read them in early 1845, and his heart bounded when he saw his name bracketed with Wordsworth and Tennyson in one of her poems. So he wrote his first letter to her: "I love your verses with all my heart, dear Miss Barrett—and this is no offhand, complimentary letter."

Into the London room that was at once her cage and her prison, the letter fluttered like a fragrant flower petal blown from an Italian sky.

> *Since the day last week when I first read your poems, I quite laugh how I have been turning and turning again in my mind what I should be able to tell you of their effect on me, for in the first flush of delight I thought I would this once get out of my habit of purely passive enjoyment, when I do really enjoy, and thoroughly justify my admiration—perhaps even, as a loyal fellow craftsman should, try and find fault and do you some little good to be proud of hearafter!—but nothing comes of it at all, so into me it has gone, and part of me it has become, this great, living poetry of yours, not a flower of which but took root and grew.*

And the man she had never met, save through his verses, rounded off his note in these bold words: "But in thus addressing myself to you—your own self, and for the first time, my feeling rises altogether. I do, as I say, love these books with all my heart—and I love you too."

She replied to Browning's letter the day after she received it, and her reply was twice the length of his original. Such a letter from such a hand!

*Sympathy is dear—very dear to me: but the sympathy of
a poet, and of such a poet. . . . Will you take back my
gratitude for it? agreeing, too, that of all the commerce
done in the world, from Tyre to Carthage, the exchange
of sympathy for gratitude is the most princely thing.*

Thus, the first buds of their immortal love began to peep
through. Meanwhile, Mr. Barrett surveyed his nine surviving child-
dren with possessiveness and satisfaction. Of the girls, Elizabeth
was approaching 40, Henrietta was 36, and Arabel 32; all three
were attractive women, and not one was married! Gay, fun-loving
Henrietta had dared to fall in love once or twice; but one scene
with her father, in which she had tentatively suggested the possibility of marriage, haunted all the girls. Mr. Barrett had lashed
himself into such a frenzy that Henrietta was carried from the room
in hysterics, and Elizabeth, who was present, had fainted. Arabel,
too, ran about the house shrieking. Nothing, however, could change
Barrett's adamant attitude, and Henrietta gave up her suitor.

Through winter and spring, Browning laid siege to 50 Wimpole Street by letter, determined to see Elizabeth, but determined,
too, to be patient. His correspondence had brought a stream of sun-
shine into her cage; her feelings, awakened at last, veered between
hope and apprehension. She was finally persuaded to fix a date for
their first meeting, face to face—Tuesday afternoon, May 20th.

Mr. Barrett knew that Browning the poet would be calling,
but to him he was just another literary figure, come to pay homage
to his distinguished daughter. Henrietta was left to do the honors.
She hurriedly introduced the visitor to sister Elizabeth and left
them together. What the two poets said to one another during
the 90 minutes of the visit no one has learned. But the following
day, Browning dispatched a note full of anxious questions: Had
he stayed too long? Had he talked too loudly?

"Indeed there was nothing wrong—how could there be?"

Facsimile Letter from Robert Browning to Elizabeth Barrett.

(Reproduced by permission of Messrs. Smith, Elder, & Co.)

LETTER FROM ROBERT BROWNING TO ELIZABETH BARRETT   *The letter reads in part: "When I come back from seeing you, and think over it all, there is never a least word of yours I could not occupy myself with, and wish to return to you with some . . . not to say all . . . the thoughts and fancies it is sure to call out of me. There is nothing in you that does not draw out all of me—you possess me, dearest. . . ."*

Elizabeth replied. "And there was everything right—as how could there not be?"

She was quickly aware that something was happening to her secure, isolated little world, something she could not understand, something she found disturbing, exciting, frightening! She sensed Browning's power over her, and she was instinctively aware that he would use that power if it ever became necessary.

Their first notes were subdued, as though both were recovering from the shock of *knowing* that they were to mean everything to each other. Then, on May 23rd, Browning cast aside wary restraint, and wrote, telling her of his love. The tempestuous words were known only to her, for his letter has never been published. But her reply contains all her misgivings, and all her unselfish honesty.

> *You do not know what pain you give me in speaking so wildly, and if I disobey you, my dear friend, in speaking of your wild speaking, I do it not to displease you, but to be in my own eyes, and before God, a little more worthy, or less unworthy, of a generosity from which I recoil by instinct and at the first glance, yet conclusively. Listen to me then in this. You have said some intemperate things . . . fancies which you will not say over again nor unsay, but forget at once and forever, having said it all, and which will die out between you and me alone like a misprint between you and the printer. . . . For me to listen to 'unconscious exaggerations' is as unbecoming to the humilities of my position, as unpropitious . . . to the prosperities of yours.*
>
> *Now, if there should be one word of answer attempted to this, or of reference, I must not—I will not see you again—and you will justify me later in your heart. Your friendship and sympathy will be dear and precious to me all my life, if you indeed leave them with*

me so long or so little. Your mistakes in me . . . I put away
gently and with grateful tears in my eyes; because all
that hail will beat down and spoil crowns as well as
blossoms. . . . You are not displeased with me? No, that
would be hail and lightning together.

She was acutely aware of her age, of her inexperience in
the world, of all the disqualifications that should have made love
for her impossible.

But Browning was not to be thwarted. He was experiencing
love for the first time. He was terrified that Elizabeth would forbid
him to see her again. At first, he called once a week; then twice.
The gaps between visits were filled with their letters. Her spirit
possessed him completely; and as for her, she was to tell him later:
"When first you entered my room, you never went away from me."

They began worrying over each other's health. Gradually,
their letters became less guarded; and in August, Elizabeth con-
fided to him the scar on her soul—the drowning of her brother,
Edward.

Again, Browning was emboldened to write of his love:

Let me say now—this only once—that I loved you from
my soul, and gave you my life, as much of it as you would
take—and all that is done, not to be altered now: it was
in the nature of the proceeding, wholly independent of
any return on your part. . . . As it is, the assurance of your
friendship, the intimacy to which you admit me, now,
make the truest, deepest joy of my life—a joy I can never
think fugitive while we are in life.

His reaffirmation of his love threw Elizabeth into a near-
panic. She was afraid that he might recklessly try to beat down
the door of her prison and saddle himself with her. Once more she
told him why she could never listen to his avowal of love.

My dearest friend—You have followed the most generous
of impulses in your whole bearing to me, and I have
recognized and called by its name, in my heart, each one
of them. . . . You once wrote to me that you had been so
happy, you should now be justified to yourself in taking
any step most hazardous to the happiness of your life—
but if you were justified, could I be, therefore, justified
in abetting such a step—the step of wasting, in a sense,
your best feelings, of emptying your water gourds into
the sand?

Your life! If you gave it to me, and I put my whole
heart into it, what should I put but anxiety and more
sadness than you were born to? What could I give you
which it would not be ungenerous to give?

This was the noble design of their love, each thinking only
of the other's good. She could never deny their love, but she tried
with all her force to reject it—for his sake. And he believed to the
depths of his soul that "I was made and meant to look for you
and wait for you and become yours forever." He had the inner
certainty that, as long as people lived, "our names will go together,
be read together."

Elizabeth then told him that the doctor had ordered her to
spend the winter in Pisa; but that her father, after first agreeing,
had changed his mind and vetoed the trip. Gradually she explained to Browning her father's eccentricities, while defending
to him her parent's righteousness and devotion to his family.

Browning could not endure her humiliations. He wrote:

You are in what I should wonder at as the veriest
slavery, and I who could free you from it, I am here
scarcely daring to write. . . . I would marry you now and
thus—I would come when you let me and go when you
bade me—I would be no more than one of your brothers—

"no more." . . . I deliberately choose the realization of that dream of sitting simply by you for an hour every day—rather than any other, excluding you. . . . And it will continue but a dream. . . .

She suddenly realized the difference between Browning's unselfish love and her father's all-demanding devotion. Suddenly, it dawned that her father was prepared to endanger her life to satisfy his need of her. Her reply came from deep within her soul:

You have touched me more profoundly than I thought even you could have touched me. . . . Henceforth, I am yours for everything but to do you harm—and I am yours too much, in my heart, ever to consent to do you harm in that way. . . . A promise goes to you in it that none, except God and your will, shall interpose between you and me— I mean that if He should free me within a moderate time from the trailing chain of this weakness, I will then be to you whatever at that hour you shall choose—whether friend or more than friend—a friend to the last in any case. . . . Only in the meanwhile you are most absolutely free—unentangled, as they call it, by the breadth of a thread. . . .

Browning's answer was immediate and exultant.

Think for me, speak for me, my dearest, my own! You that are all great-heartedness and generosity, do that one more generous thing. . . . My own now! For there it is! Oh, do not fear I am entangled—my crown is loose on my head, not nailed there—my pearl lies in my hand— I may return it to the sea if I will!

Now they could write without restraint, and they poured out their pent-up feelings in a torrent of golden words. They exchanged locks of hair. At last they were able to make plans—and marriage

was their goal. They were under no illusion that the strongest
obstacle in their path was Mr. Barrett. And they agreed that the
first step was the recovery of Elizabeth's strength. She now insisted
on being carried from her couch to the drawing room downstairs
every day, and she struggled to walk without assistance. At 40, she
was training herself for womanhood.

Despite the London winter, Elizabeth steadily regained her
strength; and occasionally, she even ventured out into the night air.

She and Robert Browning decided to go away together to
Italy, although they were by no means clear how this was to be
brought to pass. Browning wanted to put the matter directly to Mr.

ROBERT BROWNING   *This portrait by G. F. Watts is probably the best-known likeness of the famous poet.*

Barrett, but Elizabeth shrank in terror from this proposal. As she told him:

> *We should be separated from that moment, hindered from writing, hindered from meeting. . . . I should have fainting fits at every lifting of his voice. . . . I shut my eyes in terror sometimes. . . .*

Browning took his parents into his confidence, and his father offered financial help. Finally, the end of September was set as the target date. However, on September 9th, an alarming complication occurred. Mr. Barrett ordered his family to the country so that 50 Wimpole Street could be redecorated. Browning decided that he must marry Elizabeth at once, and leave for Italy.

After a frantic rush, they managed to complete all the arrangements; and at 11:30 A.M. on Saturday, September 12th, they were married at St. Marylebone Church. They had only a few minutes together; they agreed to part until Elizabeth could arrange her escape from Wimpole Street forever.

On September 19th, she had all her bags ready, and with her maid Wilson and her dog Flush, she sneaked down the stairs of her home and walked around the corner to Great Marylebone Street where Browning was waiting. They caught the five o'clock train for Southampton—and freedom.

Elizabeth well knew the blow she was dealing her father. "Set the life against the act, and forgive me for the sake of the daughter you once loved," she wrote in her farewell note to him. But the shock went deeper than she had imagined. Mr. Barrett set about to obliterate everything that could call her to his mind; he literally annihilated her memory.

Literary England applauded the elopement, and sighed for the "charming fugitives." The Brownings settled in Pisa, and letters from home conveyed some of the excitement created by their flight to seek a life together in Italy. Inevitably, there was criticism of the circumstances of their departure, but one letter from a great man of letters soothed them. Thomas Carlyle, a man not much given to romantic sentiment, wrote:

> *Certainly if ever there was a union indicated by the finger of Heaven itself, and sanctioned and prescribed by the Eternal Laws under which poor transitory sons of Adam live, it seemed to me, from all I could hear and know of it, to be this. . . . Unless I altogether mistake, there is a life partnership which, in all kinds of weather, has in it a capacity for being blessed. . . .*

At first Elizabeth enjoyed better health than she had known for years. By spring, the idyllic pair realized that she was pregnant; but in the fifth month, she had a miscarriage; but although much weakened, she recovered.

By April, 1847, she was strong enough to organize their removal from Pisa to Florence, which was from then on to be the center of their life in Italy. They were supremely happy there, and the beauty that lay all around them was reflected in their work.

Robert Browning was the perfect husband; after lunch each day, he would tuck her up in the most comfortable chair, pour eau de cologne over her hands and forehead, and fan her until she fell asleep. Her letters to friends in England were full of praise for his ministrations, and in one to her sister Henrietta, she wrote that he made her very happy:

> *. . . by saying again and again such things as can't be repeated nor forgotten, besides that never in his life, from his joyous childhood upwards, had he enjoyed such happiness as he had known with me . . . there has not been a cloud nor a breath. The only difference is from happy to happier, and from loved to being loved more. . . .*

At last, on March 9, 1849, she gave him a son. "You never saw such a fat, rosy, lively child," she boasted. They baptized him

A BEERBOHM CARICATURE   *The famous satirist, Max Beerbohm, satirizes Robert Browning by showing a group of long-haired eggheads paying homage to the master at a tea of the Browning Society.*

Robert Wiedemann Barrett Browning, remembering Mr. Barrett, who had ignored his favorite daughter's many letters, including the one informing him of his new grandson.

When the boy was two years old, they decided to visit England, taking in Venice and Paris on the way. They remained in London for two months. The moment it was known that the Brownings were in town, the great names of literature and the stage came to call.

But if Mr. Barrett had renounced Elizabeth, she refused to renounce him. Robert wrote him a straightforward letter, seeking a meeting. Mr. Barrett replied with a letter and a package. The letter contained little but abuse—the package contained every letter his daughter had written him during her five years' absence. The letters were unopened; not one seal had been broken, nor had the black-edged envelopes been slit. So Elizabeth left England with not even a word nor a glance from the father who had been so close to her for 40 years.

Back in Italy, the idyllic life of the poets continued. They had really only one serious, deep-seated difference—on the subject of spiritualism. Elizabeth was impressed by what was then a new craze; Browning treated it with scorn, particularly as manifested in the person of the 22-year-old American medium, Daniel Douglas Home, whom he regarded as a charlatan.

In 1856, Elizabeth heard that her father had had an accident that left him permanently lame. Once more she tried to heal the breach between them, but time had only stiffened his obstinacy. By now he had also disinherited his daughter Henrietta, as well as one of his sons for committing the unforgivable sin of marriage. In April, 1857, the separation of Edward Barrett and his daughter Elizabeth was made permanent by his death.

Although she had, by that time, abandoned all hope of reconciliation, his demise desolated her. She locked herself away with her grief, torturing herself with self-reproach for her disobedience and her deception. She spent days in bed, weeping and refusing to be comforted by her doting Robert and her puzzled son. She could hardly accept the brutal certainty that she was never to know her father's forgiveness. His death had killed something in her, too.

Her interest in spiritualism was renewed. She had just published her most exacting work, a poetic novel, *Aurora Leigh,* which enjoyed tremendous success in England but which drained her of much creative energy. Robert Browning had still not found popular acceptance, being regularly criticized as "too obscure," and he was sick at heart over his apparent failure.

Elizabeth lived just long enough to witness the realization of one of her great dreams—the forging of an Italian nation. In 1861, the weakness in her lungs made it impossible for her to move around. On June 29th, Robert Browning, who would not leave her bedside, noticed that her thoughts were wandering, and he sensed that she would not live through the night.

About three in the morning, she awoke from a doze and gazed at him. "You know me?" he whispered.

"My Robert—my heavens, my beloved!" she replied in a very small voice, then reached up and kissed him.

As he laid her gently down, he asked: "How do you feel?"

"Beautiful!" she murmured. It was her last word.

Browning; writing to his sister of his wife's death, said:

My life is fixed and sure now. I shall live out the remainder in her direct influence, endeavoring to complete mine, miserably imperfect now . . . I have our child about whom I shall exclusively employ myself, doing her part by him. I shall live in the presence of her, in every sense, I hope and believe, so that so far my loss is not irreparable—but the future is nothing to me now, except inasmuch as it confirms and realizes the past. . . .

Just after she died, he took a small gold ring off her finger, and placed it on his watch chain where he wore it to the end of his life.

Prince Albert and Queen Victoria

Queen Victoria and her Prince-Consort, Albert, were born for each other. They were cousins, and their mutual grandmother started her matchmaking while they were in their cradles. For an arrangement so tidily worked out by others, their marriage was an astounding success; and they remained deeply devoted until death parted them.

Unlike many royal personages who were only political pawns,

Victoria and Albert had the opportunity to meet before their betrothal. In 1836, when both he and Victoria were seventeen, Prince Albert came from his home in Coburg, Germany, to visit his aunt in London. The Princess Victoria seems to have been most impressed with him during that visit, for she wrote to her uncle, King Leopold of the Belgians:

> *He possesses every quality that could be desired to make me perfectly happy. He is so sensible, so kind, and so good, and so amiable too. He has, besides, the most pleasing and delightful exterior that you can possibly see.*

He was extremely handsome, with dark brown hair, an olive complexion, and blue eyes. He was also highly intelligent, with a deep love of the arts. She was clever, but irrational, impulsive, and very susceptible to prejudice and hearsay. Her character was strong but undisciplined.

Although everyone assumed that they would marry, Victoria developed an unexpected hesitance. A year after their first meeting, when Victoria came to the throne, she found that "the freedom, the gaiety and the excitements of becoming Queen at eighteen" drove all thought of marriage from her mind. She also came quickly under the spell of her Prime Minister, Lord Melbourne, whom she idolized. By 1839, her uncle, King Leopold, decided that his protégé Albert should force the decision. On Leopold's shrewd instigation, Albert again visited Windsor. Victoria found him irresistible. Two days later, on October 15, she asked Prince Albert for his hand, as by protocol a woman sovereign must do.

She leaves us in no doubt about her feelings for him, as she compiled an astonishing Journal of their life together. And he, in his meticulous German way, carefully bound all his letters and official papers. On the day of their engagement he wrote to her: "How is it that I have deserved so much love, so much affection," and he signed the letter "In body and soul ever your slave, your loyal Albert."

The following day he sent this revealing letter to Baron Stock-mar, friend and confidant of his family:

> *I am writing to you today on one of the happiest days of my life to send you the most joyful possible news. Yesterday in a private audience Victoria declared her love for me, and offered me her hand which I seized in both mine and pressed tenderly to my lips. She is so good and kind to me that I can scarcely believe such affection should be mine. I know you take part in all my happiness, and so I can pour out my heart to you. For the present the event is to remain a secret, and is to be announced to the nation before being communicated to anyone else, at the meeting of Parliament. What grieves me is that my aunt (the Duchess of Kent, mother of Victoria) whom this important step by her daughter touches so nearly is not to know of it. But as everyone says she cannot keep her mouth shut and might even make bad use of the secret if it were entrusted to her, I quite see the necessity of it.*
>
> *V. wishes that the wedding should take place as early as the beginning of February, to which I gladly agreed as the relations between a betrothed pair, when the fact is public property, may often appear indelicate. . . .*

He returned to Germany and faced weeks of separation until the engagement could be made public. He wrote to her: "Thinking of you makes me so happy—what a delight it must be to walk through the whole of my life, with its joys and its storms, with you at my side. Love of you fills my whole heart."

On November 23, 1839, Queen Victoria announced to the Privy Council that she would marry Prince Albert. An onlooker described her hands as "trembling so excessively that I wonder she was able to read the paper she held." The engagement was by no means enthusiastically received by her country.

In January, 1840, the House of Commons debated the question of Albert's allowance. The Government had recommended £50,000 a year—the customary sum for the sovereign's consort, man or woman. But the proposal was defeated in the House by 104 votes, and the annuity cut to £30,000. The Queen, mortified, asked Lord Melbourne for an explanation. He replied that "her marriage was liked in the country but there was no enthusiasm for it." In fact, by showing such marked partiality for the Whigs and for Lord Melbourne, Victoria had aroused the unanimous opposition of the Tory Party.

Difficulties also arose between Victoria and Albert themselves. Victoria sought to impose her feelings on her bridegroom. She told him that she and Lord Melbourne would choose his household for him. He immediately appealed. "Think of my position, dear Victoria," he wrote. "I am leaving my home with all its old associations, all my bosom friends, and going to a country in which everything is new and strange to me. . . . Except for yourself I have no one to confide in. And is it not even to be conceded to me that two or three persons who are to have the charge of my private affairs, shall be persons who already command my confidence?"

To which she tartly replied: "Once more I tell you that you can perfectly rely on me!"

This was not his only rebuff from her. He suggested that they should stay at Windsor for some time after their wedding. She replied: "I am the Sovereign. . . . I am never easy a moment if I am not on the spot . . . and everybody, including all my aunts (who are very knowing in all these things), say I must come out after the second day. . . . This is also my own wish in every way."

Albert found that only his presence and personality could overrule her stubborn nature. He arrived at Buckingham Palace on February 8. Victoria wrote in her Journal: "My dearest precious Albert looking beautiful and so well," adding that his being there

"put me at ease about everything."

Two days later they were married in the Chapel Royal of St. James's Palace. Albert wore a British field-marshal's uniform with the Order of the Garter. The Queen made her responses in a clear, confident voice. Albert, though, according to one of the bridesmaids, "was a good deal perplexed and agitated in delivering his responses." The Archbishop of Canterbury, who performed the ceremony, asked Victoria if she wished to promise to obey her husband. She did. In the afternoon the bride and bridegroom were driven to Windsor Castle. Later the Queen wrote in her Journal:

"I had such a sick headache that I could eat nothing at dinner and had to remain on the sofa for the rest of the evening."

The next morning they were up early and walking in the park. One Tory commented that this "is hardly the way to provide us with a Prince of Wales."

Victoria, at least, was ecstatic. She wrote to Baron Stockmar: "There cannot exist a dearer, purer, nobler being in the world than the Prince." Throughout her life she held fast to the recollection of him at their honeymoon breakfasts: "He wore a black velvet jacket without a cravat, and anything more beautiful—and more youthfully manly and perfect—never was seen."

It soon became apparent that she intended to exclude him from all affairs of state, to keep him as a gorgeous toy—"the plaything of the blue boudoir," one historian called him. Victoria believed that politics were the enemy of love. Furthermore, she did not wish to upset her stable relationships with Lord Melbourne and with the Baroness Lehzen—the one advising her on all political matters, and the other on all personal affairs. Within two months of her wedding she told Melbourne of Albert's dissatisfaction at his exclusion from affairs of state. She added: "I know it is wrong, but when I am with the Prince I prefer talking on other subjects." To compensate, she was a loving, attentive and tender wife in their domestic life.

When their first child, the Princess Royal, was born in November, 1840, Albert was allowed to play a slightly stronger part in state affairs. But only in the following year, when the Whigs and Lord Melbourne were defeated, did he become a trusted counselor. It took him one year longer to free his household from the Baroness Lehzen, but in September, 1842, she left England forever.

In reorganizing the royal household, Albert encountered a formidable housing problem. Buckingham Palace, Windsor Castle, Claremont (near Esher in Surrey) and the Pavilion at Brighton were the available residences, and they all presented problems. Population growth in Brighton had destroyed any hope of privacy;

the Pavilion was finally sold to the town in 1850. Claremont was too close to London, and was owned by King Leopold of the Belgians. Sir Robert Peel, the new Prime Minister, opposed Albert's plans to rebuild Buckingham Palace, although the Prince did succeed in enlarging and improving it. Finally, Victoria and Albert agreed to buy Osborne on the Isle of Wight, but they found it too small for their needs. On this site, though, they built a new house, finally completed in 1851. Here they were able to enjoy the simple life, free and informal, and Albert was extremely happy. The Queen loved to describe his strolls through the woods. He would whistle to the nightingales "in their own long, peculiar note." In 1848, Balmoral was added to the list of royal residences, partly to gratify the Scots, and partly to give the Prince the mountain air and scenery which he loved.

Albert, though, was never truly popular in his adopted country. He despised the English aristocracy and considered them dissolute. He made no attempt to create a circle of personal friends. Indeed, he was frequently tactless in voicing criticisms of English habits, customs and skills. "In England there is nothing to do but to turn rogue or marry," or similar remarks such as "No tailor in England can make a coat." These slurs did not endear him to the English public. He hated the feeling that he and his family were always on show, and were required to be agreeable, serene, smiling, and fashionably turned out. But such pressures and publicity made his companionship with Victoria even more precious to him. He drew his contentment from making her happy, and nothing was too much trouble to him if it smoothed her path. Roger Fulford, in his biography, *The Prince Consort,* writes:

> *The very strength of his devotion to the Queen and his complete satisfaction in her company deflected him from friendship. Like a domestic animal barred from the wide world he yet led his life—full, happy and complete in a narrow compass, revealing himself only to those who*

ROYAL WEDDING   *A portrait of Queen Victoria and her nine children at*
the wedding of her eldest daughter, the Princess Royale to Prince William of
Prussia.

shared his restrictions. . . . His two outstanding weak-
nesses were childish irritability over trifles and nervous
hesitation in making up his mind—an unfortunate trait
reacting unfavorably on the nervous excitability of the
Queen. But these were merely blemishes, and with a
character noble and manly, and a mind clear and earnest,
he set himself the task of molding the Queen to his
fashion.

Most historians agree on Albert's greatest contribution to
nineteenth-century England: he rid Queen Victoria of the baleful
influence of Baroness Lehzen, then set to work to cultivate her
mind and to develop her intellectual powers. Indeed, she records
in her Journal that she told the Prince: "It is you who have entirely
formed me." She had begun her reign in an atmosphere of romantic
popularity; just a girl of eighteen undertaking the onerous duties
of the monarchy, she had touched most English hearts.

The early Victorians saw fresh hope for their country in the grace and innocence of their young ruler. But this popularity was soon tarnished by her complete identification with the Whig Party. Her devotion to Lord Melbourne and her unreasoning dislike and

OSBORNE HOUSE This palace, located near East Cowes, Isle of Wight, was a favorite residence of Queen Victoria. She died here in 1901.

suspicion of Peel split the loyalty of Britain. It was Albert's task, through his admiration of Peel's great qualities, to soften Victoria's antagonism and enlist the country's sympathies.

It is difficult today to appreciate the intensity of Tory feelings against Victoria. Ladies hissed the royal carriage at Ascot. And in the eminently respectable city of Canterbury, a Conservative member of Parliament launched a public attack. No one, he said, could regret more than he the growing unpopularity of the Queen. Furthermore, he added, "the people of England would never consent that the Crown should be degraded and debased for the inglorious ease" of Victoria. But Albert's tact and diplomacy, plus the steady arrival of their nine children, gradually created the satisfying picture of a delightfully happy and united Royal Family. After only three years of marriage, Victoria wrote to King Leopold:

BALMORAL CASTLE   A royal residence built by Queen Victoria in 1854, located in Braemar, Aberdeenshire, Scotland.

I will venture to say that not only no Royal ménage *is to be found equal to* ours, *but no other* ménage *is to be compared to* ours, *nor is* anyone *to be compared, take him altogether, to my* dearest angel!

She already relied entirely on Albert's judgment and grudged every moment of separation from him. She became so completely wrapped up in him that she never became really close to her children, even in the years of her widowhood when she needed their love and companionship. Together, the Queen and the Prince Consort brought the Court to a peak of brilliance and the country

VICTORIA IN 1854 Pho
tograph of the Queen mad
in the 17th year of her reign
She was 35 years old.

to commercial prosperity. Together, they entertained foreign
royalty with magnificence unsurpassed in Europe. In one year
alone, 1844, the Queen received the Czar, the King of France, and
the King of Saxony. When Napoleon III returned their invitation
the following year, they took along the thirteen-year-old Prince of
Wales, who asked Napoleon if he might remain with him in Paris.

"I think your mother and father might miss you," said the
Emperor discreetly.

"Oh no," replied the Prince of Wales. "There are plenty more of us at home."

Because of Albert's achievement in molding the Queen intellectually and politically, historians have tended to portray her as the adoring, even clinging wife, and her uncritical adulation of him in her Journal and letters seems to confirm this view. But her character was by no means submissive, and life with Victoria's nervous and emotional temperament could not have been placid.

Albert hinted at this side of the Queen in some of his letters. One written to his eldest daughter, the Princess Royal, contains this passage:

> *For your Mama, who lives much in the past and future, perhaps more than in the present, it is a spiritual necessity to cling to moments that are flown and to recollections, and to form plans for the future. . . . This carries her, of course, into the realm of hopes and apprehensions.*

But loving him, she found it difficult, indeed almost impossible, to argue with him. When she felt she needed to complain to him, she would dissolve in tears. To overcome this barrier, he proposed that she should put her cause of complaint down on paper. She understood her own temperament. "My nature is too passionate, my emotions are too fervent," she wrote to a friend. "He guided and protected me, he comforted and encouraged me."

When her mother, the Duchess of Kent, died in 1861 at the age of seventy-four, Victoria was highly distraught and depended heavily on Albert's calming influence. As the Court was about to leave Balmoral for Windsor where her mother had died, Victoria feared that her deep grief would again overcome her. Albert wrote to her:

> *What I can do to contribute to your getting over the painful sensations which a return to Windsor under such sadly altered circumstances will be readily and cheerfully done. My advice to be less occupied with yourself and your own feelings is really the kindest I can give, for pain is felt chiefly by dwelling on it and can thereby be heightened to an unbearable extent. This is not hard philosophy, but common sense supported by common and general experience. If you will take increased interest in things unconnected with personal feelings, you will find the task much lightened of governing those feel-*

*ings in general which you state to be your great difficulty
in life. . . .*

These words were vital solace to her in the almost unsupportable blow which struck her in the winter of that same year. Albert became ill in late November, but not until December 7 did the Court doctors diagnose his illness as "gastric fever," a euphemism for typhoid. A week later, in a room filled with doctors, secretaries and servants, he died.

The public were highly critical of the doctors, arguing that for the Prince Consort to succumb to fever within a week at the age of forty-two, suggested medical incompetence. Indeed, Lord Clarendon put it bluntly. He said the royal physicians were "not fit to attend a sick cat."

Queen Victoria, however, put no blame on the doctors. She believed that Albert's death was provoked by worry over the Prince of Wales who had been involved in an escapade with a girl in the south of France. Victoria stubbornly refused to call the Prince of Wales to Windsor when his father was clearly dying. This fixation also explains her manifest dislike of her eldest son in the early years of his manhood. Shortly after his father's death, she said, "It quite irritates me to see him in the room."

There have been several accounts of the Queen's demeanor in the hours following Albert's death. Lytton Strachey asserts that Victoria emitted "one long wild shriek that rang through the terror-stricken castle." According to Roger Fulford, a footman in scarlet livery came running along the corridor with a request that the Duchess of Atholl, the lady-in-waiting, should go at once to the Queen. The Duchess met Victoria coming out of the room in which Albert had just died. The Queen sobbed: "Oh, Duchess, he is dead! He is dead!"

Victoria then saw all her children, spoke to them of their father, and dedicated herself to continue his work. Then she lay down on a sofa in a room opening out of the Blue Room where the

Prince lay. Members of the household filed past her to pay their last respects to the Prince Consort. Making a fierce effort to compose herself, she asked each one: "You will not desert me? You will all help me?"

Later, she committed her grief to paper for the eyes of King Leopold, the uncle who had done so much to bring them together. She wrote:

> *Oh, to be cut off in the prime of life, to see our pure, happy, quiet, domestic life, which alone enabled me to bear my much disliked position, cut off at forty-two— when I had hoped with such instinctive certainty that God never would part us and would let us grow old together (though he always talked of the shortness of life) is too awful.*

She mourned her beloved Prince for a score of years. Although she was in excellent health and only on the threshold of middle age, Victoria shut herself off from the outside world, hiding behind black veils and dresses, refusing all comfort and shunning all social affairs. She saw only members of her family, the private secretaries, her ladies-in-waiting, and an occasional Cabinet Minister. When she traveled by train she ordered that the platforms be kept free of people. She allowed nothing in Albert's rooms to be

FOUR GENERATIONS OF ROYALTY   Queen Victoria, age 75, is shown with her eldest son, King Edward VII (then Prince of Wales), a grandson (later King George V), and her great-grandson, Edward, on her knee. The baby would grow up to be Edward VIII who later abdicated the throne in order to marry Wallis Warfield Simpson, a commoner.

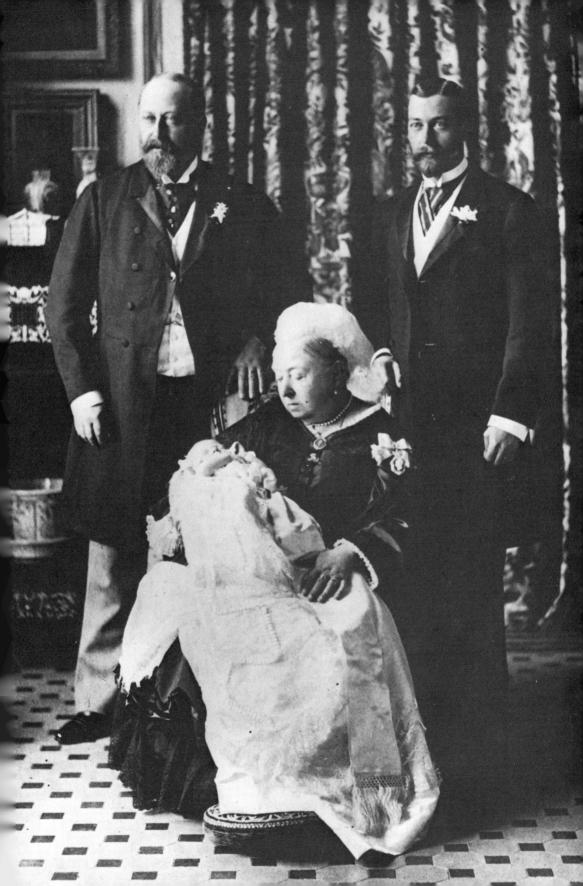

The London Gazette
EXTRAORDINARY.

Numb. 27269.   543

Published by Authority.

TUESDAY, JANUARY 22, 1901.

Whitehall, January 22, 1901.

A BULLETIN, of which the following is a copy, has been received by
Mr. Secretary Ritchie :—

Osborne, 7.8 P.M.

January 22nd, 1901, 6.45 P.M. :—HER Majesty The Queen breathed Her
last at 6.30 P.M., surrounded by Her Children and Grandchildren.

(Signed)   JAMES REID.
R. DOUGLAS POWELL.
THOMAS BARLOW.

Printed and Published by THOMAS HARRISON and JAMES WILLIAM HARRISON, Printers, at their Office
47. St. Martin's Lane, in the Parish of St. Martin-in-the-Fields, in the County of London.

Tuesday, January 22, 1901.

Price Four Pence.

touched; this order was faithfully observed until her own death forty years later. It is even said that when she signed State documents she looked at the Prince's marble bust, always close by her, and murmured to it: "Approved?"

She had a particular aversion to appearing in public, especially in London. For the next forty years of her life, she spent less than a score of nights in Buckingham Palace, preferring the peace and solitude of Osborne and Balmoral. After Albert had been dead for some years, the people began to grumble at her seclusion, and the newspapers echoed the complaints. Her Ministers tried to urge her to drive from Buckingham Palace to Westminster for the opening of Parliament. She wrote in reply:

> *To long to witness the spectacle of a poor, broken-hearted widow, nervous and shrinking, dragged in deep mourning, alone in State as a show is a thing she cannot understand, and she could never wish her bitterest foe to be exposed to.*

Yet she lived to be the center of two of the greatest acclamations ever accorded to any sovereign—the Golden Jubilee and the

ANNOUNCEMENT OF THE ROYAL DEMISE   The death of Queen Victoria in 1901 at age 82, as announced in the London Gazette.

DIAMOND JUBILEE *The procession in Queen Victoria's honor which marshalled all the pomp and panoply of British royalty is passing St. Paul's Cathedral in London. The Queen was then in the 57th year of her reign.*

Diamond Jubilee. When she died in January, 1901, surrounded by her children and grandchildren, she was laid out wearing a bridal veil and her widow's cap, symbols of her life with and without the Prince Consort.

George Henry Lewes and George Eliot

The love of Marian Evans and George Henry Lewes was devoted, loyal, and enduring. But their affair shocked Victorian England. Literary circles were agog—and she was spoken of as "the errant woman."

George Eliot—the name which Marian Evans wrote under—ranks as one of the greatest of the nineteenth-century novelists, along with Dickens, Thackeray, Scott, and Jane Austen.

George Eliot was married to George Henry Lewes in every sense but the legal one. Yet this union, which to the hide-bound society of the mid-1800s was condemned in the sight of God, proved to be of great importance to English literature; for if not for George Henry Lewes, George Eliot the novelist might never have been created or encouraged to develop. Indeed, Marian Evans chose the name *George* because it was *his* name; as for *Eliot,* she deemed that it was "a good mouth-filling, easily pronounced word."

Lewes not only encouraged her—he actually trained her. He arranged for her earliest work to be published by the then famous John Blackwood who owned *Blackwood's Magazine,* to which most of the celebrated literary figures of the day contributed.

Lewes was a distinguished journalist and critic in his own right, and already the focus of scandal at the time Marian met him. He had a reputation as an advocate of free love, and he did nothing to dispel that reputation when, in 1842, he joined other literary couples in an experiment in communal housekeeping. The previous year he had married Agnes Jervis whom he called his child-wife—she was nineteen and "one of the loveliest creatures in the world."

Along with Lewes and his wife in the experimental group was Thornton Hunt, son of Leigh Hunt, who also joined Lewes in launching the *Leader,* a weekly of literary criticism. Unfortunately, Agnes, the child-wife, fell madly in love with Thornton Hunt to whom she bore two children, one while still living with Lewes as his wife. Condoning the affair later made it impossible for him to obtain a divorce because of legal complications. Lewes thus became a victim of his own libertarian opinions. Yet his only complaint against Hunt was that the lover mismanaged Agnes' finances. It is a matter of record that George Eliot and Henry Lewes later gave Agnes a periodic allowance, and that George Eliot honored this financial arrangement even after Lewes' death. Indeed, Agnes survived the three other principals in this peculiar quadrilateral and died in 1902, at the age of eighty.

When she first met Lewes, Marian Evans was thirty-two. Until that time, her life had been lived in solemn and monotonous rectitude. She was born Mary Ann Evans at South Farm on the estate of Arbury in Warwickshire on November 22, 1819, into an England still recovering from the Napoleonic Wars. Her father, Robert Evans, a farm agent on the estate, was the dominant influence in her early life. Some of his characteristics were later to be immortalized by his daughter in *Adam Bede*.

At the age of five, she was sent to a boarding school. Even as a schoolgirl, it was remarked that she had an unusually powerful mind. When Marian was fifteen, her mother died. Two years later, the young lass was obliged to take care of the home for her father and brother, a responsibility which turned her into a serious young woman.

But her new chores did not in any way change her bent. She had a voracious intellectual appetite and, freed from the dull routine of classes, went to tutors for lessons in Italian and German. Nonetheless, it was a solitary life for a girl, shut up in a remote farmhouse in an atmosphere of strict piety, with no social contacts of her own age, and no gaiety whatever. Not surprisingly, her first letters show her to be a self-complacent prig and a bluestocking.

It is hardly surprising either that Marian Evans was slow to mature as a creative writer, for she lived in the shadow of her father. It was upon him that she bestowed all her affection, administering to his needs as a sacred duty until she was in her thirtieth year. Fortunately, the family had moved to Coventry in 1841. There she made a number of literary friendships, especially with Charles Bray and his wife and Charles Hennell. It was largely through them that her intellectual interests expanded—not always to her father's pleasure.

During the last three years of his life, Robert Evans made many demands on his daughter's time. Apart from her household duties, she had to read to him for hours on end every day. Moreover, she spent great stretches of time translating into English the works of the philosophers Strauss and Spinoza—an exacting and tedious task, even "soul-stupefying." The day of her father's death, May 31, 1849, marks the end of an arduous chapter in her life.

By this time, she was cultured, bookish, and critical, particularly critical about orthodox Christianity which had absorbed her earlier thinking, but which she had now come to reject. She was a writer of essays and treatises—far far from fiction. Now, after her father's death, she was overcome by a sense of bereavement and desolation. Her neighbors and close friends, the Brays, at once came

THE BIRTHPLACE OF GEORGE ELIOT   *This fine English provincial home in which the novelist resided up to the age of 22 is located in Arbury in Warwickshire.*

to her rescue; and a week after the funeral, they hustled her off on a trip to the Continent. She was settled into a comfortable boarding house in Geneva where she spent eight months of tranquility, and where she was able to put her life into perspective.

She was still quite unaware of her true vocation, but ideas and feelings were taking shape within her. Her letters home lost some of their smugness, and included lively character sketches of her fellow guests at the *pension*. What she needed to evoke the creative artist lying deep within her was a passionate human experience which would involve every fiber of her being.

With her warm, sympathetic nature and her keen interest in people, she found no difficulty in making friends, though few intimate ones. Unfortunately, her physical appearance did not inspire love in men—certainly not passion. She was a plain and rather ungainly woman. Acutely aware that Nature had been unkind to her, she was diffident and had a tendency to belittle herself, an attitude which persisted throughout life.

Her novels do not cloak her resentment at man's high susceptibility to female beauty. Nevertheless, Nature did, in fact, compensate for her plainness with strength of intellect and strength of character, attributes which captured the rapt attention of cultured and distinguished men. Herbert Spencer, the greatest English philosopher of the nineteenth century, who met her after she had taken up a career in journalism, writes of her in his *Autobiography*:

> *In physique, there was, perhaps, a trace of that masculinity characterizing her intellect; for though of but ordinary feminine height, she was strongly built. The head, too, was larger than is usual in women.*
>
> *Striking by its power when in repose, her face was remarkably transfigured by a smile; but with her smile, there was habitually mingled an expression of sympathy, either for the person smiled at or the person smiled with.*
>
> *Her voice was a contralto of rather low pitch and, I*

*believe, naturally strong . . . but the habit of subduing
her voice was so constant that I suspect its real power
was rarely, if ever, heard. Its tones were always gentle
and, like the smile, sympathetic . . . .*

*Conscientious and just in all relations and conse-
quently indignant against wrong, she was nevertheless
so tolerant of human weakness as to be quickly forgiving,
and, indeed, was prone to deprecate harsh judgments.
This last trait was, I doubt not, in part caused by constant study of her own defects.*

*She complained of being troubled by double con-
sciousness—a current of self-criticism being an habitual
accompaniment of anything she was saying or doing, and
this, naturally, tended towards self-depreciation and self-
distrust.*

*Her philosophical powers were remarkable. I have
known but few men with whom I could discuss a question in philosophy with more satisfaction. Capacity for
abstract thinking is rarely found along with capacity for
concrete representation, even in men; and among
women, such a union of the two as existed in her has, I
should think, never been paralleled.*

*In early days she was, I believe, sometimes viva-
cious, but she was not so when I first knew her, nor afterwards. Probably this was the reason why the wit and the
humour which from time to time gave signs of their
presence were not frequently displayed. Calmness was
an habitual trait. There was never any indication of
mental excitement, still less of mental strain; but the
impression constantly produced was that of latent power
—the ideas which came from her being manifestly the
products of a large intelligence. And yet this large intelligence working easily, of which she must have been con-
scious, was not accompanied by any marked self-confi-*

GEORGE ELIOT   A painting by F. W. Burton
made in 1865 when the writer was 46 years old.

*dence. Difference of opinion she frequently expressed
in a half apologetic manner.*

Marian, too, wrote appreciatively of Spencer: "My brightest
spot, next to my love of *old* friends, is the deliciously calm *new*
friendship that Herbert Spencer gives me. We see each other every
day, and have a delightful camaraderie in everything. But for him,
my life would be desolate enough." Spencer had everything that
Marian Evans might have been expected to seek from a man. He
was a Midlander like herself, was handsome, kindly, already a
renowned philosopher, and within a few months of her own age.
Both delighted in abstract discussion, in music, and in the arts.
It was Spencer who first tried to persuade her to try writing novels,
urging that she had keen observation, great analytical powers, unusual intuition of character, sympathy and tolerance towards
human weaknesses, wit and wide culture—all the necessary qualities, he thought. But she would not heed his counsel, refusing to
believe she could do it well.

It seemed such an obvious match of two brilliant minds that
rumor was not wanting. There was, however, one incontestable
snag—Spencer was not in love with her, nor did he have the slightest intention of being "made a drudge" (his own phrase) by marriage. "There were reports that I was in love with her and that
we were about to be married," he wrote later, "but neither of these
reports was true." And there is a sad hint in his statement that
beauty was a *sine qua non* for him, "as was once unhappily proved
when the intellectual traits and the emotional traits were of the
highest."

Indeed, it was Herbert Spencer who, in 1851, was to introduce
her to George Henry Lewes. Lewes wrote eight years later: "It was
through him that I learned to know Marian—to know her was to
love her. Since then my life has been a new birth. To her I owe all
my prosperity and all my happiness."

For her, it was not love at first sight. Two years later, she wrote: "He has quite won my liking, in spite of myself." But when she succumbed, she succumbed completely, as is shown in her letters to her friends and in the dedications of her novels: they were always addressed, with love, to "my husband."

They were as unlikely a pair of lovers as could be imagined. He was two and a half years older than she, the grandson of a once famous comedian, Charles Lee Lewes. His father, John Lee Lewes, had managed the Theatre Royal in Liverpool. Naturally enough, he gravitated towards the theatre after leaving school but he also read widely in religion, philosophy, and physiology. In 1838, he spent some time in Germany, learned the language and devoured German philosophy and literature. Then he returned to London as a freelance journalist.

Lewes was by no means prepossessing to look at. His skin was pitted by smallpox, but like Marian Evans, a smile could transfigure his face. Marian once described him "as a sort of miniature Mirabeau in appearance." And one contemporary writer noted that the "wonderful expressiveness of his eyes made one forget the unlovely rest." As a young man, Lewes was aggressive and boastful—and a little too pushing. Yet Thomas Carlyle, not the most restrained of critics, called him "the prince of journalists."

From the launching of the *Leader* in 1850 until he ran off with Marian Evans in 1854, Lewes was its literary editor and its most prolific contributor, writing book reviews, dramatic criticism, and general articles. Indeed, he was the mainspring of every periodical, including the *Fortnightly Review,* with which he was associated. Lewes was, in fact, a born editor. But because of his unfortunate marriage, he was an unhappy man, and there is little doubt that he discussed his private life with Marian.

They were now seeing each other regularly. Once they had acknowledged that they were in love with one another they must have had many anxious talks about how to arrange their future together. Certainly, in the spring of 1854, Marian Evans seemed to be preparing her friends for a shock by mentioning Lewes in terms

of affection in her letters. On July 20 came her much-quoted letter
of farewell to her three dearest friends, which ran:

> *Dear Friends—all three—I have only time to say goodbye,*
> *and God bless you. Post restante, Weimar, for the next*
> *six weeks, and afterwards Berlin. Ever your loving and*
> *grateful Marian.*

A shock it was, this decision to go off with Lewes. Her brother
Isaac promptly disowned her, and her sister Chrissie kept silent and
aloof for five years. Her close friends made no secret of their disapproval. Marian accepted all this, without complaint or rancor,
as the price she must pay for doing what she felt her future happiness dictated. Her diary for the day they went off together, however,
reveals nothing of the stress and strain which she must have felt.

> *The day was glorious and our passage (to Antwerp) per-*
> *fect. The sunset was lovely, but still lovelier the dawn as*
> *we were passing up the Scheldt between two and three in*
> *the morning. The crescent moon, the stars, the first faint*
> *blush of the dawn reflected in the glassy river, the dark*
> *mass of clouds on the horizon, which sent forth flashes*
> *of lightning, and the graceful forms of the boats and sail-*
> *ing vessels, painted in jet-black on the reddish gold of the*
> *sky and water, made up an unforgettable picture. Then*
> *the sun rose and lighted up the sleepy shores of Belgium*
> *with their fringe of long grass, their rows of poplars, their*
> *church spires and farm buildings.*

It was all ordinary enough, revealing nothing of the tension
and excitement within. But three months later, a letter from Wei-
mar to her friends, the Brays, included this passage:

> *It is possible that you have already a report prevalent in*
> *London that Mr. Lewes has "run away" from his wife and*
> *family. I wish you to be in possession of the facts which*

GEORGE HENRY LEWES

*will enable you to contradict this report whenever it
reaches you. Since we left England he has been in constant correspondence with his wife; she has had all the
money due to him in London; and his children are his
principal thought and anxiety.*

*Circumstances with which I am not concerned, and
which have arisen since he left England, have led him to
determine on a separation from Mrs. Lewes, but he has
never contemplated that separation as a total release from
responsibility towards her. On the contrary, he has been
anxiously awaiting restoration to health that he may once
more work hard, not only to provide for his children, but
to supply his wife's wants so far as that is not done by
another. I have seen all the correspondence between
them, and it has assured me that his conduct as a husband
has been not only irreproachable, but generous and self-
sacrificing to a degree far beyond any standard fixed by
the world. This is the simple truth and no flattering picture drawn by my partiality. . . .*

*Of course many silly myths are already afloat about
me, in addition to the truth, which of itself would be
thought matter for scandal. I am quite unconcerned about
them except as they may cause pain to my real friends.
If you can hear of anything that I have said, done or written in relation to Mr. Lewes, beyond the simple fact that
I am attached to him and that I am living with him, do me
the justice to believe that it is false. . . . The only influence
I should ever dream of exerting over him as to his conduct
towards his wife and children is that of stimulating his
conscientious care for them, if it needed any stimulus. . . .*

*I am quite prepared to accept the consequences of a
step which I have deliberately taken and to accept them
without irritation or bitterness. The most painful consequences will, I know, be the loss of friends. If I do not*

*write, therefore, understand that it is because I desire
not to obtrude myself. . . .*

Thus began their marriage without benefit of law or clergy, a union which endured happily until the death of Lewes twenty years later—but which was to agitate her contemporaries, embarrass her biographers, and provoke discussion on its rights and wrongs down to the 1920s. Nowadays, their decision to live together hardly raises an eyebrow, but the climate of opinion of her own time was quite different. Marian Evans, it seems, did not suffer a twinge of regret. On September 4, 1855, fourteen months after going off with Lewes, she wrote to Mrs. Caroline Bray, a disapproving old friend:

*If there is any one action or relation of my life which is
and always has been profoundly serious, it is my relation
to Mr. Lewes. . . . Light and easily broken ties are what
I neither desire theoretically nor could live for practically.
Women who are satisfied with such ties do not act as I
have done. That any unworldly, unsuperstitious person
who is sufficiently acquainted with the realities of life can
pronounce my relation to Mr. Lewes immoral, I can only
understand by remembering how subtle and complex are
the influences that mould opinion. But I do remember
this: and I indulge in no arrogant or uncharitable
thoughts about those who condemn us, even though we
might have expected a somewhat different verdict. From
the majority of persons, of course, we never looked for
anything but condemnation. We are leading no life of
self-indulgence, except indeed that, being happy in each
other, we find everything easy.*

It was, in fact, a working honeymoon in Germany. Lewes busied himself collecting material for his life of Goethe, and Marian wrote for the *Westminster Review* and translated Spinoza. They returned to England that same year; and after a number of moves, finally found lodgings together in Richmond.

The first hint that she was trying to persuade herself to attempt writing fiction occurs in her diary for August 18, 1856: "Talked with George of my novel." One morning later, she woke up and told Lewes that she had dreamed herself engaged on a story titled "The Sad Fortunes of the Reverend Amos Barton." He thought it a good title, and cautiously schooled her to the task. At last she drew up a plan for a series of sketches based on her own observation of the clergy, *Scenes of Clerical Life,* beginning with "Amos Barton."

Lewes sent her manuscript to John Blackwood with a covering letter in which he indicated that it had been submitted to him by a friend for an opinion on its merits. Blackwood was reasonably enthusiastic. There followed an exchange of letters between Lewes and himself about the new writer—Blackwood was given to understand that the name George Eliot concealed a man's identity.

Although Blackwood continued to publish her first efforts at fiction, neither Marian Evans nor Lewes would reveal to him that a woman's hand was behind the work. Even when her writing was bringing the approbation of such great novelists as Dickens and Thackeray, they insisted on keeping up the silly pretense at all costs —and one cost was a lasting quarrel with Chapman of the *Westminster Review.* The continued deception serves to show how shy, nervous, and unsure of herself was the emerging literary genius. At first it was perhaps reasonable to argue that failure as a story writer might have an adverse effect on her freelance journalism. Surely, the praise showered on her first series in *Blackwood's* must have dispeled that fear.

Soon all literary London was discussing the unknown writer of the clerical series in *Blackwood's.* But Chapman, her main source of income, suspected the truth: that his contributor, Marian Evans, was George Eliot. When he began asking her friend, Herbert Spencer, point-blank whether it was so, he received a reproachful letter from Marian. Eventually, to silence such inquiries, Lewes wrote to Chapman: "Your continuing to impute those works to Mrs. Lewes may be *meant* as a compliment, but *is* an offense against delicacy and friendship. As you seem so very slow in appreciating her feelings on this point, she authorizes me to state, as distinctly as language can do so, that she is not the author of *Adam Bede.*"

It seems a thousand pities that such a lying and pompous letter was sent at all, for despite all their efforts, the real identity of George Eliot soon became known to all who were interested. There were other embarrassments, too—not the least being the claim of a Mr. Liggins, a baker's son in Warwickshire, to be the author of *Adam Bede.* Indeed, Marian Evans felt it necessary to deny his authorship in a letter to *The Times* signed George Eliot. Other rascally characters also tried to cash in on the success of *Adam Bede,* including an unscrupulous publisher who announced a sequel to it entitled *Adam Bede Junior.*

Such irritations notwithstanding the years from 1860 until her death twenty years later brought her uninterrupted success with *The Mill on the Floss* (1860), *Silas Marner* (1861), *Romola* (1862), *Felix Holt* (1866), *The Spanish Gypsy* (1868), *Middlemarch* (1871-1872), and *Daniel Deronda* (1874-1876). There were obvious signs that her economic well-being diminished her domestic frustrations. In 1861 she wrote to a friend:

> *I have ceased to be "Miss Evans" for anyone who has personal relations with me—having held myself under all the responsibilities of a married woman. I wish this to be distinctly understood; and when I tell you that we have a great boy of 18 at home who calls me mother, as well as two other boys, almost as tall, who write to me under the same name, you will understand that the point is not one of mere egoism or personal dignity, when I request that anyone who has a regard for me will cease to speak of me by my maiden name.*

Eventually, through their courage and social tact, the union of

NOVELS

OF

GEORGE ELIOT

VOL. III.

SILAS MARNER

WITH ILLUSTRATIONS

RAVELOE VILLAGE

WILLIAM BLACKWOOD AND SONS

EDINBURGH AND LONDON

Henry Lewes and Marian Evans was accepted, at least in literary circles.

By November, 1863, Lewes and Marian moved into their final home together—the Priory in Regent's Park. Here she was to write her last three novels and her poems, and here they held the Sunday afternoon receptions which soon developed into one of the most brilliant salons of literary London. Indeed, George Eliot became a sort of Delphic oracle for young men of letters who flocked to her for advice and encouragement.

But Lewes' health was failing and causing her the deepest anxiety, although both worked on in their different fields. Life became more expansive, however, with frequent visits abroad—to France, Italy, Germany, Spain. By 1864, she managed to stop referring to "Mr. Lewes" in her letters. "My trouble now," she writes, "is George's delicate health. He gets thinner and thinner. He is going to try what horseback will do, and I am looking forward to that with some hope."

The death of George Henry Lewes, in 1878, shattered her world and she did not emerge from her stupor of grief for weeks. Immediately, she set about establishing a scholarship to perpetuate his memory. One of the first people to be allowed to see her again was John Walter Cross, a banker and ardent admirer who revered her novels. She and Lewes had first become acquainted with him in Rome eight years earlier. He was twenty-one years younger than she, but deep sympathy drew them together—his mother had died the week before Lewes. This acquaintanceship matured into friendship, and when his sister died in childbirth, George Eliot wrote him a beautiful and moving letter.

TITLE PAGE   *From first edition of "Silas Marner."*

Indeed, it turned out to be John Walter Cross who provided the final sensation in the life of George Eliot, for in 1880, he married her when he was in his fortieth and she in her sixty-first year. A series of letters written by her to Cross during her deep mourning for Lewes shows how she gradually turned to him for comfort. For instance:

> *The perpetual mourner—the grief that can never be healed—is innocently enough felt to be wearisome by the rest of the world. And my sense of desolation increases. Each day seems a new beginning—a new acquaintance with grief.*

It could be said that this bizarre marriage with Cross was her greatest tribute to Lewes, the man she loved but could not marry; that when the crutch she leaned on so heavily for a score of years was knocked away from her, she could not go on unaided. However that may be, within eight months of walking up the aisle at St. George's, Hanover Square, London, a bride for the first time at sixty-one, Marian Evans alias George Eliot was dead.

Dostoevsky and Apollinaria

Fedor Mikhailovich Dostoevsky is known to the world as one of the nineteenth century's greatest writers. His novels explore the human soul with a degree of psychological insight unequaled in his time; his plots deal with the unbridled instincts, mad desires, and passionate drives of a host of fantastic characters. Yet the most turbulent of his creations were matched by the events of his own life.

In 1849, when Dostoevsky was only twenty eight, he was led out to face a firing squad in St. Petersburg. Together with 20 members of a revolutionary literary group, he had been condemned to death for taking part in a plot against Czar Nicholas I. So it was that in Christmas week, in a temperature of 20° below, the novelist, clad only in a shirt, watched the three leaders of his group as they were blindfolded and tied to posts. He saw the firing squad, drawn up in the square, raise their rifles.

Then he blinked in amazement as a general, waving a white handkerchief, stopped the execution, and ordered the prisoners to be unbound. A new sentence was read out: their lives were to be spared by the grace of the Czar. Dostoevsky now faced four years' hard labor, and a second four years of military service in Siberia.

For some, the commutation had come too late. One of the leaders became a gibbering lunatic as he was led away; the hair of another turned white. But Dostoevsky seemed to survive the nerve-shattering experience, although there are some who believe that this event is the key to understanding the strange and disordered life he was later to lead. In any event, he was henceforth to be more concerned with literary than political revolution.

Dostoevsky was one of a family of five brothers and two sisters brought up in a wing of the Marinsky Hospital for the Poor in Moscow. The family was ruled by their doctor father whose power was absolute and unquestioned. However, Dr. Dostoevsky did not believe in corporal punishment; although he maintained rigid discipline, he never laid a hand on his children. Moreover, he was so parsimonious that he gave his sons not one penny of pocket money until they were seventeen.

The household groaned under a puritan atmosphere in which sex was a subject one didn't even mention. Because the growing brood was never allowed to go anywhere alone, Fedor's only contact with the opposite sex, until he was sixteen, was his sisters, both of whom were younger than he. Perhaps this explains his fascination with the theme of the corruption of minors which recurs throughout his work, as well as for the fact that his male characters are often involved with girls half their age. Freud sought to explain Dostoevsky's character by suggesting that he was in the grip of a powerful Oedipus complex which made him an epileptic. Dostoevsky himself admitted that during these epileptic seizures he suffered an intense feeling of guilt, followed by a brief period of lucidity, and then by loss of consciousness.

His mother's death, when he was barely sixteen, disrupted the family life. His father took to the bottle and to mistresses. Then the doctor was brutally murdered, leaving Dostoevsky an orphan at eighteen, lonely, self-conscious, and without visible means of support.

Freud argued that Fedor's epilepsy was a comparatively innocuous complaint until the time of his father's murder; that event, however, produced lasting feelings of guilt and remorse within Dostoevsky because, subconsciously, he had wished for his father's death. Freud also believed that the Oedipus complex explained a great deal of Dostoevsky's darker side, including his acceptance of suffering as a just punishment; Freud's theory would also explain Dostoevsky's rebellion against all forms of authority, a rebellion that is mirrored in his heroes who seem always to be at war with both God and Czar.

After his mother's death, Fedor and his eldest brother Michael were sent to the School for Military Engineering in St. Petersburg. Confronted with the soulless routine of military life, Fedor consoled himself with creative dreams, planning plays and novels, and shutting out the harsh realities around him.

In 1841, when he was twenty, he graduated as a junior second-lieutenant. He now had the right to live outside the school and attend an officers' class. He rented an apartment with some colleagues, and spent most of his time writing dramas and reading. Dostoevsky made the grade of second-lieutenant in 1843. He was posted to the drafting room of the Department of Engineering, but he found the work unendurable, and resigned after one year .

His tortured background, coupled with his epilepsy, made
Fedor shy and timid in the presence of girls. The story goes that

*DOSTOEVSKY   Photo of the great Russian writer
taken in 1870 when he was about 50 years old.*

on being presented to a celebrated beauty at a soirée before his graduation he fainted.

Once he had resigned his commission, he worked with a fury on his novel, *Poor Folk*, apparently prepared to stake all his hopes on its success. Although he was weary, lonely, and unknown, and without a kopeck to his name, he busied himself correcting and rewriting his first major work until he felt that his manuscript was fit to be offered. But offered to whom? He had no literary acquaintanceships. However, he was sharing quarters with Dmitri Grigorovich who had secured a toehold in the world of letters with one short article. Grigorovich showed *Poor Folk* to the poet Nekrasov who was at that time editing a literary magazine. Nekrasov finished reading the novel at four o'clock one morning, and he was so delighted with it that he insisted on visiting Dostoevsky at once. "But he'll be asleep," Grigorovich protested.

"What does that matter?" replied Nekrasov. "We'll waken him. This is more important than sleep."

The manuscript was next shown to the distinguished critic Belinsky who acclaimed it with equal enthusiasm. Before the novel's publication in January, 1846, the literary men of St. Petersburg were already heralding the arrival of a genius. "A new Gogol has appeared!" was the excited claim.

Dostoevsky wrote to his brother Michael:

> I don't think my fame will ever again reach such a peak as now. Such respect everywhere as you would not believe, and terrible curiosity about me . . . I am everywhere received as a prodigy . . .

Sudden fame went to his head, and a little money proved to be a dangerous thing. Dazzled by the unlooked-for acclaim, Dostoevsky began to show an arrogant belief in his superiority, a stance which made him the immediate target of waspish tongues. His debts multiplied, and he found himself compelled to work at a feverish pace to keep up with them. His next novel, *The Double*, published a month after *Poor Folk*, aroused active hostility. Other shorter works were greeted with disdain.

The years 1847-1849, prior to his prison sentence and Siberian exile, were spent in a dissolute round of gambling dens and brothels. Although Dostoevsky was filled with shame and remorse for his depraved behavior, there is little doubt that his experiences brought a new dimension to his novels. His characters were drawn from life, and then heightened by his great imagination.

Dostoevsky's four-year term in Omsk Prison was a period of "inexpressible, interminable suffering," as he tersely described it. By the time he had served out his sentence, his appearance was grim. A thick moustache and a wiry, spade-shaped beard cloaked his thin, stubborn mouth. His hair was light, and closely cropped over a broad forehead. His eyes were so deeply sunk into his head that they seemed to have all but disappeared. What could be seen of his face had an unhealthy aspect—ashen, freckled, and furrowed with wrinkles.

When in February, 1854, he was released and sent to Semipalatinsk as a private in a Siberian army regiment, it seemed a comfortable change. He had grown stronger, and his epileptic fits had become less frequent. But he had been so deprived of feminine society that he dreamed of being with females as the highest form of human happiness. It was in this exalted mood that he fell in love with Maria, the wife of a local government official who was steadily drinking himself to death. As Dostoevsky put it: "The mere fact that a woman held out her hand to me marked a veritable epoch in my life."

When her husband died, Fedor married Maria. But it was a marriage that was doomed from the start. His first crush was turned to nothingness when he met a woman he was destined never to marry, nor even to totally possess. Her name was Apollinaria Prokofievna Suslova, and she became the tempest of his life. She lives on in half a dozen of his most compelling novels.

Dostoevsky met her in 1861. He was then back in St. Petersburg, and once again in public favor. Radical groups were springing up everywhere. The writer who had been condemned to death now had strong appeal for the intellectual youth of Russia. Student societies deluged him with invitations to read from his works, particularly from his account of his life in prison, *Notes from the House of the Dead.*

*DOSTOEVSKY'S HOME   The writer's home in
Staraya, Russia, from a contemporary photograph.*

NEVSKY PROSPECT   *The famous boulevard in*
St. Petersburg as it looked in 1878.

After one of his readings, he was approached by a graceful
girl of 22, who told him in a low, drawling voice that she was attending lectures at the university and had been so impressed by his
works she had fallen in love with him. She had even written him
a short letter expressing her affection. Dostoevsky was struck at
once by her appearance: her large gray-blue eyes, her intelligent
face, her proud head. To him, she exuded strength and femininity.
They began to meet and to discuss literature. Apollinaria offered
him a little story of her own, which Dostoevsky published in a
periodical he was then editing.

Apollinaria encompassed all that Fedor found irresistible in women. He was 20 years older than she, but he had always been attracted to very young girls. She was exceptionally good-looking, and her every movement signaled sex to him. But more than that, her peasant background gave her qualities of earthiness and patience, and fed the nationalistic and reforming fervor that he was then experiencing.

Apollinaria typified the new generation in Russia — nihilistic and iconoclastic, with a deep idealism masked by a cynical turn of speech and casual behavior. She responded warmly to the new liberalism of the age, seeking personal freedom from all domestic, moral, and religious conventions. She was independent, proud, and self-reliant, qualities that captured the wholehearted love of the great novelist—and that wrecked her love for him, in the end.

Dostoevsky was her first love—and her first lover. She herself said later that she had given herself freely to this man of forty, with no thought of his age or appearance. Until she met him, she had been a virgin, not because of any moral scruple, but simply because she had found no one worthy of her love. But once having met him, she yielded "without question or calculation." According to a fellow-writer, the man to whom she surrendered was, at that time:

> ...either very tired or very sick, no longer young, very pale with an earthy pallor, his somber, tortured face covered, as if by a network, by some sort of extraordinary expressive shadows caused by the exertion of controlling the movements of his muscles. As though every muscle on this face with its sunken cheeks and broad high forehead was inspired by feeling and thought. And these feelings and thoughts pleaded for release, but were held back by the iron will of this emaciated yet at the same time thickset and broad-shouldered man, quiet and morose. It was just as though he were keeping himself under lock and key.

What did Apollinaria see in him? Certainly there was no physical lure for her. As she confessed to him, she had first been drawn by his insight into the wells of human character, and no doubt felt that he would understand and sympathize with her innermost self. Then there was the undoubted attraction of hero-worship, and the sense of flattery that such an unusual celebrity should be attracted to her.

But some of Dostoevsky's biographers feel that there was also a subconscious attraction to a similar nature, and that her so-far-unexpressed sexual personality responded to his eroticism—the mutual fascination of torturer and victim, in which she was the torturer and he the victim. For this girl would not concede that the woman should submit to the man in lovemaking, nor could she ever accept the potency and domination of the male.

It was in this phase of their relationship that things went wrong. Dostoevsky aroused her, but could not satisfy her; they were suited spiritually and emotionally, but not sexually. Thus, the association became complex, indeed anguished, for both. As a writer and thinker, he towered above Apollinaria; but as a partner, he disappointed her.

But if their relationship was bad for his peace of mind, it was certainly fruitful for literature. All the proud and exacting women of his later novels—Dunya in *Crime and Punishment,* Nastasya in *The Idiot,* Katerina Ivanovna in *The Brothers Karamazov,* and, of course, Polina in *The Gambler*—are really aspects of Apollinaria. Although Dostoevsky's wife Maria was still alive when his affair with Apollinaria began, she was a dying woman, and this added to his feelings of guilt and remorse.

Almost all we know of his intense love for Apollinaria has to be culled from her diary (*My Years Close to Dostoevsky*), which she kept in some detail. She married the critic Rozanov when she was forty and he was twenty-four. Rozanov records that he once asked her why she broke with the great novelist. She replied: "Because he refused to divorce his wife, who was a consumptive, as she was dying. In six months she was dead. But I was no longer in love with him."

"Why not?" Rozanov asked her.

"Because he wouldn't divorce her" was the answer.

Nevertheless, their affair lasted long after Maria's death in 1864. It is true, however, that while his wife was alive, Dostoevsky made no sacrifice whatsoever for Apollinaria who knew that he was keeping their liaison hidden from the dying woman. She knew, too, that his writing, his business, and his family all took precedence over her. She felt a deep sense of injustice; it seemed to her that she had given all for this love and he nothing.

She wrote to him:

> *Our relations were decorous as far as you were concerned. You behaved like a serious, busy person who understands his obligations after his own fashion and does not forget to enjoy himself either—on the contrary, you may have actually considered it necessary to enjoy yourself, on the basis of some great doctor or philosopher having asserted that it is neecssary for hard drinkers to get thoroughly drunk once a month.*

It seems clear that he tried to make himself her lord and master, whereas, sexually, she was the dominant force. This caused endless clashes and produced in her an overwhelming feeling of contempt and vindictiveness toward him. But every time she expressed her revulsion, his delight was heightened. Their relationship became a long drawn-out struggle. Her frustration was intensified by the shoddy nature of the affair—meetings in furnished rooms, adultery with a lover whose wife was dying, the fact that he treated her like a mistress and not like a twin literary spirit, his pathetic pretense of being the dominant partner. All this is implicit in one of her early letters to him in 1863:

*You are angry and you ask me not to write that I blush
because of my love for you. Not only will I refrain from
writing this, I can assure you that I have never written
and have never thought of writing that, since I never
blushed for my love. It was beautiful, even grandiose. I
could have written you that I blushed over our former
relations. But there should be nothing new in that for
you, since I have never concealed it—and how many
times did I want to break off those relations before my
going abroad!*

There is, of course, little doubt that Dostoevsky was not aware,
at first, of the intensity of his need for her. What began for him
as an adventure swiftly grew into a grand passion. By the early
months of 1863 he was so utterly infatuated with her that he
could not pass a day without seeing her. She had threaded herself
into his very existence. At home, a tubercular wife and a lonely
study awaited him. Outside was this girl who spelled excitement
and joy.

By the spring of 1863, Maria's condition had worsened, and
it became essential to give her a change of climate. Fedor and
Apollinaria decided to go abroad in the summer, there they could
bring their clandestine affair into the free light of day, and at last
live together without concealment.

No sooner had they made this definite decision than Dostoevsky fell afoul of the Russian authorities for a second time. One
of the articles in his periodical, *Time,* was deemed subversive; as
editor-in-chief, he had to justify it to the censors.

So Apollinaria went off to Paris alone. All summer he tried to
extricate himself from his difficulties so that he could join her,
but his affairs were in such a tangled state that he dared not
leave St. Petersburg. Publication of *Time* was suspended, and he
had to fob off creditors, contributors, and subscribers. He had to
find money for his many commitments—for Maria, for her treat-

DOSTOEVSKY'S FIRST WIFE   *The writer was married for seven years to Maria. After her death, he continued to support her son by a former marriage, though the boy's upkeep compounded Dostoevsky's financial hardship.*

ment, for his apartment in St. Petersburg, for his trip to Paris, and
for Apollinaria.

Apollinaria wrote to him until August, pleading with him to
join her in Paris, swearing that she loved him passionately. Then
the letters stopped. For three weeks there was silence.

He rushed through his affairs, collected what money he could
—which was little enough—and set off. But he did not go directly
to his loved one. Instead, true to that strange duality in his nature,
he yielded to his other great love—gambling. He stopped off at
Wiesbaden and played the tables.

For three days he tried his luck at roulette, won a large sum,
lost half of it, then managed to tear himself away with five thousand
francs safely in his pocket. His self-confidence restored, he arrived in
Paris, and promptly dispatched a letter to Apollinaria. Then without waiting for an answer, he turned up at the pension on the
Left Bank where she was staying. She was astonished to see him,
and asked him why he had ignored her letter warning him not to
come. She described this difficult interview in her diary:

> *He fell at my feet and, clasping my knees, kept saying:*
> *"I've lost you—I knew it." Having calmed down, he be-*
> *gan questioning me: What sort of man was it? An*
> *Adonis, perhaps, young and talkative? For some time I*
> *refused to answer him.*
>
> *"You have given yourself to him completely?"*
> *"Don't question me, it isn't right," I said. I told him*
> *I was very much in love with this man.*
>
> *"Are you happy?"*
> *"No."*
>
> *"How can that be? You are in love and unhappy.*
> *It this possible?"*
> *"He doesn't love me."*
>
> *"Doesn't love you!" he cried out, clutching his head*
> *in despair. "But you don't love him like a slave—tell me*

*that! I must know. You'd go with him to the ends of the
earth—isn't that so?"*

*"No, I'm going to the country," I said in a torrent
of tears, and at this point, I told him what had happened.*

Her story was a commonplace one in Paris: a handsome medical student, a Spaniard, graceful and flattering, had fascinated her,
and, following her code of independence and freedom to love, she
had given herself wholeheartedly to the youth. She found in his
embraces the healthy sensuality, the simplicity and ease which were
all absent in her relations with Dostoevsky. The Spaniard, however, cooled off quickly, no doubt terrified by the fires he had
kindled. To him, it was a mere episode; to her, it was her first real
experience of natural, uncomplicated lovemaking. She tried desperately to hold on to him, only to find that she had exchanged
the complications of an affair with an older man for the mindless
animalism of youth.

All this had been raging within her while Dostoevsky was
winning at the tables. She knew very well how her infidelity would
hurt him, but she seemed to take malicious pleasure in inflicting
this pain on him, to show him that she was no longer in his grip,
that she had no further need of him.

When her affair with the student went sour, her thoughts
turned again to her first lover. She was eager for his visit, and she
yearned to unburden herself to him. Her diary records that Dostoevsky heard her confession of infidelity with his head between
his hands and his body slumped in a chair. When she had finished,
he sat up and cried:

*"Oh, Polia, why are you so unfortunate? It was bound to
happen, your falling in love with another. I knew it!
After all, you made a mistake in loving me, because you
have a big heart. You waited until you were 23. You are
the only woman who demands no commitments of any*

sort. But think of the cost. Men and women are not the same in this respect—the man takes, the woman gives."

When he returned to his hotel, he found the cold, matter-of-fact letter from her, breaking off their affair. The letter ended: "Farewell, my dear, I wanted to see you, but what would it lead to? I very much wanted to talk to you about Russia." There was not one word of kindness or compassion for the great man she was casting from her.

Once Apollinaria realized that her Spaniard was avoiding her and had no intension of continuing the liaison, she ran to Dostoevsky for advice on how to be avenged on his rival! She read him the draft of a wounding letter she planned to send to the youth, and she discussed whether she should return to him all the money he had spent on entertaining her.

Dostoevsky dealt with all these preposterous requests tenderly and sympathetically, and even persuaded her to go on the tour that they had planned so eagerly in St. Petersburg, promising to be "like a brother" to her. She was quick to see that her unfortunate little affair had actually increased his love and desire for her. Now she proposed to use her clear domination over him mercilessly. Dostoevsky's love was to enter a phase of masochistic endurance.

They left Paris for Baden-Baden in September, and Dostoevsky promptly visited the gaming tables. In two days, he had lost all his money. He pawned his watch and she a ring; both lived in fear of the hotel manager. Dostoevsky had to send frantic appeals to Russia for money. As soon as it arrived, he was in high spirits. But his other game was faring no better. Apollinaria refused all his advances as a lover, however skillfully he tried to cloak them. Notes from her diary reveal that she was well aware of what he was about.

He is playing roulette all the time and, in general, he is very carefree. On the way, he told me he was not without hope—I made no comment on this, but I knew nothing

IN MILITARY UNIFORM
Dostoevsky, at age 27, as a junior second lieutenant of the Czar's army.

would come of it. Last evening these hopes were particularly obvious...

His daily contact with her inflamed him, and he was slowly being consumed by his unsatisfied desire for her. But he was also

ashamed of himself for wanting her physically; he was unable to keep up the role of solicitous brother. Apollinaria made no attempt to help him. Often she teased him, using her power over him to the limit, then refusing him all gratification.

After their arrival in Baden-Baden, she noted in her diary: "It seems to me I shall not come to love anybody, at any time." She was obviously intent on making him pay for the frailty of her second lover.

They traveled through Italy, with all its beckoning temptations, but they were as far from love as ever. By the end of October, they were in Turin and went on together to Berlin. There they parted: Apollinaria for Paris, and Dostoevsky for Hamburg and another frenzied spell of gambling, which cost him all his remaining funds. He wrote an appeal to her for money; she pawned her watch to send him some—which he used to travel to his wife's deathbed.

He found himself more enamored of Apollinaria than ever. It was during this period that he coined his phrase for her—he called her his "eternal mate."

Meanwhile he had to cope with certain harsh realities. First, he had to transport his dying wife back to Moscow and set her up in a new home; then he had to get busy on his new periodical, *The Epoch;* and he also had to work on his new book, *Notes from the Underground.*

THE SCRAWL AND DOODLINGS OF A MASTER   *Here is a page*
from Dostoevsky's manuscript of his novel "The Possessed."

Maria died on April 15, 1864. He wrote of her: "This was the most honest, the most noble and magnanimous woman of all those whom I have known in all my life."

But he was oppressed by a heavy sense of guilt because his heart and mind yearned not for the most honest of women but for his "eternal mate."

Yet Apollinaria was drifting farther and farther away from him, playing her power game with a dozen men, and finding nothing but bitterness. In September, 1864, she wrote: "They speak to me of Fedor Mikhailovich. I simply hate him. He has made me suffer so much, when it was possible to do without suffering."

Two years passed between their parting in Berlin and their next meeting—two years in which their correspondence was shot through with bitterness and recriminations. Third parties were brought into the exhausting fray, particularly Apollinaria's sister Nadezhda, a brilliant medical student who became the first woman doctor in Russia. Apollinaria complained to her of Dostoevsky's treatment, and Nadezhda immediately wrote to the author, demanding an answer to her sister's allegations. This produced a letter from Dostoevsky to Nadezhda, which movingly illustrated his anguish:

> *Apollinaria is a great egoist. Her egoism and conceit are colossal. She demands all from people, all perfections; she does not forgive a single imperfection for the sake of other good qualities, but she absolves herself from the smallest obligation to anybody else. To this day, she upbraids me with being unworthy of her love. She never stops complaining and reproaching me, and yet it was she who greeted me in Paris in '63 with the words: "You have come a bit too late"; i.e., that she loved somebody else, when two weeks earlier she had still been hotly protesting her love for me in her letters. It is not for loving*

another that I blame her, but for those four lines she sent to my hotel with the harsh phrase, "you have come a bit too late."

. . . I still love her, I love her very much, but now I wish I did not. She is not worthy of such love. I am sorry for her, because I foresee that she will always be unhappy. She will not find a friend or happiness anywhere. Nobody who demands everything from other people but exempts himself from all obligations can ever find happiness.

Their meeting after the two-year break was in Wiesbaden. It was the beginning of the end. Dostoevsky was still desperate with desire for her; she bestowed her favors on him like alms. Feeling their love withering away, he tried to coerce her into marrying him at once. Apollinaria rudely rejected his offer and returned to Paris.

He plunged into a mad whirl of gambling and lost everything. He was now at his lowest ebb. He was unable to pay for a meal in his hotel. He had pawned all he could. Although he had been working feverishly on two great works, *The Gambler* and *Crime and Punishment*, he could not bear to continue with *The Gambler,* for the central woman character was Apollinaria.

She returned to St. Petersburg in October, 1865, and Dostoevsky again pressed her to marry him. She had not the slightest intention of yielding to this pressure. Indeed, during her four months' stay in St. Petersburg, she forced their relationship to the breaking point.

His muddled life was now crowding in on him from every quarter. His creditors were dunning him; he had frequent attacks of epilepsy; and he faced, at last, the utter hopelessness of his tortured love affair. He decided, once and for all, to terminate the affair. So, in the spring of 1866, they said their good-byes, knowing that they were bowing out of each other's life.

According to Dostoevsky's daughter, they did meet once again, in the late 1870s, when the author's fame was at its peak. He was visited by a veiled lady who refused to give her name. She lifted the veil and looked at him for a long time. "Please be good enough to tell me your name," said Dostoevsky. The visitor dropped her veil without uttering a word, and left the house. When later he realized that his visitor was Apollinaria, he is quoted as saying: "She hasn't changed, but she has disappeared from my memory so completely that I failed to recognize her."

Bernard Shaw
and
Ellen Terry

"The ideal love affair," said George Bernard Shaw, "is one conducted by mail." But then, he was a writing machine—he must have penned a quarter of a million letters and postcards during his 94-year life span. And women always appealed far more to his imagination than to his flesh.

He dreamed of women's beauty, but he was reluctant to risk disillusionment in physical contact with them. He once declared

that the sexual act was to him monstrous and indecent, and that he could not understand how any self-respecting man and woman could face each other in the daylight after spending the night together. Shaw had no sexual experience until he was 29.

Two of his paper courtships, however, have become famous. Both were with great actresses, Dame Ellen Terry and Mrs. Patrick Campbell. He told his approved biographer, Hesketh Pearson:

> *My correspondence with Ellen Terry was a wholly satisfactory love affair. I could have met her at any time but I did not wish to complicate such a delightful intercourse. She got tired of five husbands, but she never got tired of me . . . .*

Shaw, who had built up a tremendous reputation as a music critic and then as a dramatic critic before winning fame as a playwright, tried his damnedest to break up the invincible stage partnership of Henry Irving and Ellen Terry. In his preface to *Ellen Terry and Bernard Shaw: A Correspondence Edited by Christopher St. John,* he writes:

> *To me, however, Irving's thirty years at the Lyceum, though a most imposing episode in the history of the English theatre, were an exasperating waste of the talent of the two artists who had seemed to me peculiarly fitted to lift the theatre out of its old ruts and head it towards unexplored regions of drama. With Lyceum Shakespeare I had no patience . . . .*

GEORGE BERNARD SHAW   *The Irish dramatist as a young man.*

He goes on to describe how his correspondence with Ellen Terry began, when he was a professional music critic, through a move she made to help a young musician in whom she was interested. He adds:

> ... it must be borne in mind that long and intimate correspondence can occur only between people who never meet one another . . . . Ellen and I lived within twenty minutes of each other's doorstep, and yet lived in different worlds: she in a theatre that was a century behind the times, and I in a political society [the Fabian Society], a century ahead of them. We were both too busy to have any personal intercourse except with the people we were working with . . . .

So he rarely saw her, except across the footlights, until he wrote a play for her—*Captain Brassbound's Conversion*—and they had to meet daily at rehearsals. He writes:

> By that time, Irving had passed out of her life, and indeed of his own; and Ellen's heart was for the moment vacant. I could not help speculating as to the possibility of my filling the vacancy. But Providence had other views. At our first serious meeting in the rehearsal room at the Court Theatre, Ellen and I were talking together before business began when the door opened, and a young American actor, James Carew, who had been engaged to play the part of Captain Hamlin Kearney, came in. "Who is that?" said Ellen, looking at him with quick interest. "That's the American captain," I answered. Without an instant's hesitation she sailed across the room; put Mr. Carew in her pocket (so to speak), and married him.

Shaw was a bachelor in his forties when he first met the woman he *did* marry—Charlotte Payne-Townshend, a wealthy Irish girl with a social conscience, who became sick of the social whirl and

sought out the Fabians. Shaw found himself discussing his feelings
for Charlotte with his pen-lover, Ellen.

> *We have been joined by an Irish millionairess who has
> had cleverness and character enough to decline the station
> of life ("great catch for somebody") to which it pleased
> God to call her, and whom we have incorporated into our
> Fabian family with great success. I am going to refresh
> my heart by falling in love with her. I love falling in love
> —but, mind, only with her, not with the million; so some-
> body else must marry her if she can stand him after me.*

That was in the late summer of 1896. By October, when he
was back in London, he was writing to Ellen Terry:

> *Shall I marry my Irish millionairess? She . . . believes in
> freedom, and not in marriage; but I think I could prevail
> on her and then I should have ever so many hundreds a
> month for nothing. Would you ever in your secret soul
> forgive me, even though I am really fond of her and she of
> me? No, you wouldn't.*

The remark about getting hundreds a month for nothing was
typical Shavian blarney. In fact he not only recoiled from marriage
because it would disrupt the work program he had mapped out for
himself, but he also was too honest to allow a wealthy lady to marry
a man living, as he was at the time, on £6 a week earned from the
precarious business of writing. The success of his play *The Devil's
Disciple* gave him a more comfortable income, but his fears for his
working schedule remained.

A letter from Ellen Terry at this period in his life sighs:

> *Oh, I see you two walking in the damp and lovely mist,
> a trail of light from your footsteps, and—I don't think it's
> envy, but I know my eyes are quite wet, and I long to be
> one of you, and I don't care which.*

It is certain that Miss Payne-Townshend was becoming jealous of his nonstop correspondence with Ellen. Shaw said in one of these letters:

> *She will be pretty curious about you, not only on the grounds of your celebrity, but because she has discovered that "work" and "important business" on my part means writing long letters to you.*

Shaw and Charlotte were married on June 1, 1898, at a register office in the Strand. Shaw wore a tattered old jacket while his witnesses, Graham Wallas and Henry Salt, were both immaculately turned out. He reported later:

> *The registrar never imagined I could possibly be the bridegroom, taking me for the inevitable beggar who completes all wedding processions. Wallas, over six feet tall, was so obviously the hero of the occasion that the registrar was on the point of marrying him to my betrothed. But Wallas, thinking the formula rather too strong for a mere witness, hesitated at the last moment, and left the prize to me.*

Some of the Shaw-Terry correspondence was concentrated on stage techniques. Their exchange of letters before the first night of *Cymbeline,* in which Ellen Terry played Imogen, at the Lyceum

YOUNG ELLEN TERRY   The actress made her stage debut at the age of eight in Shakespeare's "The Winter's Tale," and continued her career for more than 50 years.

SHAW'S WIFE   *Mrs. Shaw's maiden name*
was Charlotte Payne-Townshend.

on September 22, 1896, offers a vivid glimpse of the tension grip-
ping two theatrical geniuses just before a great occasion. First
Ellen to Shaw, in reply to his letter wishing her "a thousand suc-
cesses" and ending, "You will break my heart if you are anything
less than PERFECT. . . ." Her reply:

*Ah, but you are kind! But spite of all your goodness to me
I shall do nothing tonight. It's not because I've left my
efforts to chance. I've settled what I want to try for, but
I'm all earth instantly I get on the stage for this part. No
inspiration, no softness, no sadness even. Tight, mechan-
ical hide-bound. I feel nothing. I know some of myself.
In a few days it will all be different. I think it is the result
of physical weariness. My head is tired. I can't care, can't
think, can't feel. Can not. After the carefullest thinking
and practicing every detail of my blessed work, something comes upon me. (This is when things go well and
right. It has nothing to do with my will.) I feel exquis-
itely, and then, then, I realize the situation (in the play)
and all is golden.*

But no gold tonight. Only dull mud. I can't help it, dear fellow. You see it has nothing to do with me. If I ever act well, it's accident. It's divine, isn't it? There's a double movement somewhere, for all the while one is receiving this gracious dew from heaven, this fire and warmth, one is turning oneself, as it were, to be basted properly. Ah, cracked and stupid fool, to take up this man's time because he's good to you.

H. I. [Henry Irving] will be wonderful and will look his best. He comes out of that box well, I tell you! I want to act a modern part. Oh, I am so ill, and stiff, and dull.

To which Shaw replied the same day:

Now Lord bless the woman, this is too much. Pray how long, oh stupidest, do your inspirations last? From nine in the morning until twelve at night perhaps! And do they ever come twice a day? Of course not. Then, if you felt ready for Imogen at breakfast, pray what chance would you have of feeling ready for her after dinner? Rather pray that your happiness does not come one second before the call boy. Pray for it as you would pray for a bad last rehearsal, since misfortunes do not come twice running.

But mind, inspiration or no inspiration, tonight or never, Imogen must be created. Next week is nothing to me or to anyone else: Napoleon might have won the battle of Waterloo a week later. It is not your business to be happy tonight, but to carry the flag to victory. It doesn't matter whether you are tired, frightened, hurt, miserable: it wouldn't matter if you hadn't slept for a week and were heartbroken and desperate. Tonight will never come again: your enemy, his enemy, will be there in the stalls, and woe betide the Lyceum and its tradi-

tions and reputation if you do for Cymbeline what he did for Lear! If you come on with seventy-seven sharp swords sticking in your heart, I should still say you must play as if you were never to play again, even if every word drove one of the swords an inch deeper. Therefore set your heart like iron, Ellen, and fight for your side tenderly, that is strongly. Tomorrow never comes. "Cannot—tomorrow" is no answer to "Must—today."

After all, do you suppose you play the worse when you are not enjoying yourself? Ask the audience and they will tell you that you play better. Ask me, and I will tell you that every mood has its value; and that the failure of inspiration, though it may take the happiness out of a few passages that are little secrets between some half-dozen of us, gives force to other and perhaps harder passages. But whether or no, you are in for it now; and if anyone dares encourage you, WITHER him. A newspaper correspondent telling Nelson on the morning of the Nile to keep up his spirits would not be more monstrous than anyone encouraging you now. I am going to do my small duty (as a critic); and you are going to do your greater one. Who talks of happiness until the day is over? and so—avanti!

Hitherto, you have only coaxed me. Tonight you must CONQUER me. I shall fight to the last, as if you were my mortal foe, but oh, with such a longing to be conquered.

And now I think I shall go out and get some lunch.

She did not write to him for a week—and then to ask him to send her his play, *Candida*, to read. He replied by return on October 2:

This is a nice way to behave. You coax everything you

"There was a star danced + under that Was I born":
Beatrice :=
Ellen Terry :

ELLEN TERRY AS BEATRICE   The actress was photographed in
her stage costume in "Much Ado About Nothing". When she sent the
picture to Shaw, she wrote, "There was a star dancer and under that was
I born."

*want out of me—my notions about Imogen, my play,
and a beautiful notice . . . and then instantly turn on
your heel and leave me there cursing the perfidy of your
sex. However, it opened my eyes to the abject condition
I was drifting into. I positively missed your letters. I, I,
Bernard Shaw,* MISSED *the letters of a mere mortal
woman. But I pulled myself together. I will not be the
slave of a designing female. Henceforth I shall regard my
morning's mail with the most profound indifference, the
coldest calm. Let me tell you, Ellen Terry, that you make
a great mistake in supposing that I am that sort of man. I
am not: why should I be? What difference does it make
to me whether you write to me or not? You should curb
this propensity to personal vanity. My well-ordered
bosom is insensible to your flatteries. . . .*

I won't, Won't, WON'T, WON'T, WON'T, WON'T,
WON'T *let you read* Candida. *I must read it to you, if
I have to do it through the keyhole. But I too fear to
break the spell [of their non-physical relationship]: re-
morses, presentiments, all sorts of tendernesses wring
my heart at the thought of materializing this beautiful friendship of ours by a meeting. You were quite
right not to come on Saturday [when Shaw had an interview with Henry Irving]: all would have been lost. In
some lonely place, by starlight—stop! I am getting idiotic.
Miss Terry: your servant!* G.B.S.

She tried to persuade him to call her Nellen or Nell—he
would not. She signed her letter dated October 10—"your lover."
Then he wrote to her of his meeting with Charlotte, "my Irish
lady with the light green eyes and the million of money, whom I
have got to like so much that it would be superfluous to fall in love
with her." He mentioned flippantly his flirtations. This letter
(dated October 12, 1896) goes on:

... And then there are others whom I cannot recollect just at present, or whom you don't know anything about. And finally there is Ellen, to whom I vow that I will try hard not to spoil my high regard, my worthy respect, my deep tenderness, by any of those philandering follies which make me so ridiculous, so troublesome, so vulgar with women. I swear it. Only, do as you have hitherto done with so wise an instinct: keep out of my reach. You see, nobody can write exactly as I write: my letters will always be a little bit original; but personally I shouldn't be a bit original. All men are alike with a woman whom they admire. You must have been admired so much and so often—must know the symptoms so frightfully well. But now that I come to think of it, so have I. Up to the time I was 29, actually twenty-nine, I was too shabby for any woman to tolerate me. I stalked about in a decaying green coat, cuffs trimmed with the scissors, terrible boots and so on. Then I got a job to do and bought a suit of clothes with the proceeds. A lady immediately invited me to tea, threw her arms round me, and said she adored me. I permitted her to adore, being intensely curious on the subject. Never having regarded myself as an attractive man,

SHAW AT HOME   *The dramatist at the height of his fame.*

ay haif said   What say thay?   Lat thame say!

*I was surprised; but I kept up appearances successfully.
Since that time, whenever I have been left alone in a
room with a female, she has invariably thrown her arms
round me and declared she adored me. It is fate. Therefore beware. If you allow yourself to be left alone with
me for a single moment, you will certainly throw your
arms round me and declare you adore me, and I am not
prepared to guarantee that my usual melancholy forbear-
ance will be available in your case. But I am really getting idiotic. . . .*

To which she replied the next day:

*Oh, mayn't I throw my arms around you when (!)
we meet? Then I shan't play. And I can't use you any
more, so there's an end. And you are the only man I have
ever used (and I haven't used you much). . . . With your
3 (or 30) love affairs on, and the Fabian, and the "Saturday Review," and the etc., etc., etcs., you must be full up
and it's not my moment. I'll wait until you "need" me,
and then I'll mother you. That's the only unselfish love.
I've never been admired or loved (properly) but one-and-
a-half times in my life, and I am perfectly sick of loving.
All on one side isn't fair. Goodbye child.*

*Do you take snuff? I've a circular box with Napo-
leon on the outside, and a strange lady inside, but the
puzzle is to "find the strange lady"!*

ELLEN TERRY AS QUEEN KATHARINE   *The actress
played the role in Shakespeare's "Henry VIII" on January 5,
1892.*

PORTRAIT STUDY OF
SHAW AT WORK

Later that same month [October] she wrote him:

Well, I won't write today, but shall take it out in think-ing, and I shall talk to you tonight, when I come home from the theatre and have a quiet time with you. It's quite pathetic, your last card saying you want to finish your work and not write "nonsensical letters," and I sup-pose as long as I go on writing them, you'll reply so as not to make me feel "left." Well I won't post this until the end of the week so you will get some rest. You are very gentle and sweet to me. Sorry, though, you won't have the snuff-box with my picture in it.

But I've nothing you could ever "want and could get from no-one else," and I want nothing from you, dear fellow—nothing more I mean. I'm in your debt and don't mind that in the least since I love you. I want to tell you that I very nearly trotted round to you after the play the other night (the first night), but I stuck to my post like a heroine and I helped Henry with all the people, and oh, all the time I was just dying to go away to some quiet place—to you . . . most of all or something really nice. Glad I didn't now because of something you said in one of your blessed letters. . . .

In May, 1899, he started to write *Captain Brassbound's Con-version* for Ellen Terry, sketching her character from her letters to him and from her stage performances. Her son, Gordon Craig, had just made her a grandmother for the first time and Ellen had said no one would ever write a play for her now. So Shaw took the hint. And on August 4 of that year he received the most painful blow to his pride. She wrote to say that the play was not at all suitable for her, that it would not make a penny, and that the part he had written for her—Lady Cicely—ought to be played by Mrs. Patrick Campbell. He replied:

Alas! dear Ellen, is it really so? Then I can do nothing

*for you. I honestly thought that Lady Cicely would fit
you like a glove. . . . And so farewell our project—all
fancy, like most projects. . . . Silly Ellen!*

When her next letter contained the remark, "Of course you
never *really* meant Lady Cicely for me—but to be published along
with other plays," he rasped back at once:

*Oh you lie, Ellen, you lie: never was there a part so deeply
written for a woman as this for you, silly, self-uncon-
scious, will o' the wisp beglamoured child actress as you
still are. . . . Here is a part which dominates a play because the character it represents dominates the world. . . .
In every other play I have ever written—even in* Candida
*—I have prostituted the actress more or less by making the
interest in her partly a sexual interest. . . . In Lady Cicely
I have done without this, and gained a greater fascination by it. And you are disappointed. . . . Oh, Ellen,
Ellen, Ellen, Ellen. This is the end of everything.*

But it was not the end even of their remarkable correspondence, which carried on until 1920. Shaw's last letter to her was
dated March 1. During the last six years of Ellen's life—she died
on July 22, 1928—she wrote little to anyone. By 1912 the inveterate
letter-writer was involved in a regular mock-love interchange with
Mrs. Patrick Campbell; he continued that correspondence until
August 21, 1939. His last line was: "I have given up producing; I
am too old, too old, too old."

Actually, he had eleven more years of life before him. Let him
have the last word on his correspondence with his beloved Ellen
Terry, as he has had on almost every subject under the sun:

*She became a legend in her old age; but of that I have
nothing to say, for we did not meet and, except for a few
broken letters, did not write; and she never was old to me.*

Let those who may complain that it was all on paper remember that only on paper has humanity yet achieved glory, beauty, truth, knowledge, virtue and abiding love.

Woodrow Wilson and Edith Bolling

They called her "the first woman President of the United States," and yet she held no office. She happened to be the wife of President Woodrow Wilson when he suffered a crippling stroke. For seventeen months Wilson was isolated from the outside world by his wife —with the help of his doctor. Senators and Cabinet members complained that they were not even allowed to see him; all government business had to pass through the hands of Mrs. Woodrow Wilson.

She received every official document addressed to the President, and she scribbled out all orders on his behalf.

Not thirst for power, but blind devotion to her husband, drove Mrs. Wilson to shield her husband from all comers. Her decision had incalculable, disastrous consequences for the world. Although Wilson had suffered the stroke during a whistle-stop tour to persuade Americans that their country must join the League of Nations, it was during his illness and her protection that the Senate decided to keep America out of the League.

Wilson left the Presidency a broken, bitter and defeated man, a victim of his wife's overwhelming love.

Her maiden name was Edith Bolling; she was the seventh child of a Virginia lawyer who claimed descent from Pocahontas. She lived on into our own times, dying in December, 1961, at the age of eighty-nine.

Both Edith Bolling and Woodrow Wilson may have fallen in love on the rebound, for both had made successful first marriages, ended only by the death of the partner. Their love for each other too, was deep and abiding. Edith's first husband, Norman Galt, died in 1908, leaving her a flourishing jewelry business in Washington, D. C. Woodrow Wilson's first wife died during his first term as President, in August, 1914, in that fateful week when Germany invaded Belgium. "God has stricken me almost beyond endurance," wrote Wilson after his bereavement. Yet within a year he had fallen hopelessly in love again—with Edith Bolling Galt.

The matchmaker was the President's doctor, Cary Grayson, who was afraid that his patient, the lonely man in the White House, might go into decline. Grayson was engaged to marry Edith's close friend, Alice Gertrude Gordon. Noticing Edith, he arranged that his fiancée should introduce the tall, attractive, forty-two-year-old widow to Helen Woodrow Bones, a cousin of the President, who managed domestic tasks in the White House. Miss Bones and Edith Bolling Galt formed an immediate friendship; they were soon taking long afternoon walks and riding out together in Mrs. Galt's electric car—the only one in Washington. Inevitably, Mrs. Galt was invited to dine with the President and his cousin in the White House; then to drive out with them in the official car. Those around Woodrow Wilson noticed how much brighter he seemed when Mrs. Galt was in his company.

On April 28, 1915, he sent her a note offering her a book. "I hope it will give you a little pleasure," he wrote. "I covet nothing more than to give you pleasure—you have given me so much!" Two days later the book arrived, with an invitation to dine at the White House and a corsage of golden roses. The following week, another invitation to dine. After dinner, he proposed marriage.

According to her Memoirs, published in 1939, the proposal

> . . . *came to me as almost a shock. Not having given a thought to such a development, I said the first thing that came to my mind, without thinking it would hurt him: "Oh, you can't love me, for you don't really know me, and it is less than a year since your wife died."*
>
> *"Yes," he said, "I know you feel that; but, little girl, in this place time is not measured by weeks or months or years, but by deep human experiences, and since her death I have lived a lifetime of loneliness and heartache. I was afraid, knowing you, I would shock you; but I would be less than a gentleman if I continued to make opportunities to see you without telling you what I have told my daughters and Helen: that I want you to be my wife.*
>
> *"In the circumstances of the spotlight that is always on this house, and particularly on me as head of the government, whoever comes here is immediately observed and discussed, and do what I can to protect you from gossip, it will inevitably begin. If you can care for me as I do for you, we will have to brave this, but as I cannot come to your house without increasing the gossip, you in your*

*graciousness will have to come here. It is for this reason
I have talked to the girls about it, so that they can safe-
guard you and make it possible for me to see you. They
have all been wonderful about it, and tell me they love
you for your own sake, but would anyway for mine."*

They talked over his proposal for an hour; but in the end she
told him that if it had to be "yes" or "no" at once, then it would have
to be "no." She wanted time to think. They agreed to continue their
friendship until she made up her mind. The next day his cousin,
Helen Woodrow Bones, rebuked her, saying the President looked
really ill that morning. "Just when I thought some happiness was
coming into his life," she said accusingly. "You are breaking his
heart."

All through the summer months Edith struggled with her great
dilemma. All her instincts told her to say "yes," but her sense of
principle made her hesitate to marry him while he was still in office.
She did not see him for nearly two months; she even stayed away
from Washington to test the depth of their feelings for each other.
The day she returned, September 3, she found flowers to welcome
her home—and an invitation to dine at the White House on her
first night back. This is her recorded memory of their reunion:

*He came in from the Blue Room, looking so distinguished
in his evening clothes, and with both hands held out to
welcome me. When I put mine in them and looked into
those eyes—unlike any others in the world—something
broke down inside me, and I knew I could, and would, go
to the end of the world with or for him.*

After dinner, they went off for a long drive together. They
were not alone, for cousin Helen and a Secret Service man shared
the car with them. The President talked to Edith of the increasing
weight of his responsibilities, the pressures on him to join in the war

THE PRESIDENT AND HIS FIANCEE   *Two days after their announced engagement, Wilson and Edith Bolling Galt attend a Philadelphia baseball game.*

in Europe. Then he said: "So, little girl, I have no right to ask you to help me by sharing this load that is almost breaking my back, for I know your nature and you might do it out of sheer pity."

"I am proud to say," she writes, "that, despite the fact that Mr. Murphy, of the Secret Service, and Robinson the chauffeur were on the front seat, and Helen beside me in the back, I put my arms around his neck and said: 'Well, if you won't ask me, I will volunteer, and be ready to be mustered as soon as can be.'"

The following day, September 4, 1915, they announced their engagement to the President's family and staff. The only question, they thought, was when to announce it to the entire country. But they did not reckon with the White House political advisers or the malevolent voice of rumor. The President's attachment to Mrs. Galt had not gone unnoticed in Washington. Several stories were circulating. The worst was that Wilson and Mrs. Galt had even conspired to get the first Mrs. Wilson out of the way, and that she had been poisoned by the faithful Dr. Grayson. It was also said that the President had shamefully neglected his official duties for love of Edith.

And a scandal even threatened political ruin: Mrs. Mary Allen Peck claimed she had received two hundred letters from Woodrow Wilson, plus $7,500 of his own money, and was reportedly prepared to play the role of jilted lover and to publish the letters if the President married Mrs. Galt.

Two of his advisers told the President of the threatened scandal. He was horrified. He explained that his late wife had known all about their correspondence, which was completely innocent, and that the $7,500 was a loan he had made Mrs. Peck against some mortgages she held. Nevertheless, he felt that he must not expose Mrs. Galt to such hurtful publicity and slander. He sent Dr. Grayson as an emissary to release Mrs. Galt from any promise to marry. Grayson told his story, then asked her: "What shall I tell him?" She had remained silent throughout his recital. Now she said: "Tell him I will write."

She records in her memoirs:

When he had gone, I sat for hours thinking, thinking,

when, as suddenly as the blow had fallen, its weight lifted, and I saw things in their true proportions. It was our lives that mattered, not politics, not scandal. If I did not care enough for the man to share his misfortunes, his sorrows, then it was a futile love! I would glory in standing by when the world scoffed and doubted, for in the end, he would triumph and vindicate my trust. I lighted my desk light and wrote from my heart:

Sept. 19, 1915

Dearest—The dawn has come and the hideous dark of the hour before the dawn has been lost in the gracious gift of light. I have been in the big chair by the window where I have fought out so many problems, and all the hurt, selfish feeling has gone with the darkness, and I now see straight, straight into the heart of things and am ready to follow the road "where love leads."

How many times have I told you I wanted to help— and now when the first test has come I faltered . . . but the faltering was for love, not lack of love. I am not afraid of any gossip or threat, with your love as my shield, and even now this room echoes with your voice as you plead, "Stand by me—don't desert me!"

This is my pledge, dearest one, I will stand by you —not for duty, not for pity, not for honor, but for love— trusting, protecting, comprehending love. And no matter whether the wine be bitter or sweet, we will share it together and find happiness in the comradeship.

Forgive my unreasonableness tonight (I mean last night, for it is already Sunday morning) and be willing to trust me. I have not thought out what course we will follow for the immediate present for I promised that we would do that together.

I am so tired I could put my head down on the desk

and go to sleep—nothing could bring me real rest until I
had pledged you my love and allegiance. Your own Edith.

No reply came from the White House on the first day, or the
second, and she feared that the romance was over, at his wish. But
on the third day, Dr. Grayson turned up at her home. He wasted
no time on formalities. "I beg that you will come with me to the
White House," he said. "The President is very ill. It is a desperate
situation."

She hesitated, then asked: "Are you here at the President's
request?"

He replied: "No, I told him I was coming and he said it would
be unfair to you and weak in him to ask it. If you could only see
him you would not hesitate. He looks as I imagine the martyrs
looked when they were broken on the wheel."

She went with Dr. Grayson to the President's room. The cur-
tains were drawn and the room dark. She writes:

On the pillow I saw a white, drawn face with burning
eyes dark with hidden pain. . . . No word was spoken,
only an eager hand held out in welcome, which I took to
find icy cold, and when I unclasped it we were alone.
Strangely in these tense moments things are understood
with no need of words. I never asked why he had not
answered my letter, only had it reached him. He said,
"Yes."

Three months later, the day after we were married
and were sitting before the fire in our cozy suite at Hot
Springs, Virginia, my husband asked to make a confes-
sion of something that had lain heavy on his spirit. . . .
He drew from his pocket the letter which I had written
in the early hours of that September morning. The seal
was unbroken, the envelope worn on the edges from be-
ing so long in his pocket. He said: "I think I am rarely a
coward but when this letter came that Sunday morning

after a sleepless night, I could not open it for I felt the world slipping from under my feet. I was so sure, with your horror of publicity and all the rest of it, that this was the end and you would never see me again, that I could not bring myself to face the written words; so I put it here, where it has been ever since. Now with you beside me I want to open it, remembering no matter what the hurt it holds that you came like an angel of light to heal my wound."

We read it together, and what he said need not be told: only that he begged that the letter never be destroyed.

Their engagement was announced from the White House to the world press on October 7, 1915. The President was so delighted that he even wrote to Mrs. Peck saying he knew she would rejoice for him in this "blessing." Nonetheless the Mrs. Peck scandal took a long time to die. Whispers persisted that Edith bought her off with large sums, that she was on a regular Treasury salary, and that she was taken to Europe, all expenses paid, to get her out of the way.

The wedding was at Edith's house on December 18. When they went on their honeymoon, the Secret Service went too.

The honeymoon was cut short by politics, for 1916 was a Presidential election year and Woodrow Wilson was inevitably nominated as the Democratic candidate. In an exhausting campaign and a close race, Wilson won his second term. Most Americans agreed that the slogan "He kept us out of war" had helped him win. No statesman did more than Wilson to bring peace in Europe; only cruel necessities forced him and his country into World War I, in April, 1917. In his speech asking Congress to declare war on Germany he said: "It is a fearful thing to lead this great peaceful people into war, into the most terrible and disastrous

CAMPAIGN BUS   In the 1916 presidential campaign, Wilson won re-election by defeating Charles Evans Hughes.

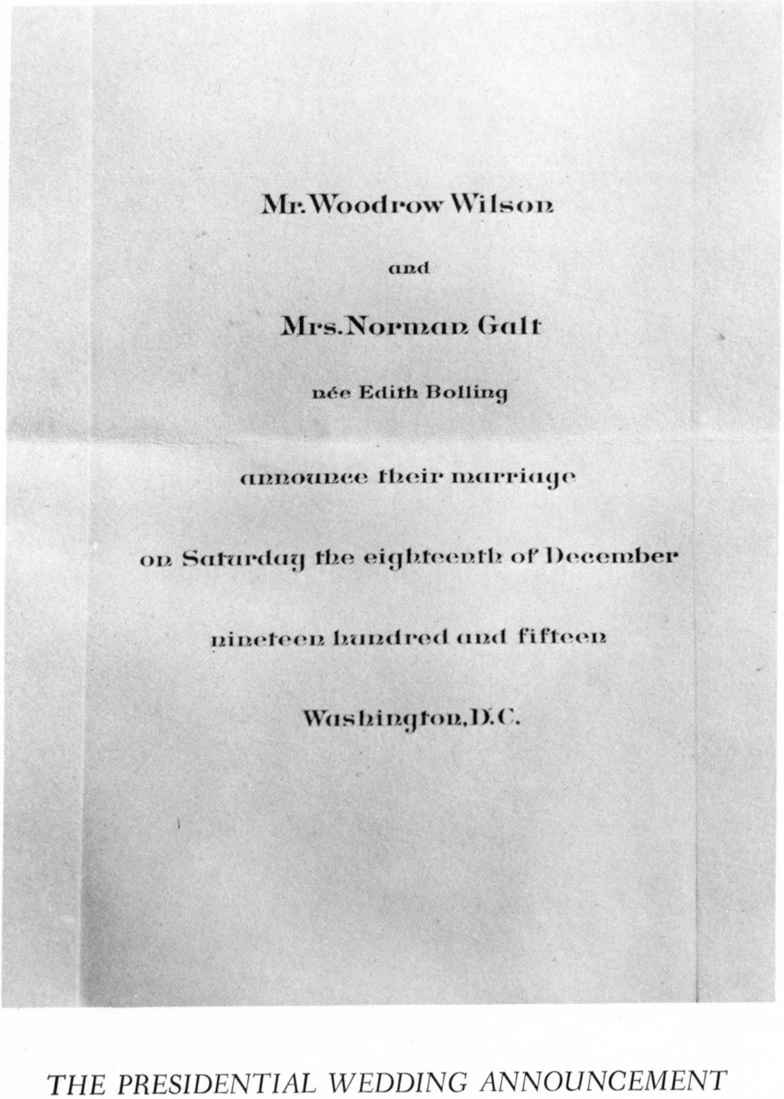

Mr. Woodrow Wilson

and

Mrs. Norman Galt

née Edith Bolling

announce their marriage

on Saturday the eighteenth of December

nineteen hundred and fifteen

Washington, D.C.

THE PRESIDENTIAL WEDDING ANNOUNCEMENT

of all wars, civilization itself seeming to be in the balance. But the right is more precious than peace. . . ."

Three weeks after the Armistice was signed, on December 4, 1918, President Woodrow Wilson sailed for Europe to work out a peace treaty and to form a League of Nations with the aim of preventing war forever. In Europe he was hailed as the Archangel of Peace. At home, however, resentment among the Senators was steadily mounting against him. It was said that the U.S.A. was becoming "a pawn in Mr. Wilson's campaign for Presidency of the Federation of the World." His opponents were so obstinate against the League of Nations that he determined to make a whistle-stop tour across the United States to the West Coast, to rouse public opinion in his favor—an "appeal to Caesar," he called it.

Although worn out from his long negotiations over the peace treaties in Paris, he set out from the White House on September 3, 1919, with his First Lady Edith, his doctor Grayson, two dozen reporters, eight Secret Service men, and a seven-car train, to travel 10,000 miles on a twenty-seven-day mission, making twenty-six major stops and ten speeches a day. His wife and doctor both pleaded with him to schedule rest days on this back-breaking crusade, but he would not. The strain of the tour proved too much for his overtaxed system, and he collapsed as the train was approaching Wichita, Kansas. The tour, which was showing signs of becoming a considerable personal triumph for him, was abandoned and the train steamed back to Washington.

The President's room was soon the center of great medical activity, with doctors and nurses constantly coming and going. The First Lady did not leave his bedside for a minute. Servants were forbidden to enter the room and all members of the Cabinet and political staff were ruthlessly excluded. Bulletins were issued regularly but were couched in the vaguest terms and gave no hint of his true condition. Not unnaturally, every kind of rumor swept around Washington—that the President was insane, was being held prisoner, was suffering from syphilis acquired in Paris. Secretary of State Lansing called a Cabinet meeting to decide whether or not the government was going to be carried on. The Constitution of the United States decrees that, in the case of the removal of the President from office, or his death, resignation, or inability to discharge the powers and duties of his office, the powers and duties should devolve on the Vice-President. Lansing complained that in this case there seemed no guide as to *who* would decide the question of the President's ability to discharge his duties. The Cabinet summoned Dr. Grayson, who was asked to explain the nature and extent of the President's illness. Grayson would say only that his patient was suffering from a nervous breakdown, that it was "touch and go" and "the scales might tip either way." Pressed for more details, Grayson would add only that "his condition is encouraging but we are not yet out of the woods." The Cabinet meeting ended with the dilemma unresolved.

One man who knew no more about the President's condition than he read in the papers was the Vice-President, Thomas Riley Marshall. He was a Washington joke, treated by his colleagues like a country grocer full of wise saws and rustic stories, but not taken seriously as a politician. As the mystery over Woodrow Wilson's condition deepened, the Cabinet members were anxious over the possibility of Marshall's having to fill the position.

Now, nearly half a century later, with the facts known, it seems incredible that the government of a major world power could possibly have been left in the untrained hands of a woman and a doctor. But so it happened. Woodrow Wilson had been ill briefly in Paris during April, 1919. His illness was diagnosed at the time as influenza, but all later evidence indicates a slight cerebral thrombosis. When Dr. Grayson examined him after his collapse on his whistle-stop tour, he realized that the President had sustained severe brain damage. Once back in Washington, Grayson hoped that rest and treatment might help his patient throw off the effects of his thrombosis. But Wilson suffered a further attack in the

White House, and hovered between life and death for several days. Only a tiny group had access to his sickroom—medical consultants, nurses, and Mrs. Woodrow Wilson. And it was she who decided that her husband would continue in his job as if nothing had happened. No one was to have access to him, no Cabinet member or officer, no senator—not even Joe Tumulty, his faithful personal secretary who had been with him since his earliest days in politics and who knew even more of his secrets than did Mrs. Wilson. The normal machinery of government nearly stopped. Urgent letters for Presidential action disappeared; documents and requests reached the White House for decision and remained unanswered.

Meanwhile, the patient's condition became worse because of a bladder blockage, and doctors urged an immediate operation. Mrs. Woodrow Wilson gave her decision to Dr. Grayson: "We will not operate. You know the real chances of recovery, so go tell the others that I feel nature will finally take care of things and we will wait."

It did, but the President was further weakened. All this time, the country was receiving vaguely reassuring bulletins. When one member of the Cabinet protested that it was terrible to lie to the public this way, Dr. Grayson replied: "I think you are right. I wish I could tell the people more but I am forbidden. The President and Mrs. Wilson have made me promise."

Three weeks after his second thrombosis, Wilson was just strong enough to sign four bills sent by Congress, the First Lady putting the pen in his quavering hand and indicating the place he should sign. As soon as his signatures were inspected by senators, rumors spread that they were forgeries, so different were they from his usual firm hand. The mutterings rumbled from the cloakrooms to the floor of Congress. One senator declared before the Foreign Relations Committee that the elected President was not in office. "We have petticoat government," he shouted. "Mrs. Wilson is President!"

It was the worst possible period for the United States to be without a President, for the country was undergoing many postwar strains. Mounted police charged down five thousand radical demonstrators in the streets of New York; race riots broke out. Labor troubles were widespread and the stock market was collapsing. The White House was silent on all these manifestations of unrest. But undoubtedly the most serious consequence concerned the League of Nations. Despite Woodrow Wilson's gallant country-wide tour, the opposition in the Senate had not abated. Had he been active, he might have taken the United States into the League, as he had promised at the Paris Peace Conferences. With his powerful influence absent, the Senate rejected his dream and voted not to join. Mrs. Wilson broke the news to the President on his sickbed. He remained silent for several minutes and then said: "I must get well."

Although Dr. Grayson decreed that it would be dangerous for his patient to be disturbed by the details of state, some White House decisions had to be made. The President's endorsement had to be given on certain documents—resignations of officials, for instance, or even the recognition of new governments in the world. But to all urgent callers pleading for personal interviews, Mrs. Wilson would reply: "I am not interested in the President of the United States. I am interested in my husband and his health."

This standstill in government had absurd consequences in foreign affairs. The British Ambassador to Washington was Viscount Grey of Fallodon, a former Foreign Secretary who came out of retirement to help Woodrow Wilson get the United States into the League of Nations. He arrived just as the President fell ill and waited for an appointment at the White House. After waiting four months and finding an entire series of his letters and requests unanswered, he returned to England without even having presented his credentials. And his departure was not marked by word, letter, or telegram. One American journalist wrote: "It seems as though our Government has gone out of business."

Dozens of bills became law without the Presidential signature, and yet *some* business was done by the White House. On some official correspondence there were penciled notes written by a woman who had managed just two years' formal schooling, and who wrote in huge characters almost like a child's. Each of these scrawls began "The President says" or "The President wants." Eventually, the First Lady condescended to receive members of the Cabinet in her sitting room. There, she gave verbal instructions which, she assured her listeners, were her husband's wishes. If her caller wanted clarification of an order she would excuse herself, go to the President's room—closing the door behind her—and return with the details required.

So the tragic farce went on, month after month. No member of the Cabinet ever saw the President, or even saw a word in his own handwriting. Washington refused to believe that Mrs. Woodrow Wilson, *née* Edith Bolling, was running the United States, or trying to do so single-handedly. Many suspected that Joe Tumulty was the power behind the throne. But they were wrong, for Edith took advice from no one. As for Tumulty, there is still extant a memorandum from him to the First Lady beginning:

> *Dear Mrs. Wilson: Please don't think I am trying to crowd you or to urge immediate action by the President, but I thought it would help you if you could have before you a list of matters that at intervals the President might wish to have presented to him for discussion and settlement.*

There followed a catalogue of dozens of important issues awaiting decision by the White House. Tumulty received no reply.

Many distinguished Americans, seeking to understand this astonishing period in their country's postwar political history, have proposed explanations. Some have suggested that the First Lady, having no previous experience of politics or diplomacy, developed a lust for power and position which she was determined would not be whittled away. The facts, however, contradict this explanation. She made no attempt to reorganize White House methods—she just

WILSON IN 1920   When this picture was taken, Wilson was
recovering from his illness and was on a pleasure jaunt with his wife.

ignored all minor problems and most of the major ones, too. No, the simple human explanation is surely the true one: she was dedicated to her husband's survival, and to insure it, she decided she had to protect him from all responsibilities and irritations. What did appointments or resignations matter, compared with that supreme need?

And she succeeded, for Woodrow Wilson not only lived out his second term as President but was confident that the Democratic Party would nominate him for a third term! He was indeed the most obstinate of men. Although his health was shattered beyond repair, he was confident that he could establish his League of Nations policy, if only he were given time. Everyone near to him realized that a third campaign would surely kill him, and the Democratic Convention nominated Governor James Cox to fight off the Republican challenge of Senator Warren Harding in the 1920 election. Cox was allowed to visit Woodrow Wilson. As he was leaving, he made this pledge: "Mr. President, we are going to be a million per cent with you and your administration, and that means the League of Nations." The country gave its verdict—a landslide victory for Harding, and thus ended an old man's dream.

Now the Wilsons had to vacate the White House to make way for President Harding. Woodrow Wilson felt that he could earn money by writing, although he was paralyzed down one side and could use only one hand. He managed to type only the dedication to his first book; that was all he wrote. It read:

A DEDICATION TO E. B. W.

I dedicate this book because it is a book in which I have tried to interpret life, the life of a nation, and she has shown me the full meaning of life. Her heart is not only true but wise, her thoughts are not only free but touched with vision; she teaches and guides by being what she is; her unconscious interpretation of faith and duty makes all the way clear, her power to comprehend makes work and thought alike easier and more near to what it seeks.

Woodrow Wilson lived until February 3, 1924. From March, 1921, when he handed over the White House to the next tenant (whom he in fact outlived), through those three long years of decline and disintegration, his First Lady, Edith Bolling Wilson, watched over him with the fierce protective care she had already shown. Rarely has any woman shown such single-minded devotion to one of history's great failures. Nor would she forgive his opponents after his death.

When the Senate appointed a delegation to attend his funeral, she noticed that Cabot Lodge, who more than anyone was responsible for the defeat of Wilson's League of Nations policy, was to attend. She wrote to him:

> *As the funeral is private and not official and realizing that your presence would be embarrassing to you and unwelcome to me, I write to request that you do not attend.*

Cabot Lodge complied with her request.

In 1957, four years before her own death, she still referred to Cabot Lodge as "that stinking snake." During the years left to her after her husband's death, nothing was ever too much trouble if it was to honor the memory of Woodrow Wilson. She was always willing to assist in dedicating a bridge or a school to him.

And she concluded her published memoirs with this dedication in a black mourning border:

To My Husband
WOODROW WILSON

who helped me build from the broken timbers of my life a temple wherein are enshrined memories of his great spirit which was dedicated to the service of his God and humanity.

William Randolph Hearst and Marion Davies

Marion Davies was just another young blonde in the Ziegfeld Follies of 1918 when she first met William Randolph Hearst, the Napoleon of American journalism. She was eighteen. He was fifty-five, father of five sons. That meeting sparked off one of the most remarkable love affairs in twentieth-century America.

Hearst, the multimillionaire owner of a chain of newspapers which operated throughout the country, was regarded by the general public as an outsized personality to be treated with deference, skepticism, even fear. He had been happily married for fifteen years. His wife Millicent was devoted to him, organizing the parties and salons which his position in public life made necessary, and helping him in his multifarious activities.

How could it happen? How could a man like Hearst, well established in middle life, and without a long record of "little affairs," fall for a scarcely mature chorus girl like Marion? For fall he did—and hard—as the next thirty years were to prove. What was the chemistry that joined them together for three decades, utterly faithful one to the other, despite all the sniggering and ribaldry which was never too loud, of course, and never uttered in public because Hearst wielded tremendous power through his newspapers. There was a major family explosion, and the intervention of his well-meaning friends. But Hearst never budged. Probably the best explanation came from Hearst himself in answer to one of his inquiring friends. "I'm not saying it's right," he said. "I'm saying that it *is*."

Marion, on her part, idolized her eccentric millionaire but never kowtowed to him. Often she lost her temper with him, screaming abuse into his embarrassed and perspiring face while he tried desperately to calm her.

In one important matter, however, he would not give way to her. He would do anything in the world for Marion—except divorce his wife. And he maintained his refusal in face of the stormiest scenes. Not all Marion's wiles nor all her rages could shake that decision. He was influenced in standing firm not only by his wife's spotless reputation but undoubtedly in fear of a sensational divorce case, and the damaging effect of the publicity on his growing sons.

So from 1922, when he began his association with Marion Davies, until his death in 1951, the fiction of a respectable marriage was maintained without open conflict between the parties. Indeed, his newspaper editors were to receive, to their excruciating embarrassment, suggestions from both women on how to run their papers!

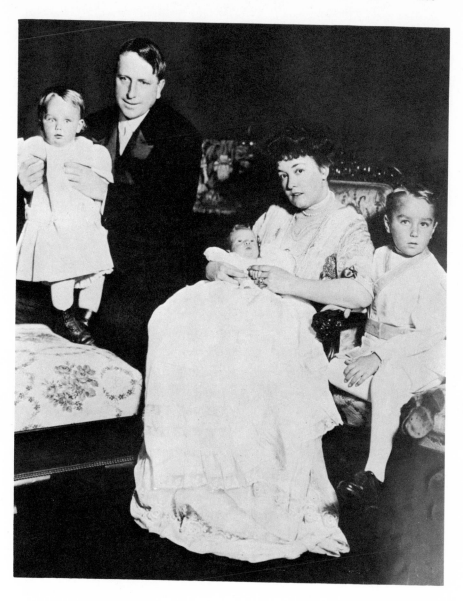

THE HEARST FAMILY   William Randolph Hearst,
wife Millicent, and their three children.

Needless to say, the Hearst press was careful to publicize the activities of both Marion and Millicent.

Rival newspaper groups, too, were discreet enough not to stir up any scandal. They all solemnly recorded the social engagements and philanthropic interests of the only Mrs. William Randolph Hearst.

Although their marriage as such had become a sham and mere social pretense, a genuine affection seemed to exist between William Randolph and Millicent. For years after the parting, he would call her on the telephone nearly every day and she continued to the very end to refer to him as "Willie" or, half in jest, as "the old scoundrel." But nothing, no one could break the bond that tied him to Marion. She proved to be much more than "a little blonde." She was utterly uninhibited, much given to short drinks and shorter oaths, but warm hearted, lovable, reveling in fun and luxury, and above all, delightful company.

Hearst set out to buy Marion success. He formed International Films and devised million-dollar extravaganzas around her, too often ludicrous in effect. His very determination to create a great screen star of her ruined any chance she might possibly have had of making it in her own right. He compelled her to study elocution and languages, but absolutely refused to allow her to play the role that came most naturally to her—that of a tough blonde. She herself wanted to play the Sadie Thompsons, but had to settle for sweet young things like Peg o' My Heart. He was forever on the set, training her, directing her, and in the end, smothering her. Her name will be remembered not as a screen idol but as a millionaire's darling. There were concrete compensations nevertheless, for she did become rich in her own right.

That Marion Davies was not just a gold digger, however, was convincingly shown during the great depression of 1938 when Hearst found himself in financial difficulties. She immediately came to his rescue, turning over to him her five-million-dollar fortune—even her diamonds, rubies, and emeralds. Hearst, of course,

A VERY YOUNG MARION DAVIES   *One of the first of her professional photos.*

weathered the storm and made a successful comeback. Marion's supremely selfless gesture touched the magnate more deeply than anything anyone else ever did for him. Yet she did even more for him—she showed him how to be a human being instead of a money-making machine. It was, in a sense, for his sake that she finally accepted the inevitable—her failure to achieve success as an actress. Convinced that her lover's overeagerness to make her a world star would always prevent her from becoming one, she retreated to Hearst's princely estate at San Simeon.

In addition to the famous castle, San Simeon contained four chateaux, a private zoo, a railroad and airport, and other wonders. La Casa Grande, dominating the hilltop overlooking the broad blue bay below Big Sur, is probably the most opulently magnificent roof a man ever put over his head, and at the same time the most revealing of any of Hearst's countless possessions. It was, perhaps, his attempt to create a shrine to beauty as well as a twenty-million-dollar monument to his mother, who remained first in his affections until her death in 1919. The truth is that Hearst had a strong mother complex and, in fact, delayed marrying until the comparatively late age of forty because he could find no one during his shy, romantic years to compare with his mother Phebe, his ideal woman. That she was a remarkable and gifted woman is attested by all who knew her. Witty, intelligent, and attractive, she exercised great restraint in her relations with her only child. When he insisted that she share his home after his marriage, Phebe was too sensible to be persuaded, and continued to pursue her own activities in California while he was making his fabulous way in New York.

MARION DAVIES AS "FOLLY"   She was 23 years old when she starred in "April Follies", a Cosmopolitan Paramount-Artcraft picture released in 1920.

Hearst, at his most appealing, once wrote to his mother: "I think California is the best country in the world, and always will be. . . . I am going to save up and build a cabin down at the ranch just big enough for you and Millie and the baby and me." That letter must have struck a chill in the hearts of both women, and would certainly have brought a chuckle to everyone else who knew Hearst's background, for the "ranch" was the epitome of extravagance, as lavish a home ever built for one man, and the need to "save up" could hardly be taken seriously.

Hearst had started out in life with certain obvious advantages. His father, the great mining magnate, had passed on to him several million dollars and a newspaper, the San Francisco *Examiner*. All his young life had been spent in sumptuous homes or apartments —his father once built a mansion in Washington for the express purpose of dwarfing the White House.

William Randolph certainly inherited his father's penchant for extravagant home building. In his own last phase, surfeited with mere mansions and chateaux, he took to collecting palaces and castles. He bought an estate at Sands Point on Long Island as part of a settlement with Millicent in 1929, when she was his wife in name only. They called it St. Joan; it included not only a castle but a lighthouse! Four years earlier, he had shocked all Wales and much of England by reaching across the Atlantic with his acquisitive hands and buying, sight unseen, the medieval keep of St. Donat's which for nearly a thousand years had kept watch over the Bristol Channel. One day, leafing through a magazine, Hearst happened to see a photograph of a room of St. Donat's. When he discovered it was "a genuine part of British history," he simply cabled his London representative asking to be informed if St. Donat's ever came on the market. It did, four months later, and Hearst bought it within twenty-four hours. However, it took him three years to get around to a tour of inspection.

We are told that he arrived at St. Donat's at ten o'clock one night and beheld his possession bathed in moonlight. He was so

MARION DAVIES IN "THE ZIEGFELD FOLLIES" OF 1916   Two years later, this girl was to capture the heart of the world's richest newspaperman.

MRS. WILLIAM RANDOLPH HEARST   *As she appeared in 1937.*

thrilled by the spectacle of the ancient pile that before he would sit down to dine, he insisted on being conducted, by the light of a lantern, through the dungeons and cobwebbed passages. Still, when he discovered that its plumbing and heating systems were also antiquated, the thrill quickly wore off. Nevertheless, Hearst was not one to give up easily; he soon had almost as many baths installed to serve St. Donat's 135 rooms, as he had in his luxuriously appointed American homes. His agents scoured the London auction rooms for furnishings and silver. No expense was spared. By the time he paid his next visit, three years later, St. Donat's had been converted into a museum worth crossing the Atlantic to see.

There were many other domestic extravaganzas: Wyntoon, for instance. This was another of Hearst's munificent importations—an entire Bavarian village set up on the scenic acres of his mother's summer retreat in the high sierras of California, background music supplied by the roaring McCloud River in the canyon below. It was at Wyntoon that his five sons had learned some of the skills of the outdoor life—riding and swimming. It was at Wyntoon that he played croquet with Marion Davies and his retinue of hangers-on, sycophants, and jesters. It was at Wyntoon, too, that he sought peace in his old age. Ironically, he was to leave it four years before his death to settle down finally in a rented house, so to speak—Marion's two-million-dollar palace in Beverly Hills.

In contrast to William Randolph Hearst's lavish background, the girl who was to share his king-sized life came from a modest middle-class family, the daughter of a Brooklyn judge. Born Marion Douras, she was educated at a Roman Catholic convent in New York. But by 1916, as Marion Davies, she was dancing in the chorus of "Chu Chin Chow" where she was spotted by Florenz Ziegfeld.

How did she first meet Hearst? There are many versions of this fateful encounter. Perhaps it would be as well to take Marion's. "It was in 1918," she told her friends with disarming frankness. "I was in the chorus before that. I used to hold up the backdrop.

HEARST IN THE PUBLIC EYE   *Watching the Fifth Avenue parade of the 27th Division's return from World War I are (left to right) Al Smith, Mayor John Hylan of New York, Hearst, and Franklin D. Roosevelt (then Assistant Secretary of the Navy).*

Did you know I studied ballet when I was four years old? At the same school as Marilyn Miller, but she was a much better dancer. In one of Ziegfeld's shows I had seventeen dance numbers, all on my toes. It was hard work, but I loved it.

Then I made a movie which my brother-in-law, George Lederer, directed. It was called 'Runaway Romany' and it was a flop; but Mr. Hearst saw it and he told his film company to sign me up. They gave me five hundred a week. Oh, I was living!"

The most intriguing version, however, is that Hearst's wife Millicent actually took Marion home and introduced her to her husband as a dancer worthy of a part in one of the big films he was then financing.

But Hedda Hopper, Hollywood's "all-knowing" columnist in its halcyon days, insisted that Hearst happened to drop in at Ziegfeld's Follies one night, saw Marion dance—and was back every night for the following two months. Then he asked her to supper, and that was that.

It is perfectly in character that while not one of his many newspapers dare make mention of his own affair, Hearst's greatest scoop as a newspaperman was about someone else's love story. It was Hearst himself who beat the press of the world with a cable in 1936 announcing that King Edward VIII would abdicate the throne of England to marry Mrs. Simpson. Nothing he had ever achieved as an editor gave him quite as much delight as this coup.

Apparently, the big man could not—and certainly would not —see that he was a living contradiction of one of his own memoranda to his staffs:

> *A good many people who object to the attention that newspapers give to their private affairs forget that their affairs have become a public interest and reached public importance through their own fault entirely, and through no fault of the newspapers. A newspaper's right and duty is to print public facts in which the public is interested, whether the individuals concerned are public or private.*

This double standard—some, more tersely, would call it hypocrisy—ran through much of Hearst's business and professional life. Rules were for lesser men—and they included Presidents and ex-Presidents of the United States. All this notwithstanding, Hearst became the most successful journalist of the twentieth century— that is, if success it to be measured in material terms. He had a

MARION DAVIES IN "OH, BOY"   Miss Davies, the central
figure, and her chorus girls in a scene from the 1919 musical in the
Princess Theatre.

formula. That formula was that sex and crime, lavishly illustrated,
can sell newspapers to the masses. He backed his formula with all
his millions, and he exploited to the fullest the most sensational aspects of love, hate, and maudlin sympathy. Everything, including
decency and accuracy, had to bow before the great god Circulation;
and Hearst, its high priest, brought many human sacrifices to that
altar.

He invented many novel rites, too. It was he who put over the colored comic strips in a big way. Indeed, it was the battle of the comic strips that introduced a new term to the language, and ushered in a new crass era in journalism. Hearst and his greatest New York rival, Joseph Pulitzer, were locked in a desperate circulation war over Sunday colored supplements. The hero of a Pulitzer comic strip, a yellow-shirted boy, was a major attraction of the Sunday *World*. So Hearst proceeded to buy over the artist for his *Morning Journal* only to have Pulitzer buy him back.

This tug-of-war between the tycoons went on until the artist, R. F. Outcault, inventor of the colored comics and the character Buster Brown as well, found himself with a king-size salary. For both newspapers now ran a Yellow Kid strip, while the other New York papers looked on which supercilious sneers. The editor of the New York *Press* characterized the struggle as "yellow journalism," and the term stuck.

Had Hearst and Pulitzer confined themselves to a circulation war, the reputation of the United States Government would not have been dragged into their dubious activities. Unfortunately, they managed to provoke a shooting war between the United States and Spain over Cuba. In what must surely be one of the most disreputable episodes in American history, the two publishers vied with one another in promoting full-scale war out of a Cuban revolution. Ostensibly for the liberation of that Spanish possession, the real reason for the attack was the disruption of the United States trade with Cuba, following the collapse of the sugar industry.

The Spanish-American War is usually held to be Hearst's war, in part, because of his much quoted telegram to Frederic Remington, an artist, whom he ordered to Cuba with the statement: "You supply the pictures, I'll supply the war." It was Hearst's war, too, because of the part his press played in whipping up public fervor by a disgraceful succession of distorted news stories and faked atrocities. Hearst himself went to the front, and he sent off several highly colored and highly opinionated despatches under the by-line "W. R. Hearst."

The war ended in victory for the Cubans—and Hearst. His New York *Journal* was first to publish the terms of the peace treaty; and Hearst reached the summit of his prestige and popular acclaim. As he set his own sights on the White House, this lifelong Democrat then proceeded to tell his party what its policies ought to be. He had spent half a million dollars on his newspaper's Cuban war effort, and he was prepared to pour out all his treasure to maneuver himself into the presidency.

In 1902, he bought his way into Congress, but he showed his contempt for the House by attending the sessions only half a dozen times in as many months. He scorned the professional politicians, convinced that his money and newspapers could get him anything he wanted. By 1904, he was all set to be president, and he succeeded in having his name placed before the Democratic Convention, but he was routed for the nomination. In 1906, he actually ran for governor of New York, and was again beaten by the highly-respected and formidable Charles E. Hughes.

Eventually, after fruitlessly spending over a million and a half dollars on his political ambitions, he was forced to conclude that his role thereafter was to be kingmaker rather than king.

The activity in which Hearst did minimum harm to other people was his art collecting. He had developed his enthusiasm for art through his mother during their frequent tours of Europe together Indeed, she had launched him on his collecting mania with a set of her own tapestries. Every year for the next fifty, he spent a million dollars on his collections; and by the end of that period, he owned at least 20,000 different items. He had each acquisition photographed and documented. His collections of English furniture and Gothic tapestry were unrivaled in the world. Primarily concerned with decorative arts—painting interested him least and then only the representational of the most realistic kind—he was utterly relentless and often ruthless in going after anything he really wanted, however hopeless the pursuit seemed to be. At one time he decided he really wanted the Spanish monastery at Sacramenta,

GRECIAN TEMPLE   *One of the gorgeous
buildings at San Simeon.*

HEARST CAMPAIGN FOR GOVER-
NOR   *Defeated two years earlier in his
bid for the presidential nomination, Hearst
ran for governor of New York in 1906. He
was roundly beaten by Charles Hughes, a
defeat which marked the end of his political
efforts.*

that town's only place of worship. To attain his desire, Hearst supplied the town with a new church, built a road down the mountain-
side, added a rail link so that he could dismantle the monastery

stone by stone, and then have it packed and transported to the U. S. A. The cost of that project was $400,000—a formidable sum in those years.

Still, that was not much more than he had paid for a Van Dyck, when after a tiff with his wife, he needed some ego satisfaction. He confessed to her afterwards: "I've done a terrible thing. I've just bought a picture—and paid $375,000 for it."

Millicent Hearst's reply remains a classic: "When I'm upset," she said, "I just go out and buy a hat."

In 1937, Hearst decided to sell off most of his immense collection, both because he needed cash reserves and because he wanted to avoid inheritance taxes. The public sale of part of his treasures was conducted like a Hollywood spectacular. Gimbels department store in New York was chosen. The sale drew a crowd of 100,000 in the first week—takings grossing half a million dollars. It was a bazaar on the grand scale: Egyptian statuettes went for 35 cents each; Benjamin Franklin's eyeglasses fetched $325. Rich collectors, like John D. Rockefeller, Jr., came from all over to buy up rare exhibits for museums of their choice. Gimbels put on a masterpiece of salesmanship, with Hollywood-style backdrops and lighting to give the antiques suitable settings. Standing in the middle of that conglomeration assembled from every part of the world and from all periods of history, Mrs. Hearst could not resist asking: "How could one man buy all these things?"

A dealer made the shrewd answer: "He bought as if he thought he would live forever."

OUT RIDING   *Hearst, and Marion Davies go riding in a cabriolet*

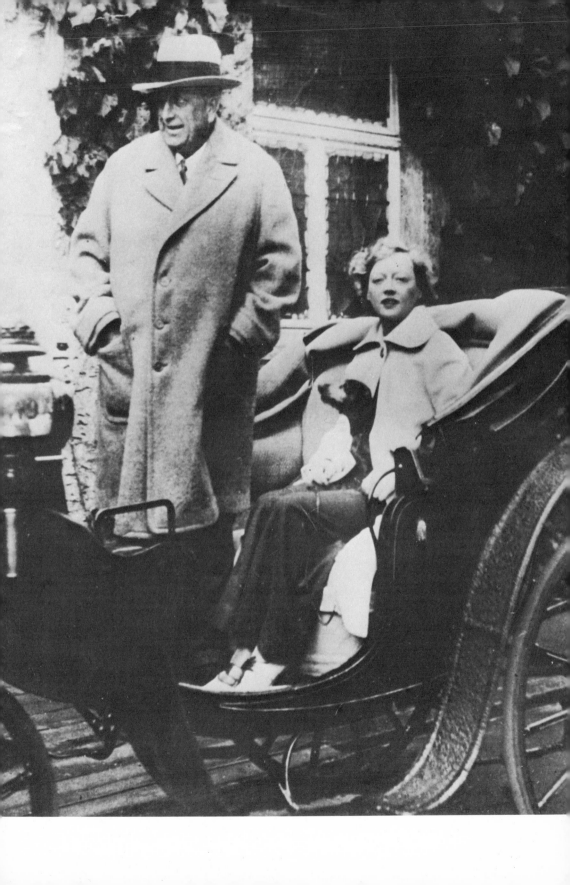

WILLIAM RANDOLPH HEARST AT DINNER   The fair-haired woman
in the polka-dot dress (back to camera) is Marion Davies. The dining room, once
the interior of a Spanish Church, was brought from Spain to Hearst's castle in
California, piece by numbered piece. Reconstituted with infinite care, this ancient
church became one of Hearst's many dining rooms.

Indeed, the word *death* was never allowed to be mentioned
in his presence. But mentioned or not, Hearst could not buy immor-
tality. In the spring of 1947, he had a heart attack, and the doctors
urged him to leave the rarefield air of his mountain fastness Wyntoon and take it easier in the gentler atmosphere of Beverly Hills.

Obediently, he went to Marion's place, her rambling three-storied, palatial residence at 1007 Beverly Drive. Complete with spacious gardens, patio, and swimming pool, she had bought the palm-girt house herself. She had sold it to Hearst when he was hit by the Great Depression, but he later gave it back to her by deed on condition that he have "tenure for life." In his latter days, the ruthless, hard-driving tycoon was replaced by a sentimental old man, too often on the verge of tears. The house in which he waited to keep his appointment with death, like all his other dwellings, held a vast fortune in paintings, eighteenth-century English furniture, and rare silver. The concession to modernity was in the main hall which connected two wings of the H-shaped building: here were four life-sized portraits of Marion Davies, painted during her years in the cinema.

Although his mind remained strong and active, his body was palsied; and Hearst chose to withdraw from society to a suite on the second floor of the house where his world had now dwindled to a bedroom, sitting room, and an office. His life was largely prolonged by the skill of a man who spent much of the outsized fees he got from Hearst on research involving vivisection. It was the final irony, for Hearst had campaigned against vivisection all his active life.

As always, Marion was his sure and loyal comforter, rearranging her daily routine to meet his trying new needs. First, she dealt with household problems; then with her own affairs. In the early afternoon, she often shopped in Beverly Hills; later in the day, she would give a small cocktail party, or a dinner party in the evening for a few friends. Although this might not seem like the quiet life, compared with the life she was used to Marion was living like a recluse. At night, she would remain alone with Hearst, reading or sewing, an enormous change from her wild days and wilder nights.

She was, in fact, preparing to play out the noblest scene of her extraordinary life. The curtain rose on that scene one Monday evening when Hearst complained of great pain in his leg. The doctors decided to give him a blood transfusion, and they asked Marion

AIRVIEW OF HEARST'S CASTLE   *The estate of San Simeon lies*
nestled like a giant jewel on the wooded slope of a mountain overlooking the
Pacific Ocean.

to distract him by keeping up a running conversation while they were setting up their equipment. She did far more. She talked away through the wee small hours reminiscing about their life together, chatting on and on with the man on the high, canopied bed—the "Citizen Kane" of real life—who was flanked on one side by two framed pictures of his favorite dachshunds, and on the other side by a picture of Marion at the height of her beauty. Her photograph, inscribed "To W. R. from Marion," was followed by a quotation from *Romeo and Juliet* which ran: "My county is as boundless as the sea; my love as deep; the more I give to thee, the more I have, for both are infinite."

Throughout that long, long night she sat by his bedside. When the dawn broke, she rose to leave for a few minutes. William Randolph Hearst, the man who had everything, puckered up his lips to kiss her, and passed out of the world with a grimace. The stunned Marion was given a sedative—she had barely slept for forty-eight hours. As she put it. "The doc came at me with that little old needle, and one, two, I was out."

And while she was "out," some remarkable things happened. The doctors immediately called two of Hearst's sons, Bill and David. They had been staying in the guest house during their father's last illness. With them was Richard Berlin, Hearst's top executive, who immediately took charge of the situation. Apparently, after Hearst's heart attack in 1947, a master plan had been worked out for just such an eventuality. Now with the speed and efficiency of a Hearst newspaper operation, the plan was put into action.

HEARST'S HOME IN SAN SIMEON   The architectural style of this fabulous castle in California is Gothic. Every brick, every piece of sculpture is authentic. Brought from Europe piece by piece at fantastic cost and re-created with great care, the entire home is itself a gigantic masterpiece of art.

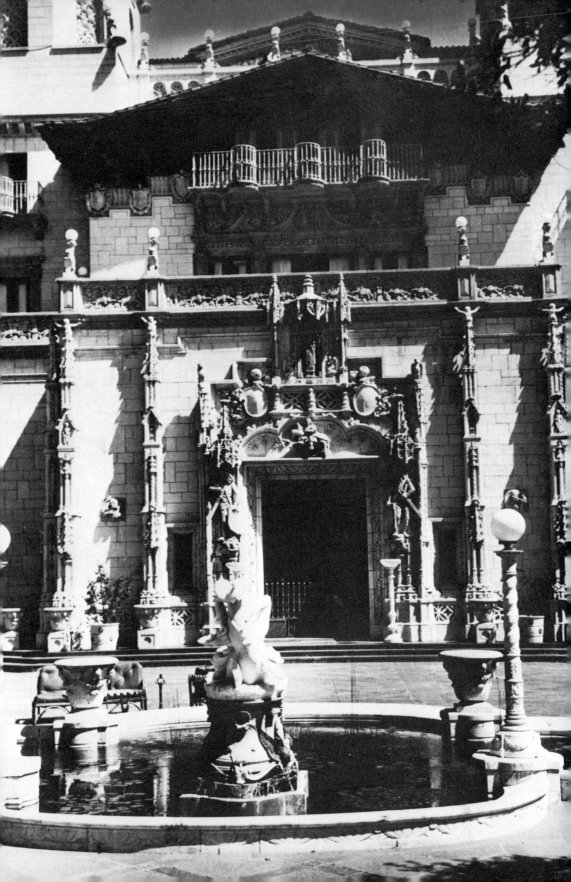

The Beverly Hills undertakers were notified, and within the
hour their hearse arrived at the gates from which the usual guards
had been withdrawn. They conferred with Berlin and the doctors,
then removed the body for embalming, while two of Hearst's serv-

BEACH HOME OF MARION DAVIES   Today a 110-room luxury hotel, this was at one time the private beach house of the actress. The third story gable in the center of the building was the sun-filled sitting room of Miss Davies' private suite.

ants stood guard over the corpse. The undertakers then placed the body in a copper casket which was covered with a blanket, loaded it into the hearse, and drove off to the International Airport where the casket was placed aboard a hired plane. Four of Hearst's sons

MARION DAVIES WITH HEARST DURING WORLD WAR II
They are shown leaving the California State Guard Military Ball held at the
Hollywood Palladium in 1942.

then boarded the aircraft, and took off at once for San Francisco
and Millicent Hearst.

An hour after Hearst died, back at 1007 Beverly Drive, Marion
Davies had been roused with difficulty from her drugged sleep. She

threw on a dressing gown, and staggered down to his bedroom. In an interview which has become famous, she later described the experience: "He was gone. I asked where he was, and the nurse said he was dead. His body was gone, whoosh! like that. I didn't even know whether he was dead when they took him. Old W. R. was gone; the boys were gone. I was alone. They didn't even let my say goodbye. Do you realize what they did? They stole a possession of mine. He belonged to me. I loved him for thirty-two years, and now he was gone. Yes, I couldn't even say goodbye."

Marion spent that night, the most agonizing of her life, with her close friend Constance Talmadge, the film actress. When the phone rang, she accepted the not wholly unexpected call from San Francisco. It was Bill Hearst, Jr., on the line.

Marion, some time later, told Constance Talmadge how the conversation went. "I asked him when the services would be. 'Look,' I said, 'you wouldn't let me say goodbye to him. At least you can tell me when the services will be, so I can pray for him down here.' He said the whole thing was now up to his mother. I found out about the funeral by reading the paper the next morning."

Then she added: "I will never understand this if I live to be a thousand years. I couldn't believe they would do this to me."

Marion behaved with great dignity. All who saw her were impressed, even moved by her bearing. And her summing up of the grisly business was: "For thirty-two years I had him, and they leave me with his empty room." Fortunately, she had no lack of friends or condolences and she sought no pity.

In San Francisco, Mrs. Hearst decided on a large and formal funeral. Hearst's body was taken to the Chapel of Grace in Nob Hill's Episcopal Cathedral where he lay in state for two days. The casket was framed by banks of roses, and was provided with a glass window for those who wished to look at him—and there were hundreds who were curious about the legendary figure. Known by, but remote from, the millions during his lifetime, he was now a lifeless reminder that "sceptre and crown must tumble down." He lay in death only a few blocks from the house of his birth.

The staff of his first newspaper, the *Examiner*, decorated the chapel with an American flag made of flowers, the stars composed of forty-eight gardenias and the stripes of red and white carnations.

On the day of his funeral, 1,500 people packed the cathedral, thousands more lining the streets outside. The high and the mighty

ST. DONAT'S CASTLE

attended. A score of police on motor cycles escorted the twenty-two limousines to Cypress Lawn Cemetery where the body was committed to the Hearst family mausoleum.

In Beverly Hills, Miss Davies rose at 10:30 that morning. Just before the funeral service began at 11:00, she took Hearst's dachshund to her room, telling her nurse: "I meant to go to church this morning, but I will just stay here alone. He knew how I felt about him, and I know how he felt about me. There is no need for dramatics."

But the Hearst spectacular was not yet over—there were sensations to come. As soon as the news of his death reached his lawyers, they filed his 125-page will for probate so that, as they explained it, his empire could carry on without disastrous interruption. The will set up three trusts to distribute an estate estimated at $400,000,000. One trust fund gave his wife the income from $6,-000,000 worth of shares in the Hearst Corporation. A second trust fund provided for his sons, already drawing large salaries as Hearst executives. The third trust fund was for charitable, scientific, and educational purposes. The bequest also directed that a memorial be built "to my beloved mother" which would contain part of his art treasures "for the public enjoyment." The will did not, however, make provision for Marion Davies.

Any sense of relief that the family may have felt after that happy discovery was short-lived, for a trust fund, dated November 5, 1950, had given Miss Davies a lifetime income from 30,000 shares in Hearst Corporation Preferred, the principal to go to his sons after her death.

W. R. had left one sting after death. He had drawn up a voting trust agreement which stipulated that Marion was to have sole voting power in the Hearst Corporation. Under this agreement, her 30,000 preferred shares were pooled with the 170,000 owned by Hearst, which more than made up for her omission from his will *because that arrangement gave her absolute control of his interests.*

The discovery of this document was nothing less than a

HEARST AT THE WARNER STUDIOS   *Joan Blondell upstages Mayor Kelly of Chicago on her left and Mayor Frank Hague of New Jersey on her right. Clinging to Mayor Hague is Marion Davies. To Mayor Kelly's right is Louis B. Mayer, and at the far left stands Hal Wallis, production chief of Warner Studios. The year is 1935.*

*A MULTIMILLIONAIRE SITS ALONE   A rare glimpse of William
Randolph Hearst playing patience in his California castle, San Simeon. His
chair dates back to the Tudors. The intricate woodwork and the silver can-
delabra are typical of the myriad art treasures in this fantastic estate.*

bombshell. The executors immediately contested it, alleging that
"it had never been executed and therefore might as well never have
existed."

A long and bitter legal battle now seemed likely. Marion was
quoted as saying: "I don't like the idea of a fight. I'm not the fighting type. This is very unpleasant for me, and I don't know what's
going to happen, but I don't believe in disregarding W. R.'s wishes."

The lawyers shuttled to and fro among the dozen or so repre-
sentatives of both sides, and they finally came up with a compromise. A joint statement declared:

> *Despite the numerous stories printed since Mr. Hearst's
> death indicating dissension between Miss Davies, the
> voting trustees, and the Hearst estate, there has in fact
> been no conflict between them and all questions as to
> their respective interests have been the subject of amic-
> able discussion and have all been amicably resolved. . . .
> Miss Davies has relinquished all rights she may have
> to act as voting trustee for the stock of the Hearst
> Corporation for the reason that there is question as to
> when her right would commence. This question would
> have to be clarified by long court proceedings which all
> parties deemed unnecessary and undesirable.*
>
> *Miss Davies has every faith in the intentions and
> abilities of Mr. Hearst's sons and the other directors and
> executives of the Hearst enterprises to ensure the contin-
> uity of Mr. Hearst's editorial policies, the furtherance
> of which would have been Miss Davies' only purpose in
> serving as a trustee. . . .*

When Marion heard that the compromise had been signed by everyone involved, her comment was: "Well, I've sold my power for a dollar a year. Maybe I was wrong, but it's all over."

Not quite all over. Marion, too, had a sting left.

On October 31, 1951—ten weeks after Hearst's death—she was married to Captain Horace G. Brown, Jr., of the Merchant Marine, in Las Vegas. Her wedding outfit consisted of a blue sweater, dark blue slacks, blue suede shoes, and a camel's hair coat. She wore dark glasses, and blandly gave her age as forty-five, although the year of her birth is reported to be 1900. The newly-weds breakfasted on turkey sandwiches and champagne; then flew off on a chartered aircraft for a Palm Springs honeymoon. It was said that the bridegroom bore a remarkable resemblance to W. R. Hearst in his palmy days.

King Carol and Madame Lupescu

It could have been the plot of a Ruritanian romance so beloved of Hollywood in the 1930s. Here is the Crown Prince who, because of his love for a commoner, falls afoul of his father, the King. Then banishment. Then the triumphant return to take his rightful place on the throne. Then war, flight, exile with the loved one by his side. Then marriage. Finally, death ends all. Close-up, with the tragic widow snipping a lock of the royal hair.

CROWN PRINCE CAROL AS A YOUNG MAN

But this was no film script. It all happened to Carol II of Greater Romania, the darling of prewar gossip columnists who knew him as "the playboy King." Carol's exploits with his red-haired mistress, Madame Lupescu, kept European newspaper and magazine readers agog—and eager for more.

Woman trouble plagued Carol from boyhood. In women he sought the attention and affection so lacking in his own family. King Ferdinand was a cold, austere figure who neither loved nor was loved by his son. Carol's beautiful mother Queen Marie turned to lovers for the warmth and understanding her husband never gave her. Not unreasonably, this alienated her firstborn, who adored her until he found out about one of her many affairs.

Marie, a granddaughter of Queen Victoria and also of Czar Alexander II, tried to arrange a marriage for Carol with a daughter of the Russian Royal Family; but Rasputin, whose influence at the Russian Court was then paramount, frustrated all her plans. In 1917, when he was twenty-four, Carol found consolation in the arms of Zizi Lambrino, a general's daughter, whom he determined to marry. There was no hope of having the wedding ceremony performed in Romania, so Carol smuggled Zizi over the frontier into Russia, and they were married in the Cathedral Church of Odessa.

The news caused a sensation in Bucharest. Queen Marie wrote of the marriage that it was "an almost insurmountable grief, a staggering family tragedy which suddenly hit us a stunning blow for which we were entirely unprepared. . . ." King Ferdinand even issued an order for Carol's arrest, for he was regarded as a traitor to his dynasty for marrying a commoner.

But this was only the first in a lifetime of scandals for Carol. Every possible pressure was put on him to abandon Zizi; but in the end, nature succeeded where family and politicians failed. Zizi was pregnant, her beauty faded—and so did Carol's love.

When their first child was born, on January 20, 1920, Zizi had not heard from Carol for weeks. After he was told he was the father of a boy, he sent flowers with a terse note: "Please call him Mircea," the name of his brother who had died in childhood. Legal machinery was put into operation; and by a decision of the highest court in Romania, the marriage was declared unconstitutional and therefore null and void. Zizi was paid off, and Carol was sent on his travels.

He first went to bid farewell to the officers of his regiment in the northern town of Bistritza. There his roving eye was caught by the lovely and vivacious wife of Captain Tempeanu, a comrade-in-arms. Her name was Elenutza, and she was destined to run like a thread through the fabric of his life. Her maiden name was Lupescu.

King Ferdinand and Queen Marie, anxious to erase the memory of the Carol-Zizi affair from the public mind, sent the troublesome Crown Prince on a world tour that would keep him out of the limelight for a year. However, just before he left, Carol slipped into a little jewelry shop in Bucharest and bought a small but costly brooch which he sent to Elenutza as a token of his interest. His father, by this time, would not trust him an inch, and had the Court's secret servicemen report Carol's movements back to him. Within a day of the purchase, Ferdinand knew about the brooch as well as the name of the woman for whom it was bought. At once, the security services were ordered to build up a secret dossier on the Tempeanus. The file on Captain Tempeanu was routine and uninteresting: it simply noted that he had been a fellow officer and friend of the Crown Prince for five years. But Elenutza was linked with a file on her family that reached back into the nineteenth century.

MAGDA LUPESCU   *An early picture of the internationally famed beauty. She was quite a young woman when this photo was taken.*

CAROL AND HIS BRIDE   *The youthful heir to the crown*
of Romania poses with Princess Helen of Greece.

Her grandfather was a member of an Orthodox Jewish community who, after fleeing from a pogrom in Poland, had taken refuge in the Romanian town of Jassy. Her father opened an apothecary's shop in that town and married a Viennese Roman Catholic. The mixed marriage threatened to ruin him so it seemed wise to change his name—which he did—to Lupescu. He then started a new business in another district of Jassy. Elenutza, his only child, was born in 1897 and educated in a Catholic convent in Bucharest. Nevertheless, her Jewish ancestry was to later provide a useful weapon for her enemies.

King Ferdinand's hope that he had bought himself some peace of mind by packing Carol off abroad soon proved vain. The Prince's roistering and drunken behavior brought protests to Bucharest from many quarters, not least from the British authorities in India who found his notoriety a nuisance there. Carol received a sharp command to proceed at once to Japan, where he was to convey a message from the Romanian King to the Son of Heaven.

His conduct in Singapore en route caused further indignation; and although he calmed down a little after he reached Tokyo, his parents realized that the tour was destined to create more trouble than it cured. So he was ordered to return home by the most direct route. Queen Marie decided it was high time to arrange a suitable marriage for him. The unlucky victim was Princess Helen of the Greek Royal Family, then in exile. Like many another loveless royal couple, theirs was not to reason why; and on March 10, 1921, Carol of Romania and Helen of Greece were married in the Metropolitan Cathedral of Athens.

The honeymoon was a fiasco. Helen was timid and unemotional; Carol, fiery and demanding. After a week, Carol suddenly discovered an interest in botany, and went off on his own "to collect flowers." Although it had been arranged that the happy couple were to end their honeymoon with an idyllic cruise through the Aegean, Carol became impatient to get back to Romania. He commanded a Romanian state vessel to transport them to Constanza on the Black Sea, and a royal train to take them to Bucharest.

In the capital, they received the usual ecstatic welcome from street crowds eager to cheer royal honeymooners; but Helen sat sulking in their open carriage, and Carol leaned back with indifference. There followed a fortnight of official junketing which finished off what little was left of their marriage.

It soon became evident that Carol had sired another child. Helen was installed in the rambling Pelesh Castle, with its hundred and fifty rooms and a thousand drafts, while Carol went a-roaming. As before, the father was not present at the birth. His child Michael was born on October 25, 1921.

Helen could well be called one of the world's most unlucky royal princess—her grandfather, George I of Greece, had been murdered; her cousin, the Czar of Russia, had been murdered; her uncle was ex-Kaiser Wilhelm of Germany; and her husband was Carol. Before her marriage was a year old, she was requesting permission to return to her parents in Athens. She was allowed to go for four months.

Carol seized the opportunity to woo Elenutza and install her as his mistress, telling his friends that Helen had gone off to Greece to alienate him from his son Michael. And—perhaps the unkindest cut of all—he began to call his new mistress Helena. He took little trouble to conceal his liaison, and the scandal quickly assumed political importance. Through all the hubbub, Helena Tempeanu maintained a discreet silence and, with a minimum of fuss and publicity, organized a divorce from the cuckolded captain. Her former husband's reward was a comfortable senior appointment in the provinces. She resumed her maiden name, and henceforth was known to the newspapers and magazines of the world as Madame Helena Lupescu.

The strained situation of the Crown Prince's marriage could not continue indefinitely. It was brought to boiling point over the funeral of Queen Alexandra in England. For that state occasion, King Ferdinand insisted that his country be represented by the Crown Prince. His government, fearful of an international incident if Carol went abroad, suggested that Queen Marie, a member of the British Royal Family, would be a much more suitable representative. Ferdinand would not change his mind. He ordered Carol to attend the ceremonies, and asked his son for his word of

PRINCESS HELEN AND HER SON MICHAEL

honor that he would cause no trouble and would return within a month. There was a furious scene between father and son, which ended with Carol agreeing to go—but he went straight from the palace to Madame Lupescu and arranged for her to go on ahead and wait in Paris.

Carol behaved with decorum at the funeral, although there were lurid stories of his boisterous behavior in London night clubs after it was over. One unconfirmed report stated that in consequence, he had been reprimanded by Buckingham Palace. He arranged a rendezvous with Helena Lupescu in Milan; and from there, he wrote to his father and to his wife that he had no intention of returning to Romania. The letters caused a roaring sensation in Bucharest. The King despatched a court official to Milan with a personal message for his son. Carol replied that he no longer wished to be regarded as a member of the Romanian Royal Family. In the presence of Madame Lupescu and the court official he renounced his succession to the throne.

The Crown Council of Romania met on New Year's Eve to discuss Carol's attitude; and on January 4, 1926, issued this communiqué:

> His Royal Highness, Prince Carol, heir to the throne, having informed His Majesty in writing of his irrevocable renunciation of the succession to the throne and all prerogatives appertaining to that rank, including that of membership of the Royal Family, His Majesty the King has deemed himself compelled to accept this renunciation and to summon a Council at the Castle of Pelesh. In communicating his high decision, His Majesty appealed to all men of eminence in the country who were present to help him in its execution and in the proclamation of his grandson, Prince Michael, as Heir to the Throne.

Carol reacted to the proclamation by opening his campaign

CAROL AND MICHAEL   *The King of Romania mounts the stairs of a chapel to place a wreath on the grave of King Ferdinand, his father on the occasion of the requiem held on the fourth anniversary of the former monarch's death. Michael, the young heir presumptive, attends the ceremony.*

for a divorce from the lonely Princess Helen. She herself was opposed to such a step, and suggested a meeting between them in Italy. Carol at first agreed to see her there and then, but ducked out of the arrangement at the last moment. He and Helena Lupescu moved to Paris, and later set up house in the suburb of Neuilly.

Carol's first wife, Zizi, who was living in Paris at the time, promptly filed suit against him in the French courts claiming ten million francs for support of their son. The judge found for Carol, declaring that the annulment of the marriage decreed by the High Court of Romania was legally binding internationally.

The dispute dragged on in Portugal, the country in which Carol finally established residence after his abdication. In 1957, the Portuguese Supreme Court declared Zizi's son, Mircea, to be the legitimate son of Carol. Victory it may have been, but it came four years after the royal father's death.

In 1927, King Ferdinand was a dying man. A powerful group of Romanian politicians, faced with the prospect of the infant Michael succeeding to the throne, intrigued to bring Carol back to seize power and thus avoid a regency.

The King died on July 27—his last reference to his son Carol a joke: "Excellent for what he is but, like a Swiss cheese, full of holes."

The government moved fast. Within an hour, Michael was proclaimed king and a regency of three was established to run the country. Neither Queen Marie nor Princess Helen was included.

The public was uneasy, and a People's Party was set up for the purpose of proclaiming Carol king. He was still in Neuilly with Lupescu, but living in much more modest circumstances. Messages reaching him from Romania convinced him that absence was making the hearts of his people grow fonder of him. The snag was that his estranged wife was now the Queen Mother, and it was most unlikely that Romanians could be persuaded to accept his mistress as well as himself.

He wrote again to his wife, begging her to reconsider her attitude concerning a divorce. Her reply was cold and formal—a complete rejection of his request. After this rebuff, Carol and Lupescu moved to Nice, where they were regular visitors at the casino.

Suddenly a new figure appeared on the scene, Barbu Ionescu, a Romanian who had made a fortune in London, and was now an international figure with business interests all over Europe. He offered to back Carol's bid for the throne and managed to get the Prince's signed messages smuggled into Bucharest. They announced that Carol would not be deaf to any reasonably supported request for his return to claim his heritage. Ionescu reported a favorable response to the messages, and invited Carol and Madame Lupescu to stay at his home in Godstone, Surrey. They did so; but unfortunately, Carol could never resist the lure of London's West End. Once again, he became the magnet of publicity seekers, and again there was a hint from Buckingham Palace for him to behave more discreetly. The Home Office did more than hint—Carol was given forty-eight hours to leave the country. Apparently the Foreign Office had discovered the maneuvering to put Carol on the throne of Romania. Carol and Helena Lupescu had no option but to leave the country. They proceeded to cross the Channel to France, and from there made their way to another Ionescu home, this one in Belgium.

This setback merely sharpened Ionescu's determination. Events in Romania greatly helped his campaign. Queen Marie and Princess Helen had quarreled over the education of the infant King. The wretched Helen suddenly found herself the target of every foul rumor and vituperation, while Carol was emerging as a much-wronged man. Helen could not hold out against the forces now assailing her. Her marriage with the exiled Prince was finally dissolved at a secret session of the Romanian High Court on June 21, 1928. The grounds for divorce—incompatability.

Carol and Lupescu celebrated the good news by giving a dinner party for Ionescu and his other supporters. Now that his chances of returning as ruler were growing, "the playboy Prince" lived a quiet and respectable life—he had been caught by scandal too often. In Bucharest, the tide was running for him. The world economic crisis helped to sweep the National Peasant Party to power. The new Prime Minister, Maniu, was a strong advocate of Carol for king. Maniu proposed to Queen Marie—once more the power behind the throne—that he send an invitation to Carol to become king, but on two conditions: (1) that Carol must submit to parliamentary control; and (2) that Madame Lupescu should not return with him.

Neither Queen Marie nor Maniu expected Carol to swallow the second condition. To their amazement, word came back from

France that Carol had agreed to both conditions without demur. A newspaper owner who visited the couple in Paris reported that Madame Lupescu told him: "My enemies are putting about the lie that I am a wicked woman. What I now do will no doubt convince them that I have lost my lover. But the choice is mine alone. I hereby renounce our perfect love."

However, Carol had no intention of allowing her to make this sacrifice. Once supreme power was his, let them outlaw Madame Lupescu if they dare!

In June, 1930, the two went to Switzerland with the full spotlight of publicity on them. They dined at a restaurant in Berne, and then bade each other ostentatious farewells. Carol traveled to Paris; Madame Lupescu, to Lucerne.

Meanwhile, word was spread in Romania that Prince Carol was on his way home. He landed at an airport outside Bucharest at 8 a.m. on Sunday, June 8, wearing the uniform of the Royal Air Force. He was accorded a triumphant procession into the capital. He spent the rest of the day with the Regency Council and the Cabinet. Overriding all proposals, he would not budge from his stand that he be proclaimed king immediately. In the end, the question was put to a meeting of delegates from the National Peasant Party, the party in power, and there was an overwhelming vote in Carol's favor.

Prime Minister Maniu reported the verdict to Carol but added his own recommendation that Carol state emphatically that he had

IRON GUARD PARADING   *These two shots show the Romanian army of Hitler's Nazis in their heyday. In the lower picture, the Fascist commander, General Antonescu, reviews his Romanian stormtroopers.*

no intention of bringing Helena Lupescu to Romania. Carol merely pointed out that she was *not* in the country and that she had renounced their love in the presence of a distinguished fellow countryman. With that, Maniu had to remain content.

That same afternoon, Carol drove through a huge crowd to Parliament, where without opposition, the Act of 1926 was declared invalid, and Carol II was proclaimed king. The proclamation also stipulated that his accession was to be retroactive to the death of his father Ferdinand. Thus the reign of Carol's son, King Michael, was obliterated from the records! Romania was proving itself a comic-opera state indeed.

The first move in the farce was the proposal that Carol's divorce from Princess Helen be annulled in order to allow her to stand by his side at the coronation ceremony!

While the Prime Minister went ahead with his preparations on that basis, Helena Lupescu returned by train to Bucharest. All plans for a coronation ceremony were hastily abandoned. Instead, Carol immediately set up his mistress in a two-storied villa just outside his palace grounds. And Helena behaved most discreetly—she never attended functions nor accompanied the King on his official journeys.

It was hardly to be expected that Carol would make a good and wise king. He did not. His reign was marked by confusion and compromise. But he was not helped by a new force sweeping through Europe in the 1930s—the force of fascism. And fascism was no respecter of kings. The Romanian version was known as the

NUPTIALS   Ex-King Carol of Romania is married to Madame Helena Lupescu at a Greek Orthodox ceremony in his Estoril villa in Lisbon, Portugal, on August 18, 1949. It was the second marriage in their 25-year romance. They had previously been married "in extremis", in Brazil, two years before when Madame Lupescu was believed to be near death.

Iron Guard; and at the time of Carol's accession, the Romanian fascists had mustered nearly half a million members.

Carol decided to try to suppress the organization. That was unfortunate for him, since it later appeared that the Iron Guard was backed by the Nazis of Berlin. Carol's Prime Minister, Ion Duca, on his way to spend the New Year with his King, was blown to bits.

Nor did Carol's love life with Madame Lupescu endear him to his subjects. It was said that her clothes allowance was about $50,000 a year, and that her jewelry was insured for a quarter of a million dollars. In addition, and at enormous cost, Carol had a tunnel built under the palace grounds leading from her villa into that wing of the palace in which his private suite was situated.

They both became increasingly prickly about insults, real or imagined. The Chief of the Romanian General Staff was demoted and sent to a frontier post because his wife had been rude to Lupescu. He was replaced at once by one of her creatures.

Discontent was rife. Even Ionescu, who had financed and promoted Carol's bid for the throne and had received lavish government contracts as reward, was visited by the secret police, and stripped of all his royal gifts and emoluments. Soon the only people who could make a killing were those who had initially ingratiated themselves with Lupescu. The wits were beginning to call her the "uncrowned Queen of Romania."

Then in January, 1936, came Carol's disastrous visit to London to attend the funeral of King George V. To begin with, there was trouble over his accommodations. He felt slighted because, as a reigning monarch, he was not put up at Buckingham Palace. Later stories went around that he had been living it up in West End night spots on the eve of the funeral. All Fleet Street chuckled over a picture of the procession which showed Carol accompanied by a man in white, said to be a masseur, whose job it was to sober him up so that he could march with the distinguished mourners. The story of Carol's hangover was not published in Britain; the

American press, however, suffered no such qualms. Of course, the story got back to Bucharest. In consequence, King Carol II found himself involved with the British in yet another public scandal.

Lavishly financed by Germany, the Iron Guard could now boast two million members. By 1937, it was the second strongest political group in Romania. The organization changed its name to the Fatherland Party. Carol's inept moves to deal with the menacing situation even disgusted Madame Lupescu; and in January, 1938, she went abroad without warning. When she reached Paris, she renounced her liaison saying, "This is a final break with His Majesty."

Her dramatic gesture did the trick. Within a few weeks, Carol, thoroughly goaded, issued an edict declaring the Iron Guard to be an illegal movement. He ordered the organization to disband, and demanded the immediate surrender of all its arms to military posts throughout the country.

Helena Lupescu was so overjoyed, she telephoned her congratulations to Carol. Within two days, she was back with him in Bucharest. England was pleased, too; and Buckingham Palace sent him a formal invitation to make a state visit to London later in the year. Emboldened and flattered by this support, Carol went further —he declared that fascism was treason in Romania.

But there was one country that had no congratulations for him. For the moment, Germany was, however, too busy annexing Austria to deal with Carol. He would come later.

That was a summer of Hitler crises in Europe. In July, Queen Marie died. Carol's petty and spiteful nature had found a dozen ways of humiliating her; but the one that hurt her most was his ban on national celebrations for her sixtieth birthday. Although he made a great show of grief over her death, he was too late to reach her deathbed. He sold her house and pocketed the money.

On November 15, 1938, he arrived in London for his state visit, wearing a plumed helmet and a white cloak. He spent three days in England hoping for a loan and for improved trade. He got

IN BERMUDA   *The King and his lady love out for a ride in an open carriage in 1941.*

CAROL IN PORTUGAL   Seated
in the lofty shell-pink livingroom of
his home, Casa Mar y Sol, at Estoril,
Carol seems to be content with his
peaceful life, living simply, spending
most of his time with his stamp collection or in gardening.

IN MEXICO   Former King Carol and
Madame Lupescu attend a French Theatre
festival in the Palacio de Bellas Artes in
Mexico City.

PRINCESS HELENA OF RO-
MANIA   *The wife of King
Carol poses in her sitting room at
Casa Mar y Sol in Portugal, in
June, 1947. Upon their marriage,
the King conferred the title upon
her.*

neither. During his absence, widespread rioting broke out in Romania, with Jews as the main target. Banners appeared in the streets bearing the legend: "Kill the Jewess Lupescu."

On his way home, Carol stopped over in Paris, trying again, unsuccessfully, for a loan. In despair, he went to see Hitler in Berchtesgaden where he was pointedly told that his treatment of the Iron Guard had been brutal and ill-advised. Hitler forcefully indicated that he wanted the Iron Guard leader Codreanu released from prison at once.

Far from taking this advice, Carol had Codreanu and a dozen Iron Guard leaders shot "while attempting to escape." The King turned dictator, and clamped a reign of terror on Romania.

Then, in July, 1939, when all Europe was teetering on the brink of World War II, Carol decided he needed a holiday, and with Madame Lupescu went off cruising on his yacht *Luceafarul*, better known to Britain as the *Nahlin*. It was the same yacht used by the Prince of Wales for his fateful cruise of the Aegean with Mrs. Simpson. Helena had been so moved by the Englishman's love story that she talked Carol into buying the yacht for themselves.

Within weeks of the return from their holiday, Europe was at war. Carol had hasty consultations with Prime Minister Calinescu, and then announced that Romania would remain neutral. Before the month of September was out, Calinescu was assassinated in the center of Bucharest. The Iron Guard had answered back.

WIDOWED   Arriving for her husband's funeral services in the pantheon of St. Vincent's Roman Catholic Church near Lisbon, Magda Lupescu is the very picture of grief.

Soon Hitler's propaganda machine was turned full blast on "the Jewess Lupescu." Carol finally gave way, and in March, 1940, announced a blanket amnesty for all his Iron Guard prisoners. Now he went crawling into the Nazi camp and appointed Horia Sima, the new Iron Guard chief, as his Minister of Culture. Sima was quick to persuade Carol to enact fiercely anti-Semitic laws.

To add to his dismay, Carol suddenly found himself facing an ultimatum from Soviet Russia ordering him to hand over the rich province of Bessarabia. He turned to Hitler for advice, and was told sharply to comply with Moscow's demand. The Ruritanian big shot who was playing at being king and dictator was now a marionette jerked about by his masters.

Carol made a big deal of announcing that Romania had joined the Rome-Berlin Axis as a satellite of the Third Reich. Any hope that this gesture would save his country from further depredations was rapidly dissipated when Hungary demanded the return of Transylvania, the richest wheat belt in Europe. Berlin supported the demand, and there was nothing Carol could do but obey orders.

Ruthlessly and effectively, all Carol's powers were stripped from him by Hitler's puppet, General Antonescu. Finally, in September, 1940, the King was given an ultimatum demanding his abdication. He went through the solemn ritual of penning his last message to his sorely-tried people.

> *Times of great disturbance and anxiety are passing over my beloved country. For ten years since I assumed my place of high duty as King of my Fatherland, I have striven incessantly day and night. With deep love I have worked to do all that my conscience dictated for the good of Greater Romania. Now days of terrible hardship are overwhelming my country which is faced with the gravest dangers. Because of the great love I bear for my country and in which I was born and reared, I wish to prevent these dangers by passing today to my son, the Crown*

Prince Michael, whom I know you love very dearly, the heavy burden of kingship. In making this sacrifice for the salvation of the Fatherland, I pray God that it shall not be in vain.

In leaving my beloved son to my people, I ask all Romanians to protect him with their warmest love and loyalty, so that he may find all the support that he will need so much in the difficult task which will henceforth rest on his young shoulders.

I pray that my country may be protected by the God of our fathers, and He may grant her a glorious future. Long live Romania.—Carol Rex.

A special train of three coaches waited for him and Helena Lupescu at a Bucharest yard, and one hundred pieces of royal luggage were loaded aboard. At midnight, they began their long journey into oblivion. Just before they crossed the Romanian frontier at Timisoara, the train ran into an Iron Guard ambush and bullets ripped into their coach. Carol flung Helena to the floor, holding her down while the engine driver put on all speed to race clear of the assault. No one was hurt. Half an hour later, the train halted at a customs post in Yugoslavia. After a brief respite in neutral Switzerland, authorization came from Berlin permitting the exiles to reside in pro-Axis Spain.

Thanks to Helena's prudence, the couple was well off. She had crammed one of their many suitcases with banknotes from almost every country in Europe.

Carol spent most of his time in Spain scheming to escape into neutral Portugal. Eventually the two managed to reach Estoril. There they led a useless, almost comic existence. Some time later, they got to Mexico City, where they tried to run a night club.

When he read of the liberation of his country by the Russians, Carol realized that there was no future for monarchy in Romania. At last he was prepared to make the grand gesture to his faithful mistress, now fifty years old. First came the mysterious announcement that Helena Lupescu was dying of an incurable disease; then the statement followed that her marriage to Carol would take place immediately. The civil ceremony was held in Rio de Janeiro on July 7, 1947, and the ex-King solemnly proclaimed that henceforth she would be known as Princess Helena. The "incurable disease," however, did not prove fatal. Some twenty years later, she was still living in Coyoacan, a suburb of Mexico City.

The last years of Carol's life were unremarkable. In 1949, the devoted pair were married a second time in Portugal where they now made their home. The ex-King, however, never lost his insistence on protocol, and he proved extremely touchy about any slight to his Princess Helena. He died in 1953, and was buried in the pantheon of the Augustine monastery in Lisbon which contains the royal tombs. On the evening before his interment, he lay in state in an open coffin, the cross of the Orthodox church clasped in his hands.

Helena, thickly veiled and in deep mourning, tiptoed into the pantheon, looked into the open coffin, and taking a small pair of scissors from inside her cloak cut a lock of hair from his forehead. Then she bade farewell to the turbulent lover who became her quiet husband. "Adieu, amour de ma vie!" she said.

Lord Mountbatten and Edwina

England, in the early nineteen-twenties, was caught up in a frenzied reaction to four lean years of war. It was the era of the "bright young thing," of the girl in a short skirt and the man in plus-fours, the era of the society whirl and the social struggle. To be young and rich was very heaven; and two young socialites who seemed to be specially favored by the gods were Dickie Mountbatten and Edwina Ashley.

Dickie—as Lord Louis Mountbatten was called by his Smart Set friends—was the great-grandson of Queen Victoria. He was related to most of the crowned heads of Europe. His father, formerly Prince Louis of Battenberg, had renounced his German titles in July, 1917, and changed his name to Mountbatten, becoming the first Marquess of Milford Haven. The senior Prince Louis had already acquired British nationality and had made a distinguished career in the Royal Navy. He had become First Sea Lord in 1914, but had been forced to resign because of popular feeling against his German background. Restitution was done to him in 1921, a month before his death, when he was promoted Admiral of the Fleet on the Retired List. Dickie's mother was Princess Victoria, a daughter of the Grand Duke of Hesse and of Princess Alice, a sister of King Edward VII.

Born on June 25, 1900, Dickie was the youngest of four. He was christened Louis Francis Albert Victor Nicholas of Battenberg. He was first known as "Nickie," but there was another Nicholas in the family—Czar Nicholas of Russia—so young Prince Louis became "Dickie," and the nickname endured.

He was educated for the Navy. At thirteen, he went to the Royal Naval College at Osborne, and later to Dartmouth. In July, 1916, Dickie joined Admiral Beattie's flagship, H.M.S. *Lion,* and the following February went with Beattie to the new flagship, H.M.S. *Queen Elizabeth.* Later he served on submarines and escort vessels. After the war, he went to Cambridge. At the university, his closest friends were his royal cousins, the Princes Albert and Henry, who later became King George VI and the Duke of Gloucester.

With such connections, Dickie was soon a welcome guest at the best homes in London. And it was at a dance in Claridges Hotel in the summer of 1921 that he was introduced to Miss Edwina Ashley.

Edwina was born in November, 1901, and christened at Romsey Abbey in Hampshire. King Edward VII, one of her godparents, had suggested the name Edwardina for her; this was tactfully adapted to Edwina. Few girls could have had a better chance in life: her father was an aristocrat linked by blood to the oldest families in England, and her mother was one of the richest heiresses in the world. Her grandfather was the fabulous Sir Ernest Cassel, a German Jew whose first job in England had paid him fifteen shillings a week, but who had proceeded to earn such a vast fortune that he actually lent money to China, Mexico, and Uruguay. He founded the Bank of Egypt, the National Bank of Turkey and the State Bank of Morocco. He doted on his daughter, Maud, and when she died before him, he focused his love on his granddaughter, Edwina. He planned to leave her the richest girl in England.

This was the silver-spoon background of the well-matched couple who danced their first evening at Claridges. They next met during Cowes Week, and went together to the round of parties and dances. Then Mrs. Cornelius Vanderbilt invited Edwina to join a party on board her yacht, *Atlanta,* for a cruise around Belgium and France. "If you come," she told Edwina, "you'll balance my numbers, because I have at the moment a spare man—Dickie Mountbatten."

The moonlight hours on deck were irresistible to the lovely girl of nineteen and her handsome escort only sixteen months older. By the end of the cruise they were hopelessly in love. Dickie took Edwina to meet his parents. A few weeks later, they were both guests at Dunrobin Castle in Sutherland when news came that Dickie's father had suddenly died. A week later, Sir Ernest Cassel also died. Out of her grandfather's estate, which was valued at £7,500,000, Edwina was left £1,400,000—but she would not receive her inheritance until she married or came of age. The young couple's carefree life together was nearly halted at the very start.

In October, Dickie was to leave England for a tour of Austroasia as aide-de-camp to the Prince of Wales. He begged Edwina to go to India in time to join the royal party.

"But what do I do for my fare?" asked the heiress. "I have nothing left of my allowance."

Young Mountbatten himself was barely getting by on his naval pay and allowances. Edwina finally raised her fare from her great-aunt. She traveled to India second-class in a four-berth cabin; when she got to Bombay, she hadn't enough money to buy even a second-class rail ticket to Delhi. She booked a room at the Taj Mahal Hotel, where she called Dickie and reported her predicament. He managed to contact an Indian Army colonel in Bombay who produced enough money to get her to Delhi. Once there, she had no problem, as she was a guest of the Viceroy, Lord Reading.

Dickie and Edwina were immediately caught up in durbars, parades, garden parties, pig-sticking tournaments, tiger shoots, horse races and State functions. Occasionally, they managed to slip away alone to wander around New Delhi, then being built, and to look at the foundations of the magnificent new house for the Viceroy, where they were later to celebrate their silver wedding anniversary. Dickie, immersed in his duties as aide-de-camp, could not afford much time for romance, so a sympathetic Prince of Wales gave him the key of his private sitting room. Dickie proposed to Edwina in one of the rooms of Viceregal Lodge, and they announced the engagement the night the royal party left India. Edwina had to make her own way back to England—in a cargo boat!

When Dickie returned from the exhausting royal tour, Edwina took him to meet her family on their 6000-acre estate in Hampshire. She also showed him their magnificent stately home, Broadlands, on the River Test, with interiors designed by Robert Adam, and parks laid out by Capability Brown. Broadlands had first been made a showplace by Palmerston, Queen Victoria's great Prime Minister, but Edwina was later to embellish it for the honeymoon of the future Elizabeth II and Prince Philip. Indeed, Elizabeth and Philip began their married life in the same bedroom as did the Mountbattens.

Edwina Ashley and Lord Louis were married on July 18, 1922, at St. Margaret's, Westminster, before 1,200 guests including Princess Andrew of Greece (four of whose daughters were brides-

DICKIE MOUNTBATTEN AND FIANCEE   *This portrait study was
made on the occasion of the engagement of Lieutenant Lord Louis Mountbatten, R.N., and the Honorable Cynthia Annette Ashley, elder daughter of
First Lord Mount Temple, P.C.*

maids), the Princess Royal and her daughters, the Duke of Con-
naught, the Duke of York, Princess Mary and Viscount Lascelles,
Queen Alexandra and, finally, the King and Queen. The Prince of
Wales was Dickie's best man, officers of the battleships *Renown*
and *Repulse* formed the guard of honor, and a gun crew drew the
bridal car from the church. Four strong men were needed to lift
the wedding cake into Brook House for the reception.

Their five-month honeymoon took them on a rapid motor tour
of Europe and a more leisurely exploration of the United States.
Dickie and Edwina then returned to England to cope with life on
an income of £45,000 a year after taxes. Lord Louis, now a naval
lieutenant, played hard but worked even harder. The Mountbattens were central figures in the Prince of Wales' high-living set—
they were regularly featured in society columns and in slick magazines. The birth of their first child, Patricia, in 1924, put only a
temporary curb on their social activities. Edwina, who seemed to
have everything a girl could ask for, was burning up her energies
in the pursuit of purposeless pleasure.

*THE BEST MAN   At the wedding of his good friend, Lord
Mountbatten to Miss Edwina Ashley, the Prince of Wales enters St.
Margaret's Church, Westminster.*

Voices were raised in criticism. The Mountbattens were seen as typically selfish examples of the "idle rich"—especially objectionable in Britain's hungry thirties. Dickie was talked about, even in his own naval circles, as a show-off. After a tour of sea duty, he enrolled for a signals course for officers at Portsmouth; he rented Adsdean, a large house twenty-five minutes' fast driving away in the center of pleasant parkland overlooking Chichester Harbor. Dickie drove to classes in a large and shining Rolls-Royce. On the license plate were his initials, "L. M.," and on the hood stood a silver signalman holding two flags—a gift from the Prince of Wales. He also owned an outsize power-boat, for which members of the Royal Yacht Club at Cowes blackballed him.

Meanwhile, Edwina was winning a bubble reputation as one of the best-dressed women—in an England where the dole queues were lengthening every year. Even in that earlier era of mini-skirts, Edwina's skirt length was considered daring. At her all-night parties, guests had a choice of caviar, pâté de foie gras, roast pheasant, or woodcock—always with champagne. This reckless and ostentatious way of life could obviously not last forever, and the abdication crisis stopped the Fort Belvedere Set (as the Prince of Wales and his followers came to be called) in their tracks.

Dickie was quixotic enough to volunteer to accompany his close friend, now the Duke of Windsor, into exile. The offer was not accepted, and Lord Louis Mountbatten was almost immediately appointed personal naval aide-de-camp to another of his cousins, King George VI.

Gradually, even their sharpest critics realized that the pampered darlings of society were developing social conscience. Polo and parties were not enough for Dickie, and fashion and fun could not satisfy Edwina. When the superficial routine of a society gadfly began to depress her, she took to travel and exploration. Thus, before she was thirty, she traveled by train across Russia, then to China and back via San Francisco. The following year she sailed on the

BRIDAL PICTURE   *Lady Edwina is flanked by her husband,*
Lord Louis Mountbatten and the Prince of Wales.

crew of a schooner trading in copra among the remote islands of the South Pacific. Later, she made an archaeological tour of the Middle East.

By the spring of 1929 she was expecting their second child, Pamela, who was born prematurely while Edwina and Dickie were in Spain. Even with their income, the Mountbattens were strained by the £17,000 annual upkeep of Brook House, in Mayfair. In May, 1933, they sold the site. The house was pulled down and a block

NEWLYWEDS   *Lord Louis Mountbatten and his bride leave St. Margaret's Church on July 25, 1922.*

of flats and offices replaced it, with a two-story penthouse which in
the years before World War II was rented to them as their London
home. This became England's most sensational dwelling, a showplace almost on the Hearst scale. The Mountbatten penthouse was
designed to Dickie's own specifications and was decorated without
counting the cost. It had five reception rooms overlooking Hyde
Park, every conceivable refinement of furnishing devised by a Long
Island friend, and even an elevator from a private entrance in Upper
Brook Street. The Mountbattens moved in during 1936. Three
days after the outbreak of war in 1939, they closed the penthouse
forever.

If the Mountbattens had lived out their marriage according
to the pattern of their first 15 years, they would have earned no
place in the history books. But after 1938, the rich couple who had
been living for their own selfish interests and pleasures became
transformed into two dedicated and responsible people who made a
tremendous impact on our time. For Edwina, the metamorphosis
probably began with a remarkable visit she made to the Far East.
She determined to explore the Burma Road from Lashio to Yun-
nanfu. Lady Mountbatten was the first individual not involved in
the construction work to make the complete journey in a truck.
On this tour she saw profound human misery and degradation,
and she developed deeper attitudes and concerns.

By the time she returned to England, she had matured from
a society gadabout into a highly intelligent and determined humanitarian. She found her country gripped by the Munich crisis. While
her husband took command of a flotilla of destroyers, she turned
her talents towards reorganizing the nursing services. She herself
took a full course in first-aid training. The old life was gone forever. She closed the Mayfair penthouse, packed her two daughters
off to stay with the Vanderbilts in the United States, joined the
London branch of the St. John Ambulance Brigade, and trained
as a nurse at Westminster Hospital. When France fell, she was
ready to handle the critical situation which faced London. She set

BASEBALL FANS   *Lord and Lady Mountbatten visit the*
Yankee Stadium and pose with Babe Ruth and Col. Ruppert on
October 6, 1922.

about organizing ambulance services for the pathetic ramshackle
shelters, especially for those in the East End, and she visited the
shelters three or four nights a week throughout the Blitz. Lady
Mountbatten, immaculate in her black uniform with white collar
and gloves, became for thousands of embattled East-Enders one of
the most familiar and comforting figures of that historic defiance.
Meanwhile, her husband was winning his reputation as a leader of
men on the destroyer *Kelly,* which was finally sunk in the defense
of Crete. Later, he became head of Combined Operations, and she
became Superintendent-in-Chief of the St. John Nursing Division.

The most illustrious period of their life, though, was still to come. In the autumn of 1943, Lord Louis was appointed Supreme Allied Commander in South-East Asia. Edwina remained in London to carry on her invaluable work. At the end of 1944, she was invited by the Viceroy of India, Lord Wavell, to advise on hos-

HORSEY SET   *In 1924, in Deauville, France, Lord and Lady Mountbatten, with the Prince of Wales and other members of the British nobility, spend a day at the races.*

pitals and medical units throughout the SEAC military area. Her tour took her to the front in Burma and as far as Chungking in China. By the time her visits of inspection had ended, she had traveled 20,000 miles and talked to patients in 170 hospitals. One practical result was the transfer of 500 nurses of the Voluntary Aid Detachment to India.

While Germany was crashing to defeat, Edwina and her organization were involved in the rehabilitation of millions of refugees and prisoners of war. Then she dealt with similar problems in the Far East. She carried out a fantastic tour of Japanese-dominated zones of Burma, Siam, and Indonesia, risking her life daily to visit POW camps in remote jungle areas. For this outstanding example of her courage, energy, and endurance she was created a Dame Commander of the Royal Victorian Order.

The Mountbattens had assumed another—and as it turned out, dynastic—responsibility, the upbringing of their nephew, Prince Philip of Greece. Philip was the son of Prince Andrew of Greece and Princess Alice, Lord Louis' sister. Philip's father had died in Paris during the war, and his mother was living a life of seclusion in a Greek convent. The boy was, to all intents and purposes, an adopted son of the Mountbattens; indeed, he was to take their name and become a British subject. They sent him to a preparatory school at Cheam in Surrey, and then to Gordonstoun in Scotland —a program which Philip followed in turn with his own son, now the heir to the throne. Indeed, historians have noted that, by her marriage in 1947 to Philip Mountbatten, Duke of Edinburgh, the Princess Elizabeth changed her surname from Windsor to Mountbatten. Thus she succeeded to the throne on February 6, 1952, with the Mountbatten surname even though two months later, by a special Order in Council, she resumed the style of Windsor for herself and her descendants.

Dickie and Edwina emerged from the war loaded with honors and titled Viscount and Viscountess Mountbatten of Burma. Yet

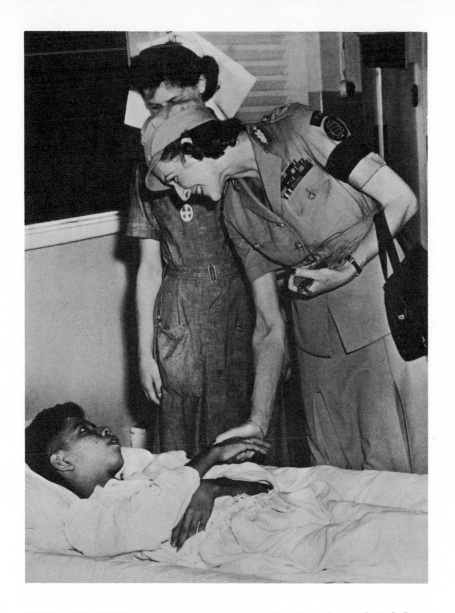

WELFARE WORKER   As chairman of the St. John and Red Cross
Services Hospital Welfare Department, Countess Mountbatten of Burma
visits a hospital to cheer up a wounded recruit.

AT HOME IN ENGLAND   The Earl and Countess Mountbatten stand
before their residence estate, Broadlands, in Romsey, Hampshire, which consists
of 500 acres of land, lawns and gardens. The Countess inherited Broadlands in
1939 from her father, First Lord Mount Temple, P.C.

an even more exacting task awaited them. The postwar Labor Government decided to free India from the British Raj, and the Government chose Lord Louis as the Viceroy to negotiate the transfer of power. Lady Mountbatten's comment on hearing that her husband had been selected for this most delicate and responsible of assignments was: "If anyone can succeed in India, I think Dickie can." And when his tremendous mission had been brought to a triumphant conclusion, he remarked: "I could never have done it without Edwina."

The tribute paid to her work at that time by Pundit Nehru is so remarkable that it is worth quoting in full:

> *The gods, or some good fairy, gave you beauty and high intelligence, and grace and charm and vitality—great gifts —and she who possesses them is a great lady wherever she goes. But unto those that have, even more shall be given: and they gave you something that was even rarer than those gifts—the human touch, the love of humanity, the urge to serve those who suffer and who are in distress. And this amazing mixture of qualities results in a radiant personality and in the healer's touch.*
>
> *Wherever you have gone you have brought solace, and you have brought hope and encouragement. Is it surprising, therefore, that the people of India should love you and look up to you as one of themselves and should grieve that you are going? Hundreds of thousands have seen you personally in various camps and other places and hospitals, and hundreds of thousands will be sorrowful at the news that you have gone.*

Much has been written about her selfless and devoted work among the refugees from the Punjab bloodbath which followed the partition of the country between India and Pakistan. Again and again she visited their camps until the refugees knew her personally. She spent days personally meeting their processions,

NAGA TRIBESMEN   In Assam, India, Earl Mountbatten meets with the wild
Indian Tribesmen who came to pay him homage. The Nagas arrived, mostly on foot,
from the Himalayas bordering on Tibet. Some of the headhunters took 14 days to trek to
Government House. This state reception was typical of the Imperial duties performed
by Earl Mountbatten and his viscountess.

DUTIES OF A VICEROY　　*Viscount Mountbatten and his wife walk through the devastated village of Kahuta, near Rawalpindi, which had been ravaged by riot.*

and supervising their feeding and welfare arrangements. She picked up their children with affection. She spent hours in their sick bays, comforting the patients, bathing their foreheads, changing their bandages. She did not shrink from infectious cases. By the end, she had become a legend, even a goddess, to them. For this outstanding work, she was awarded the O.B.E. For his own services, her husband was granted an earldom.

Their mission over, it was difficult to imagine what other tasks were left for them. Lord Mountbatten himself ended all speculation by returning to his old love, the Royal Navy. The former Viceroy was appointed Rear-Admiral in command of the First Cruiser Squadron, Mediterranean Fleet, and his Vicereine took second place to the wife of the Naval Commander-in-Chief. Then they turned attention to their finances, which were greatly depleted by their mission to India. Lady Mountbatten accepted legal advice to promote a private bill in order to break her share of her grandfather's trust and draw capital to augment her ever-diminishing income. Unfortunately for the Mountbattens, the bill became a controversial political issue and cost them a good deal of popularity. Eventually, the private bill was withdrawn. The Labor Government shortly introduced their own bill to the same effect; this bill became law in November, 1949.

THE VICEROY AND THE MAHATMA   *Ghandi talks things*
over with the Mountbattens.

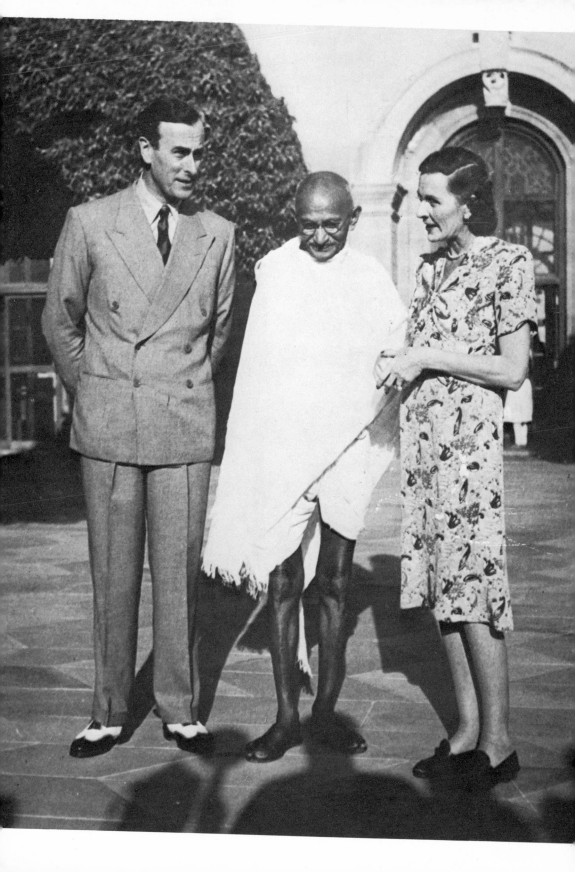

DAY OF INDEPENDENCE   On August 15th, 1947, Earl Mountbatten, Viceroy of India, hands over the instruments of India's independence to Mr. Nehru who became India's first Prime Minister. Lady Mountbatten stands on the dais.

RIGHT HONORABLE EARL MOUNTBATTEN OF BURMA   As a Colonel
of the Life Guards, the Earl is privileged to use after his name Knight of the Order of
the Garter, Privy Councillor, Knight Grand Commander of the Order of the Star of
India, and Knight Grand Commander of the Order of the Indian Empire.

In 1955, Winston Churchill made amends for the disgraceful wrong done to Dickie's father in World War I by appointing Admiral the Earl Mountbatten of Burma as First Sea Lord, a post he held until 1959 when he became Chief of the Defense Staff. The following year, 1960, saw another great occasion when Edwina and Dickie attended the wedding of their daughter Pamela to the interior decorator Mr. David Hicks. According to one of the women guests: "Edwina was dressed in gold and looked perfectly radiant. All the signs and lines of age, and the worn look, had disappeared. I don't know what she did, but she was fresh and beautiful." This despite thousands of hours spent under tropic suns, and despite the strain of her nonstop round of social activities. Dickie, too, was still charming and youthful-looking. The Mountbattens were one of the most handsome couples in England. Both were nearing sixty.

Queen Elizabeth, who was shortly expecting her third child, was not at the wedding, but the Queen Mother and Princess Margaret were. So, too, were Prince Philip and Prince Charles, the Duke and Duchess of Gloucester, and the then Duchess of Kent. Princess Anne was a bridesmaid for the first time in her life.

Four days after the ceremony, Edwina was off again, this time on a tour of the Far East as Superintendent-in-Chief of the St. John Ambulance Brigade and chairman of the Save the Children Fund. Her ten-week itinerary included Cyprus, India, Singapore, Malaya, North Borneo, Hong Kong, and Korea. On Thursday, February 18, 1960, she arrived at Government House in Jesselton, North Borneo, from Singapore, and appeared in excellent health and spirits. That night she was a guest at a dinner party, and the next morning she inspected an Army Training Center. At night, there was another dinner organized by the St. John Ambulance Brigade. Edwina looked pale and shaky. She made only a short speech, then offered her apologies and went back to Government House.

On Saturday she canceled her morning engagement and stayed in bed, but insisted on making three scheduled appearances in the afternoon and appearing at an evening reception for 120 people.

She went to bed late that Saturday night and fell into a deep sleep, from which she never woke up.

On Sunday morning Lord Mountbatten received the staggering blow of Edwina's death. The news all but broke his heart—even a year later he told a close friend: "There is nothing left in life for me but work." The Queen decreed a week of family mourning. Lord Mountbatten announced that "at Lady Mountbatten's special wish expressed in her will, the private funeral will take place at sea. The Board of Admiralty have made H.M.S. *Wakefield* available for this purpose, and she will sail from Portsmouth on Thursday afternoon."

Edwina's body was flown back to lie at Romsey Abbey the night before the funeral. The next day, a group of mourners huddled round a flag-draped coffin on the *Wakefield's* quarterdeck when the vessel hove to south of the Nab Tower—Lord Louis and Prince Philip in naval uniform, Patricia and Pamela with their husbands, Prince Philip's mother wearing her grey nun's habit, and some of Edwina's closest women friends. The Archbishop of Canterbury read the Committal to the Deep. Then, with the wailing of the bo's'ns' pipes, the bier was tilted forward, and the coffin slid into the waters. Lord Louis, his high spirits and jauntiness gone forever, kissed a wreath of white roses, and threw it after her into the sea.

THE LAST SALUTE   *Earl Mountbatten, grief stricken, casts a wreath of white roses into the sea, after the casket of his beloved wife has been laid to rest in the deep. On shipsboard, in the forefront, stands Prince Phillip, husband of Queen Elizabeth.*

The Duke of Windsor and Wallis Simpson

The love affair of the Duke and Duchess of Windsor shook the throne of England, forced King Edward VIII to abdicate, and split the country into pro-King and anti-King factions. It was unquestionably the most discussed romance of the twentieth century.

When first they met, the present Duke of Windsor was Prince of Wales and the heir of King George V; the Duchess was Mrs. Ernest Simpson, the American wife of an English businessman. At

20, she had married a lieutenant in the United States Navy. In 1925, after eight years of marriage, she obtained a divorce from him on grounds of incompatibility. Two years later, she met Ernest Simpson; and when his marriage ended in divorce, she married Simpson in London.

In his autobiography, *A King's Story*, the Duke has described the Simpson's apartment in Bryanston Square:

> *Everything in it was in exquisite taste, and the food, in my judgment, unrivalled in London. Having been raised in Baltimore, where a fine dinner is considered one of the highest human accomplishments, Wallis [Mrs. Simpson] had an expert knowledge of cooking. But, beyond all that, she had a magnetic attraction for gay, lively, and informed company.*
>
> *I travelled a good deal during this period, but, whenever I was in London, I liked to drop in at Bryanston Court for tea or cocktails, where one met young British and American men of affairs, foreign diplomats, and intelligent women. The talk was witty and crackling with the new ideas that were bubbling up furiously in the world of Hitler, Mussolini, Stalin, the New Deal, and Chiang Kai-shek.*

The Duke and Duchess differ about the date of their first meeting. In *A King's Story*, the Duke records that it was in the winter of 1931. The Duchess, in her autobiography, *The Heart Has Its Reasons*, gives the year as 1930. But there is no doubt about the occasion. Mr. and Mrs. Ernest Simpson were invited to meet the Prince of Wales and his brother, Prince George—later King George VI—at a weekend hunting party at Burrough Court in Melton Mowbray, Leicestershire. It is interesting to compare their first impressions of one another, as set down in their autobiographies.

THREE GENERATIONS OF BRITISH ROYALTY *Photographed in 1909 aboard the royal yacht were King Edward VII, George, Prince of Wales (later George V), and young Prince Edward.*

EDWARD, PRINCE OF WALES   This official portrait
shows the 17-year-old prince in his garter robes after his investiture in 1911.

The Duchess of Windsor writes:

The Prince of Wales, as I remember, had on very loud-checked tweeds. His younger brother was similarly dressed, but his clothes were more conservative in pattern. I remember thinking, as I studied the Prince of Wales, how much like his pictures he really was—the slightly wind-rumpled golden hair, the turned-up nose, and a strange, wistful, almost sad look about the eyes when his expression was in repose. But I was surprised on seeing him for the first time to discover how small he was. . . . I realized then that he could not be more than two inches taller than I, and I am five feet five.

What attracted me at once about the two brothers, and especially the Prince of Wales, was their utter naturalness. The thought was afterwards to occur to me that it was decidedly unimaginative on my part to expect them to be anything else. Still, the notion that they would be imposingly formal and reserved was in the back of my mind, and to find that Royalty lights a cigarette in much the same way as other people do and employs much the same gestures and mannerisms and in addition could be highly agreeable was for me an astonishing revelation.

Here is the Duke of Windsor's account:

I had gone to Melton Mowbray with my brother George for a weekend's hunting. Mr. and Mrs. Simpson were guests in the same house. It was one of those weekends for which our winters are justly infamous—cold, damp, foggy. Mrs. Simpson did not ride and obviously had no interest in horses, hounds, or hunting in general. She was also plainly in misery from a bad cold in the head. Since a Prince by custom is expected to take the lead in

*conversing with strangers, and having been informed
that she was an American, I was prompted to observe
that she must miss central heating, of which there was
a lamentable lack in my country and an abundance in
hers. . . . A mocking look came into her eyes. "I am sorry,
sir," she said, "but you have disappointed me."*

"In what way?"

*"Every American woman who comes to your coun-
try is always asked that same question. I had hoped for
something more original from the Prince of Wales."*

During the next few years, they met occasionally at dinner
parties in London or on weekends in the country. They remained
distant acquaintances until, according to the Duke:

*. . . one day she began to mean more to me in a way that
she did not perhaps comprehend. My impression is that
for a long time she remained unaffected by my interest
. . . presently and imperceptibly the hope formed that one
day I might be able to share my life with her, just how
I did not know.*

What qualities did the Prince of Wales find in Mrs. Simpson
which were not present in the other women who fluttered around
him? Clearly, she gave him sympathy and understanding for the
official side of his life. With her, he could discuss the problems
that beset the heir to a throne, as well as his visions of the British
monarchy in the new and troubled age then dawning. He is reported to have said that she was "the only woman who has ever
been interested in my job."

*INVESTITURE OF THE PRINCE OF WALES   The
ceremonial procession is proceeding through the grounds of
Carnavon Castle. The year is 1911. The Prince, in the third row
center, is accompanied by his mother, Queen Mary, and his
father, King George V.*

The Prince was obviously attracted to mature women, and particularly Americans. Perhaps their combination of enthusiasm, informality, and reverence for royalty intrigued him. His previous favorite had been an American whose background was rather similar to Mrs. Simpson's. She was Thelma, Viscountess Furness, one of the celebrated beauties of the 1920s whose husband was the head of a famous shipping line and one of the wealthiest men in Britain. However, they had gone their separate ways. Thelma's association with the Prince of Wales lasted four years.

It was Thelma—as she was later to recall wryly—who claimed the honor of introducing Mrs. Simpson to the Prince of Wales. Wallis had been recommended to Thelma as a vivacious companion, suitable for her circle around the Prince. Indeed, when Mrs. Simpson was presented at Court, she borrowed Thelma's train and feathers to grace the occasion.

In 1934, Viscountess Furness was obliged to go to New York to deal with family matters. She was reluctant to leave, and the Prince was equally reluctant to be deprived of her society. Thelma talked it over with Mrs. Simpson in a much-quoted conversation, which is said to have gone like this:

"Thelma, the little man is going to be so lonely."

"Well, darling, you look after him for me while I'm gone. But see that he does not get into mischief."

When Thelma returned, she found that the Prince's interest in her had cooled—and she was soon to realize why. "Wallis Simpson of all people! I knew then that she had looked after him exceedingly well."

In *The Heart Has Its Reasons*, the Duchess of Windsor has this to say of that fateful period:

> *Thelma returned in the early spring. Something had happened between her and the Prince. She was back at the Fort [Fort Belvedere, the Prince's country home near Windsor Great Park] once, but the former warmth and*

easiness of their relationship was plainly gone. One after-
noon she came to Bryanston Court. It was an unhappy
call. She told me the Prince was obviously avoiding her
—she couldn't understand why. He would not speak to
her himself on the telephone. No more invitations to the
Fort were forthcoming. Finally she asked me point-blank
if the Prince were interested in me—"keen" was the word
she used.

This was a question I had expected, and I was glad
to be able to give her a straight answer. "Thelma," I said,
"I think he likes me. He may be fond of me. But if you
mean by keen that he is in love with me, the answer is
definitely No."

As Wallis' friendship with the Prince ripened, the life of the
Simpsons became submerged in the royal round. Mrs. Simpson
noted that her husband's interest in the Prince tended to diminish
as hers increased. This was hardly surprising; although Simpson
continued to accept weekend invitations to Fort Belvedere, he must
have realized that his wife was the magnet. Both the Simpsons were
guests at the wedding of Prince George to Princess Marina (later
the Duke and Duchess of Kent), and Wallis was presented to King
George V and Queen Mary—"the only time I ever met his father
and mother."

Gradually, it began to dawn on the Prince that Wallis Simpson was essential to him, and he began to think ahead to the day
when it might be possible for him to marry her. How did this come
about? The Duchess of Windsor faces this question with remarkable candor in her autobiography:

Searching my mind I could find no good reason why this
most glamorous of men should be seriously attracted to
me. I certainly was no beauty, and he had the pick of the
beautiful women of the world. I was certainly no longer

very young. In fact, in my own country I would have been considered securely on the shelf.

The only reason to which I could ascribe his interest in me, such as it was, was perhaps my American independence of spirit, my directness, what I would like to think is a sense of humor and of fun, and, well—my breezy curiosity about him and everything concerning him. Perhaps it was this naturalness of attitude that had first astonished, then amazed, and finally amused him. Then, too, he was lonely, and perhaps I had been one of the first to penetrate the heart of his inner loneliness, his sense of separateness. . . .

I had no difficulty in explaining to myself the nature of the Prince's appeal to me. Over and beyond the charm of his personality and the warmth of his manner, he was the open sesame to a new and glittering world that excited me as nothing in my life had ever done before. For all his natural simplicity, his genuine abhorrence of ostentation, there was nevertheless about him—even in his most Robinson Crusoe clothes—an unmistakable aura of power and authority. His slightest wish seemed always to be translated instantly into the most impressive kind of reality. Trains were held; yachts materialized; the best suites in the finest hotels were flung open; aeroplanes stood waiting. What impressed me most of all was how all this could be brought to pass without apparent effort; the calm assumption that this was the natural order of things, that nothing could ever possibly go awry. . . . It seemed unbelievable that I, Wallis Warfield, of Baltimore, Maryland, could be part of this enchanted world. It seemed so incredible that it produced in me a happy and unheeding acceptance.

When did Wallis and the Prince "cross the line that marks

the indefinable boundary between friendship and love?" The Duchess cannot answer that question with certainty: "Perhaps it was one evening strolling on the beach at Formentor in Majorca. How can a woman ever really know? How can she ever really tell?"

The Prince's determination to marry Mrs. Simpson, coupled with his accession to the throne, catapulted the nation into crisis. He was well aware of the many difficulties in his path. He knew that he could expect maximum opposition from his father, who held the power of veto. By Act of Parliament, the sovereign has absolute authority over the marriages of all members of the royal family. There could be no doubt that the King would use it to forbid his son's marriage to Mrs. Simpson.

FORT BELVEDERE   *The royal country home in Berkshire.*

King George V was the embodiment of the old virtues of kingship—sincerity, devotion to duty, acceptance of the teachings of his church, especially on divorce. In his eyes, it was deplorable that the heir to his throne could ever contemplate marriage to a woman whose two former husbands were living. But he uttered no word of warning or protest to the Prince. And Queen Mary, who was also uncompromising in her views and had a deep sense of duty to the Crown, was too unbending to win her son's personal confidences.

So the Prince of Wales had to go his own way. Lacking the capacity to cement deep and enduring friendships, he tended to surround himself with amusing acquaintances. He resented any interference and disdained well-meant advice. Those who studied his life noted that his natural charm and grace and his consideration for others seemed to turn sour toward the end of his long wait for the throne.

In January of 1936, King George died. The Prince was at his bedside. As her act of submission to the new sovereign, the Queen Mother took her son's hand and kissed it. It was later noticed, however, that the new King preferred to spend the period of mourning with Mrs. Simpson at Fort Belvedere rather than to comfort his mother at Sandringham.

The morning after his father's death, the new King set a precedent by flying from Sandringham to London to deal with the formalities of his accession to the throne. He was proclaimed Edward VIII, and he made the interesting and significant pledge before the Accession Council that he was "determined to follow in my father's footsteps" (in striving to uphold constitutional government) "and to work as hard throughout my life for the happiness and welfare of all classes of my subjects."

Proclamation of a sovereign is a colorful ceremonial in which gloriously appareled heralds and pursuivants follow a fanfare of trumpets in announcing the new monarch to the citizens of the capital city. Here again, King Edward was responsible for a startling innovation. Not only did he arrange for Mrs. Simpson to observe the ceremony at St. James' Palace, but she was present to watch him proclaimed. When she wondered if all this pomp and ceremony meant the end of their carefree chapter, he was quick to reassure her that "Nothing can ever change my feelings for you." The strength of his feelings was shortly to be put to the test.

A few months before his accession, a General Election had returned to power the Conservative Party led by Mr. Stanley Baldwin, who became Prime Minister. When, on May 27, 1936, it was announced in the *Court Circular* that Mr. and Mrs. Ernest Simpson had dined at St. James' Palace as guests of the King, with Mr. and Mrs. Stanley Baldwin also present, it was clear that the testing time would not be long delayed. It became even clearer when Mrs. Simpson's name appeared again in another *Court Circular,* but this time without her husband's.

Still, the newspapers of Britain, by tacit agreement, refrained from linking the King and Mrs. Simpson in print, although, of course, the American press was by no means so reticent. There was plenty to write about. When his day's duties had ended, the King would drop in on Mrs. Simpson at her London apartment. Meanwhile, Mr. Simpson had plainly come to the conclusion that, though there might be a future for his wife in this relationship, there was none for him, and he moved out. This is what *The Heart Has Its Reasons* has to say about that difficult period in the developing drama:

> In the meantime Ernest had gone off to New York again. It was now made unmistakably clear to me that he had found a new emotional centre for his life. There was another woman. The details are unimportant: the situation became known to me through one of those coincidences that are stranger than fiction—a letter meant for Ernest that was inadvertently addressed to me.

However, she was consoled by the King, who, early in the

summer of 1936, chartered Lady Yule's yacht, the *Nahlin,* for an Adriatic cruise. Mrs. Simpson was one of a party of nine. Mr. Simpson was not invited.

At this time, she sounded out the King about the wisdom of beginning divorce proceedings. According to her book, he said gravely that it would be wrong for him to attempt to influence her either way, that only she could make the decision. "You can only do," he finally said, "what you think is right for you."

But he did arrange for her to see his solicitor, Sir George Allen, who asked: "Are you quite sure, Mrs. Simpson, that you want a divorce?" She assured him that her mind was made up. He explained that he did not handle divorce cases, but some weeks later he called her to say that Mr. Theodore Goddard would take her case. Mrs. Simpson's petition was put down to be heard at Ipswich Assizes on October 27. The fat was in the fire.

The love affair now became the urgent concern of Church and State. It was referred to—in the unpublicized discussions—as the "King's Matter," and the Archbishop of Canterbury, Dr. Cosmo Lang, saw himself facing the distasteful possibility of officiating at the coronation of a sovereign who was married to a woman with two husbands still alive.

The Prime Minister calculated that, if Mrs. Simpson was granted a decree nisi in October, it would become absolute just before the coronation, which had been fixed for May. Clearly, someone with the necessary authority had to take a hand before the matter had gone too far. Astonishingly, that someone was the King's mother, Queen Mary.

She had avoided all mention of the subject in her conversations with her son, but she viewed the prospect of his marriage to Mrs. Simpson with concern and anger. It was entirely in character that Queen Mary should put her responsibilities to the institution of the Crown before her maternal feelings. She let it be known that it was her wish that the Government should act.

The way was clear for Mr. Stanley Baldwin to speak to the

King on behalf of the country. He was, however, in a considerable dilemma about the form his intervention should take, for although Parliament had decreed that the King has the power to regulate the marriages of his children and other members of the royal family, it had no power to regulate the marriage of the King. And there was no precedent in British law for Baldwin to follow—the situation was unique.

It was, indeed, the greatest crisis over the authority of the monarch since the days of James II. The Prime Minister sought an audience with the King, and it was arranged for October 20— one week before the hearing of Mrs. Simpson's divorce petition. The talk lasted all that day, and an agreement was reached: that King and Premier must settle the issue between themselves.

It is possible that both parties failed to appreciate the determination of the other. But neither was in any doubt about the scandalous possibilities of newspaper coverage of the divorce hearing, which would be in open court before the world. So far, the name of Mrs. Simpson had barely received a mention in the British newspapers, but it was expecting too much of the editors to suppress all mention of the divorce.

Consequently, the King invited Lord Beaverbrook to the palace, and he, in turn, secured the support of Lord Rothermere, who called together the London and provincial newspaper proprietors. All agreed to confine their reports to the bare facts of the divorce hearing. This gentleman's agreement was upheld 100 percent in England, but such restraints could not be applied to the American press. Indeed, on October 26, the eve of the hearing, Hearst's *New York Journal* announced:

> *Within a few days, Mrs. Ernest Simpson of Baltimore will obtain her divorce decree in England, and some eight months thereafter she will be married to Edward VIII, King of England. King Edward's most intimate friends state with the utmost positiveness that he is very deeply*

and sincerely enamoured of Mrs. Simpson, that his love
is a righteous affection, and that immediately after the
Coronation he will take her as his consort.

Normally, a report of this significance would, if incorrect, be repudiated at once by the Court. But this time there was no comment—and no reaction in the British press. The following day, Mr. Norman Birkett, K. C., rose before the assize judge at Ipswich to open the case of Simpson *vs.* Simpson, and he at once called the petitioner. The swarms of reporters packing the court in out-of-the-way Suffolk craned forward to see Mrs. Simpson make her way to the witness-box. If they expected sensational evidence, they were disappointed, for the proceedings were routine, and the husband did not appear.

However, Mrs. Simpson was required to read a letter she had written to her husband about a fortnight before she set out on the summer cruise on the *Nahlin.* The letter complained that he had been staying at a hotel with a lady and had not, as he had said, been absent on business. She therefore requested him to move out of their home.

Mr. Birkett asked for a decree nisi with costs. Mr. Justice Hawke then broke his silence. "I suppose," he said, "that I must come to the conclusion that there was adultery in this case."

The hearing over, the reporters tried to scurry from the courtroom to see Mrs. Simpson leaving. They discovered that they were locked in, and they did not get out until Mrs. Simpson had been driven off toward London—where she dined that night with the King. Here is her own description of the occasion:

The evening started off as a happy reunion. But it was
not long before I realized that something was troubling
David. Beneath his gladness over my having successfully
cleared the hurdles at Ipswich, I detected a certain reser-
vation, a suppressed anxiety. Bit by bit, as he described
his own activities over the previous days, the reasons for

ENGLAND LEARNS OF THE KING'S ROMANCE
Scene on a London street corner on December 3, 1936.

his worried air came out. Several disturbing and impor-
tant things had happened.

 A week before, the Prime Minister, at his request,
had been to see David at the Fort. David had been taken
aback by Mr. Baldwin's desire that the request for an
audience be kept private. David told me, with obvious
distaste, that the Prime Minister's purpose in seeking the
interview was to express his concern over the divorce and
to suggest pointedly that the King use his influence to
persuade me to drop the proceedings. . . . For the first
time I was frightened. David tried to reassure me and
minimized the importance of the Prime Minister's call.
He said: "Don't be alarmed, I'm sure I can fix things."
David's reassurance notwithstanding, I was still con-
vinced that we had not heard the last of Stanley Bald-
win. . . .

How right she was. But the next threat to their future did not
come from the Prime Minister. It came in the form of a letter from
the King's private secretary, Major Alexander Hardinge. Before
delivering the letter, Major Hardinge took the precaution of showing a draft to Mr. Geoffrey Dawson, editor of *The Times*. Dawson,
who was a powerful force in the Establishment and a determined
opponent of the King's marriage plans, approved of what Major
Hardinge had written. The letter was sent off to Fort Belvedere in
a red dispatch box marked "Urgent and Confidential." The King
opened it after visiting the Fleet and was shocked to read:

Sir, With my humble duty.

 As your Majesty's Private Secretary, I feel it my
duty to bring to your notice the following facts which
have come to my knowledge, and which I know to be
accurate:

 (1) The silence of the British press on the subject of

your Majesty's friendship with Mrs. Simpson is not *going to be maintained. It is probably only a matter of days before the outburst begins. Judging by the letters from British subjects living in foreign countries where the press has been outspoken, the effect will be calamitous.*

(2) The Prime Minister and senior members of the Government are meeting today to discuss what action should be taken to deal with the serious situation which is developing. As your Majesty no doubt knows, the resignation of the Government—an eventuality which can by no means be excluded—would result in your Majesty having to find someone else capable of forming a government which would receive the support of the present House of Commons. I have reason to know that, in view of the feeling prevalent among M.P.s of all parties, this is hardly within the bounds of possibility. The only alternative remaining is a dissolution and a General Election, in which your Majesty's personal affairs would be the chief issue—and I cannot help feeling that even those who would sympathize with your Majesty as an individual would deeply resent the damage which would inevitably be done to the Crown, the cornerstone on which the whole Empire rests.

If your Majesty will permit me to say so, there is only one step which holds out any prospect of avoiding this dangerous situation, and that is for Mrs. Simpson to go abroad without further delay, and I would beg *your Majesty to give this proposal your earnest consideration before the position has become irretrievable. Owing to the changing attitude of the press, the matter has become one of great urgency.*

The King's immediate reaction to the letter, which he read in

a cold fury, was that Hardinge was, in effect, passing on an ultimatum from the Government. He determined to have it out with
Baldwin forthwith. At last, he realized the need for a wise counselor by his side, and he called in an old acquaintance, Sir Walter
Monckton, K.C., whom he had known at Oxford a score of years
before.

Mrs. Simpson had to be shown the letter from Major Hardinge, but the King asked her to read it alone. She tells us, in *The
Heart Has Its Reasons,* that she was stunned.

> *This was the end I had always known in the back of my
> mind was bound to come. . . . Clearly, there was only one
> thing for me to do: it was to leave the country immedi-
> ately as Hardinge had implored, and so I told David
> when he returned a few moments later. Almost peremp-
> torily he said: "You'll do no such thing. I won't have it.
> This letter is an impertinence."*
>
> *"That may well be. But just the same I think he's
> being sincere. He's trying to warn you that the Govern-
> ment will insist that you give me up."*
>
> *"They can't stop me. On the throne or off, I'm going
> to marry you."*

He would not listen to her renewed entreaties. "I'm going to
send for Mr. Baldwin to see me at the palace tomorrow. I'm going
to tell him that if the country won't approve our marrying, I'm
ready to go."

This was, she writes, the first time he had mentioned to her
that he had ever entertained any thought of stepping down from
the throne. And this, the Duchess of Windsor conceded, was the
fateful moment that toppled a king. If she had held fast to her decision to leave England at once, the crisis might have been resolved.
What kept her from going? In her own words: "The fundamental
inability of a woman to go against the urgent wishes of the man she
loves."

THE KING GIVES UP HIS THRONE   *Mrs. Simpson's picture graces a London newsstand, as residents gobble up the latest editions. The clamor for newspapers was so great that the presses could not keep up with the demand.*

INSTRUMENT OF ABDICATION

I, Edward the Eighth, of Great Britain, Ireland, and the British Dominions beyond the Seas, King, Emperor of India, do hereby declare my irrevocable determination to renounce the Throne for Myself and for my descendants, and my desire that effect should be given to this Instrument of Abdication immediately.

In token whereof I have hereunto set My hand this tenth day of December, nineteen hundred and thirty six, in the presence of the witnesses whose signatures are subscribed.

SIGNED AT
FORT BELVEDERE
IN THE PRESENCE
OF

KING EDWARD VIII   *The monarch is shown during his first radio broadcast after he ascended the throne, the setting similar to his abdication broadcast, eleven months later.*

The decisive meeting between the King and Prime Minister was held on the evening of Monday, November 16. In the end, the King asked Baldwin to consider whether he could marry Mrs. Simpson and, by Act of Parliament, enable her "to be the King's wife without the position of Queen." This request converted the "King's Matter" into a constitutional issue involving the House of Commons.

Mr. Baldwin replied that he would have to place the proposal before the Cabinet and seek the opinion of the Dominion Prime Ministers before he could give the sovereign an answer. The King agreed. On December 2, Mr. Baldwin reported to the King that such legislation would not be acceptable.

This spelled defeat for the King, who withdrew from London to Fort Belvedere. The following day, the London newspapers lifted their veil of silence, and the crisis was fully discussed in the leader columns. On December 4, Mrs. Simpson left England for the South of France, and on Thursday, December 10, 1936, the King announced his decision to abdicate.

The following day, King Edward addressed his final words to those who had been his subjects. At 10 P.M. he told the nation in a broadcast:

> *You must believe me when I tell you that I have found it impossible to carry the heavy duty of responsibility and discharge my duties as King as I would wish to do, without the help and support of the woman I love. I now quit altogether public affairs and I lay down my burden.*

As Prince Edward, he went to Portsmouth where the destroyer H.M.S. *Fury* was waiting to carry him across the Channel, free at last to live out his life with the woman for whom he had given up so much.

THE DUKE AND DUCHESS OF WINDSOR *A photographic study by Cecil Beaton on their wedding day, June 3, 1937, in Monts, France.*

THE WINDSORS IN 1951   The Duke and Duchess during one of
their many Mediterranean cruises along the French and Italian Riviera.

THE WINDSORS IN THEIR PARIS HOME   *The Duke, a habitual armchair-percher, tends to sit on the arm even when the rest of the chair is empty.*

ROYAL RECOGNITION   The first official meeting of Queen Elizabeth and the
Duchess took place in 1967, 30 years after the Windsors' marriage. The occasion was
the unveiling of a plaque in memory of the Duke of Windsor's mother, Queen Mary.
Left to right are Prince Philip, the Queen, the Queen Mother, the Duke and Duchess
of Gloucester, and the Windsors. The Duke of Gloucester is the Duke of Windsor's
only surviving brother.

Index

Aberdeen, Scotland, 182
Aboukir Bay, 128
Actium battle, 38
Adam Bede, 197, 209
Adam Bede Junior, 209
Adam, Robert, 346
Adsdean, 350
Aegean, 321, 338
Aeschylus, 150
"Agamemnon," 125
Age of Reason, 150
Ajaccio, Corsica, 95
Albert, Prince, (consort of Queen
    Victoria), 171-194
  death, 187; influence on Victoria,
  177-178, 185; marriage, 175; views on
  England, 177
Albert, (Prince of the Two Sicilies),
    128
Alexander, (son of Cleopatra), 27, 31
Alexander II, Czar, 317
Alexander the Great, 36
Alexandra, Queen, (England), 322,
    349
Alexandria, Egypt, 27, 32, 34, 40, 47,
    49
Alice, Princess (Greece), 344, 356
Allen, Sir George, 384
Anastasius, Emperor, 50
Andrew, Prince, (Greece), 346, 356
Anne, Princess, (England), 367
Anthemius, (Justinian's architect), 60,
    63
Antioch, 30, 31, 50, 62
Antonescu, General, 328-329, 340
"Antoniad," 39
Antonina, 49, 60, 62
Antony, Mark, 21-46

at Antioch, 30-31; in Athens, 30;
death, 42; marriage to Cleopatra, 31;
marriage to Octavia, 29; Persian cam-
paign, 31-32; peace treaty at Brindisi,
29; reunion in Alexandria, 27
Apollinaria, 218-234
April Follies, 283
Armistice, W. W. I, 269
Ascot, 182
Ashley, Edwina, *see* Mountbatten,
    Lady Edwina.
Assam, India, 361
Athens, 29, 30, 34, 322
Atholl, Duchess of, 187
"Atlanta," 345
Augustine Monastery, Lisbon, 342
Aurora Leigh, 168
Austen, Jane, 195
Austroasia, 345
Autobiography (Herbert Spencer), 199

Baden-Baden, Germany, 228, 231
Baker Street, London, 151
Baldwin, Prime Minister Stanley, 383
    385, 388, 390, 394
Ballearics, 130
Balmoral Castle, 177, 182-183, 186, 191
Baltimore, Maryland, 380
Bank of Egypt, 345
Bank of England, 152, 154
Barras, Paul, 91
Barrett, Arabel, 157
Barrett, Edward M., Sr., 148, 149, 151,
    152, 157, 161, 163, 165, 167, 168
Barrett, Edward M., Jr., 150-152

DATE DUE

1-30-85			
GAYLORD			PRINTED IN U.S.A.